How To Change
Painful Feelings Into
Positive Action

WHEN ANGER HURTS

Matthew McKay, Ph.D.,
Peter Rogers, Ph.D., and
Judith McKay, R.N.

MJF BOOKS
NEW YORK

Published by MJF Books
Fine Communications
Two Lincoln Square
60 West 66th Street
New York, NY 10023

Copyright © 1989 New Harbinger Publications, Inc.
5674 Shattuck Ave., Oakland, CA 94609

Library of Congress Catalog Card Number 93-77373
ISBN 1-56731-028-1

This edition published by arrangement with New Harbinger
Publications, Inc.

Manufactured in the United States of America

MJF Books and the MJF colophon are trademarks of Fine Creative
Media, Inc.

10   9   8   7   6   5   4

"I would like to congratulate you on the very lucid manner in which you have developed and presented your approach to a complex problem."

Ray H. Rosenman, M.D., author of *Type A Behavior and Your Heart* and director of cardiovascular research at SRI International

"(The techniques) you described were very sensitive applications of what we had in mind in the formulation about the escalation process. I particularly like the idea of T time, checking in and rechanneling.... Nice job."

G. R. Patterson, Ph.D., author of *Families* and research scientist at the Oregon Social Learning Center

"What has been learned can be unlearned. The authors present techniques to both reduce stress and learn how to turn away from anger-triggering thoughts. They also show how conflicts start and how to modify your behavior so that a simple discussion doesn't turn into a thermonuclear war. The book is particularly helpful for those concerned with family violence—especially parental and spousal abuse."

The Discriminating Librarian, Small Press Reviews

"*When Anger Hurts* is a reevaluation of current myths on anger, its origins, and its control by three professionals with impressive backgrounds.... This is a valuable book."

Small Press

For Our Children

Dana, Noah, Jordan, and Rebekah

Èlan and Becky

Contents

I

Understanding
Anger

1

How To Use This Book

Anger has enormous costs. The impulse that felt so right at the moment, so justified, becomes in the quiet hours another source of guilt and regret. What seemed so worthy of blame passes. What remains are the scars, the hurt, and the alienation.

If you are often angry, every one of your relationships may be affected. Marriage can become a minefield. Distance grows. Walls thicken. Children may become hardened, resistant, while carrying deep feelings of worthlessness. Co-workers may withdraw or sabotage you, bosses become critical. A bitterness may grow with certain friends.

And anger affects your health. A 25-year followup study of law students who had taken a test measuring hostility revealed a startling fact. Twenty percent of those who had scored in the top quarter on the hostility scale had died, compared to a death rate of only five percent for students who had scored in the lowest quarter on the same test (New York Times, 1989). Frequent anger is damaging to your body and increases the death rate from nearly every cause.

When Anger Hurts

This book is for people who are concerned about their anger, who've grown tired of the emotional and physical toll that anger takes. It's for those who want less anger in their relationships, who seek better ways of expressing needs and solving problems.

This is a self-help book—which means that you are in for a lot of work. You can't achieve anger control without learning and practicing crucial coping skills. A passive reading of the text may prove disappointing. Nothing will change in your life.

A real change in your experience and expression of anger can only be achieved by doing the exercises, trying the techniques, and practicing your new skills on a daily basis. Whether you are learning stress reduction or a system to alter your anger-triggering thoughts, the book can only help if you master each step and then apply what you've learned to real events in your life.

The work will pay off. The skills you'll learn in this book can help you achieve important benefits:

1. The ability to control destructive anger venting. And the chance to protect and rebuild relationships that have been damaged by venting in the past.
2. A reduction in the frequency and intensity of your physiological anger response. There is a wealth of scientific data that anger damages your health (see Chapter 3). The less anger you experience, the longer you live.
3. A change in the beliefs, assumptions, and attitudes that trigger chronic anger. As you learn to restructure anger-triggering thoughts, you'll find that fewer and fewer things upset you.
4. Identification of the stresses and needs that lie *below* your anger. When you're clear about the real problem, you can move past anger to decision making.
5. The ability to cope effectively with your stress. Instead of exploding when stress exceeds your tolerance threshold, you can employ specific relaxation tools.
6. Greater effectiveness in meeting your needs. Anger generates resistance and resentment in others. You may get short-term cooperation. But in the long run your needs will be ignored and you will be avoided. Problem solving and communication tools can help you get what you want *without* anger.

When Anger Helps

Despite its costs, anger can be adaptive. It's a warning signal that something is wrong. Just as physical pain can be a warning ("this stove is hot—move your hand right now"), anger can warn you of imminent trauma. Anger can provide the energy to resist emotional or physical threats. The following exceptional situations are examples of when anger helps:

1. Perhaps the most obvious situation in which anger can be helpful is that of *physical threat* or actual attack. Anger can mobilize you to defend yourself or escape.

A few years ago Iris, a middle-aged woman living in New York, heard footsteps following her as she was returning home alone from the theater. She was frightened, of course, but then she became angry at the thought of being victimized. She slowed down. Then, when the footsteps came near, she whirled around and shouted at the top of her voice, "Get away from me you son of a bitch—or I'll kill you!" The would-be attacker fled.

2. Anger can be adaptive when your *boundaries are violated.* This type of infringement can take a variety of forms. At work, Sally's boss often asked her to bring him coffee, although food service is not part of her job description. Jim's boss expects him to put in hours of unpaid overtime each day. A personal boundary can be violated by relatives or friends who drop in without calling, by a neighbor who consistently borrows tools, or by a lover who demands a kind of sexuality you find repulsive.

Anger can help you mobilize your resources to set appropriate limits. You don't need to get hostile or aggressive with your boss. But you can learn to be very assertive. In your personal life, anger can help you set limits and give you the strength to resist threatening demands.

3. Many people struggle with the task of *separation and individuation*. Some children live most of their lives in the shadow of intrusive or abusive parents. And even when the child thinks she's escaped by marrying and having her own family, the intrusiveness continues.

Penny is a case in point. When she and her husband and newborn baby moved to the other coast, they thought they had bought a measure of independence. Not so. Weekly telephone calls full of interrogation and criticism were followed by overlong visits where Penny's mother completely "took over." Finally, Penny (supported by her husband) took the risk and confronted her mother. She didn't yell and scream. But her controlled anger allowed her to communicate the intensity of her need to raise this child *her* way. Penny's mother felt hurt and angry. But eventually she learned to appreciate her daughter as an individual.

Adolescence is a trying and troubled time for all concerned. Richard was a fairly "good" boy. When he got to high school he started using the nickname "Gandi" (short for Gandalf), and his parents noticed a change. He began to have and voice opinions. He was openly critical of the president and made disparaging remarks about capitalism. When his Republican parents objected to these new political values, his first response was sullen withdrawal. After a while his anger energized him to take bolder action. He told his parents off: "I have a right to my beliefs. Lay off or you'll have a cold war right in your house." His parents were shocked, but decided to give him "more space."

Chris and Sandy met and fell in love. After a whirlwind courtship they moved in together. It was wine and roses for a couple of weeks, but soon Chris began to feel trapped.

Sandy kept demanding more and more attention until Chris felt drained. In the end, Sandy was following him around like a lost puppy. This was the last straw. Fully experiencing his anger enabled Chris to set firm limits. Eventually, the couple had to separate entirely. However nourishing it had been at first, the relationship was stifling both of their lives and not allowing them to grow.

4. One of the most difficult problems to deal with is *sexual or physical abuse* as a child. Sexual molestation, whether by a parent, grandparent, sibling, or next door neighbor, is a devastating experience. Equally devastating is physical or continued verbal and emotional abuse. Children who experience these kinds of maltreatment are traumatized and carry huge reservoirs of grief and anger into adulthood.

For survivors of child abuse, recovery means allowing more and more of the child's buried feelings to surface. First the pain, the humiliation, the sense of wrongness. Next comes the anger and a realization that one's innocence was violated. Finally the deep feeling of grief. If ever the words "legitimate," "valid," or "appropriate" could be used in connection with anger, this is the best example.

For victims of child abuse, catharsis in a safe therapeutic environment is an essential requirement for "moving on." Getting in touch with the victimized child's anger is a major step in the recovery process.

5. Anger helps overcome the *fear of asserting your needs*. Many people believe they don't have a right to ask for what they want. They don't deserve to be happy. Without the mobilizing effects of anger, they would simply never have the courage to communicate their needs.

Cindy is a case in point. She was always being put down, even as a child. Her family's message was: "You're not important." "Your sister needs braces on her teeth, she's going to be in the school play. Your teeth are OK. So what if they're a little bit crooked." "We're sending your brother to college, he's the bright one. You'll get a job till you get married."

There came a time when Cindy finally stood up for herself. Her anger strengthened and supported her as she confronted her parents. In a loud voice she told them that she was finished being second best, finished with the "Cinderella shit." Some things started to change. For one, her mother apologized. And her father offered to pay for books and tuition at the local community college.

How To Use This Book

While anger can serve vital functions to protect and defend the integrity of the self, it is too frequently an instrument that destroys and abuses. Chronic anger does not make you strong and safe. It weakens you. It encourages attack. The truth is that anger begets anger. The more you shout, the more you invite shouting. The more you rage, the more you invite rage.

There are two kinds of anger: anger at yourself and anger directed toward others. Anger at yourself triggers depression and damages your self-esteem. Self-directed anger is not within the scope of this book. If this is a significant issue for you, it is suggested that you read *Self-Esteem* (McKay and Fanning 1986) for a thorough cognitive behavioral treatment of the problem.

This book is focused on anger directed toward others. Whether you tend to vent your feelings (*anger-out*) or silently seethe (*anger-in*), you will find help here.

Chapters 2 through 4 contain basic information about what anger is and isn't and what it costs you physiologically and interpersonally. Chapter 5 shows how anger is *always a choice*. You can control anger by controlling your anger-triggering thoughts. Chapter 6 explores the issue of responsibility. For the angry person, someone else is always responsible for the pain. Anger control means taking responsibility for *everything* that stresses, hurts, or frustrates you. Chapters 7 through 14 are skill-building chapters. It's vital to apply the information in these chapters—not just read them. Do the exercises, try the techniques, find out what works best for you. Chapters 15 and 16 focus on the special problems of anger with children and spouse abuse. Chapter 16 has been designed to function on its own, as a component of a spouse abuse treatment program. To this end, key strategies presented at length in earlier chapters are summarized in a section on anger control. For professionals, an appendix contains a protocol for leading Response Choice Rehearsal groups.

Your Anger Journal

Keeping an anger journal is a recommended part of using this book. You will be instructed at various points to observe and record specific aspects of your anger. For example, you will be asked to monitor the patterns of chronic tension in your body, your physiological anger response, and your anger-triggering thoughts. You'll track the most frequent targets of your anger. You'll notice and record the images and remembered scenes that most incite you.

The journal is important because it enables you to apply the book to your specific situation. Rather than passively reading about stress, you will explore the patterns of tension in your own body. Instead of absorbing abstractions and concepts, you will learn about your own trigger thoughts and anger imagery.

Coping with anger is an active process. And the time to start the process of change is now. Buy yourself a spiral notebook. Put it on your desk or bedside table (wherever you're more likely to use it). Today and every day until you've worked your way through all the chapters in this book, make the following notations.

1. The number of times you got angry in the last 24 hours.
2. How aroused you felt when you were at your angriest during the past 24 hours. Use a scale of 1 to 10, where 1 is minimal arousal and 10 is the most anger arousal you've ever felt.
3. How aggressively you acted when you were at your angriest during the last 24 hours. Again use a 1 to 10 scale, where 1 is minimal aggression and 10 is the most aggression you have ever displayed.

A typical entry might look like this:

Dec. 4   4 times.   Arousal 6.   Aggression 2.

Dec. 5   3 times.   Arousal 7.   Aggression 5.

Monitoring your anger in this way may teach you quite a lot about yourself. But it will also provide you with a measure of your progress. Over the weeks you will be able to observe yourself change both the frequency and intensity of your anger. Seeing progress documented in this way will be enormously reinforcing for your efforts.

2

The Myths of Anger

Anger, Shakespeare's "full hot horse," has been both praised and maligned, but mainly misunderstood. Whether it is "the sinew of the soul" (Thomas Fuller, *Of Anger*) or that which "resteth in the bosom of fools" (*Ecclesiastes*), anger has been the subject of speculation and discussion from the beginning of time.

Have you ever gotten angry and had a friend reassure you that "it's good to get it out?" Have you been to a therapist who advised you to stop holding your anger in? Have you sometimes had the feeling that anger is inevitable, that you better find a way to let off steam before you burst? These are all common experiences. But these common sense beliefs about anger, accepted even by mental health professionals, have turned out to be, in a word, wrong. This chapter examines the four basic myths of anger and describes some of the research that is now uncovering the truth.

Myth 1: Anger is a biochemically determined event.
Myth 2: Anger and aggression are instinctual to man.
Myth 3: Frustration leads to aggression.
Myth 4: It's healthy to ventilate.

Each of these myths supports the unfortunate conclusion that anger and aggression are a *necessary* part of being human. By suggesting that anger and aggression are determined by instinct and biology, that they are basic to human adaptation, these myths make anger seem inescapable. The end result is an era in the history of psychology during which the expression of anger has been encouraged and even praised. People are assumed to be naturally angry. And they are told that letting anger out is the royal road to mental health.

The truth is that anger is rarely inescapable and seldom necessary. But that's getting ahead of the story. Right now it will be helpful to examine, one by one, the myths of anger.

Myth 1: Anger Is a Biochemically Determined Event

It is a common belief, mainly held by the biomedical community, that anger is largely a biochemical process. Specifically, anger is thought to be the result of hormonal changes or activity in the limbic system (e.g., the hypothalamus and amygdala).

Anger and Hormones

Some researchers have linked the hormone prolactin (which stimulates the production of mother's milk) to high levels of anger. Kellner et al. (1984) found that women with hyperprolactinemic amenorrhea (a condition characterized by increased levels of prolactin in the blood and absence of menstrual periods) had higher hostility scores than women with normal prolactin levels. When hyperprolactinemic women were given a prolactin-lowering drug, a significant and progressive decrease in hostility followed. In a related study, postpartum women who had high prolactin levels were significantly more hostile than a control group and equally as hostile as hyperprolactinemic women.

Testosterone has also been linked to hostility. Scaramella and Brown (1978) found that testosterone correlated with aggressive behavior. Konner (1962) found that male prison inmates with the highest levels of testosterone had the earliest age of first arrest. However, testosterone levels have also been found to be subject to environmental influences. When a monkey was introduced into a cage where rival males had established dominance, Konner noted that the newcomer exhibited a rapid drop of plasma testosterone. On the other hand, when a male subject was placed in a cage of females in heat, testosterone levels rose sharply.

Norepinepherine has long been implicated in the anger picture. Friedman et al. (1960) reported that aggressive, hostile individuals were found to excrete more norepinepherine than the passive and anxious subjects to whom they were compared. However, this research suffers from the "chicken-egg" problem. It is unclear whether the secretion of norepinepherine is a product of anger, or whether the subjects were angrier because they had higher levels of norepinepherine in their system.

There is no question that hormones are associated with emotion. But although physiological arousal may be a necessary component of any emotional response, it usually cannot, by itself, make you angry. Your cognitive awareness and interpretation of an emotion-provoking event or situation is a second, equally important component.

The work of Stanley Schachter best demonstrated the importance of the cognitive point of view. Building on the research of Maranon (1924), Schachter proposed a "two-factor" theory of emotion. According to this theory, the labeling (or attribution) of an emotion is based on a physiological change *plus* a cognitive interpretation of that change.

In a classic series of experiments exploring this point of view (Schachter and Singer 1962), subjects received what they thought to be vitamin injections. Actually, the injections were adrenalin. One group of subjects was told that the "vitamin" would produce certain side effects, such as heart palpitations and tremor (which are real side effects of adrenalin). Other groups were led to expect no side effects or ones not usually associated with adrenalin.

While waiting for a "vision test," each subject sat in a room with another person who was actually a confederate of the experimenters. In some cases, the "stooge" appeared euphoric and silly, throwing paper airplanes, laughing, and playing with a hula hoop. In other cases, the stooge acted annoyed and angry, finally tearing up a questionnaire he was supposed to fill out.

The purpose of the study was to see whether subjects under these different experimental conditions would assign different emotional labels to the physiological sensations produced by the adrenalin. The major finding was that subjects who did not expect the arousal produced by adrenalin, and thus had no way of explaining the physiological changes they were experiencing, tended to use the emotion displayed by the confederate as a label of their own feelings. They too expressed euphoria or anger, depending on the model provided them by the stooge. In contrast, subjects who were told to expect side effects were less likely to share the confederate's feelings.

Many other experiments (Schachter 1971) have lent support to the notion that cognitions tend to override the effects of sheer arousal. Anger authority Ray Rosenman (1985) concluded that "It is primarily the perception of an event that determines the emotional response and hence the psychophysiological consequences.... Anger is a cognitive response that is associated with personal appraisal and interpretation."

Carol Tavris, author of the seminal book, *Anger—The Misunderstood Emotion*, agrees that hormonally induced arousal is not enough to *cause* emotion. "It needs a psychological component before heat is transformed into hostility, uncertainty into fear, general distress into depression or rage. Adrenalin does not become the anger hormone until it is attached to a provocation, perception of injustice, or some interpretation of events" (Tavris 1982).

Anger and the Limbic System

The area of the brain that neurologists believe governs violent behavior is the limbic system. This system is located in the oldest part of the brain and includes among other components the amygdala and the hypothalamus. The amygdala, in particular, has been fingered as a major culprit in aggressive behavior.

Elliot (1976) has suggested that brain diseases affecting the limbic system may result in something called the "dyscontrol syndrome." He believes that this syndrome has "an important cause of wife and child battery, senseless assaults, motiveless homicides, self-injury, dangerously aggressive driving, domestic infelicity, divorce," and so on. Vivid case histories of the dyscontrol syndrome have been cited that involve brutality of all kinds, sexual assault, and recklessness. The syndrome also appears to be implicated in the tragic case of Charles Whitman, the "Texas Tower" murderer of 17 people. After his death, an autopsy revealed a tumor the size of a walnut located in his amygdala.

Although the limbic system, and particularly the amygdala, is identified with aggression, Rosenman (1985) points out that the relationship is not a straightforward one. "...The amygdala's existence does not necessarily mean that the brain is programmed instinctively for aggression. Thus, its stimulation in animals does not elicit aggressive behaviors *unless they were previously learned.* Moreover, its stimulation in human subjects variously causes anxiety, depression, anger, fright, and horror...."

Other researchers agree. Deschner points out that the amygdala evaluates incoming stimuli for their life-threatening or life-enhancing potential.

These primitive "good-bad" evaluations seem to control access to the anger programs in the hypothalamus. Fortunately, incoming stimuli must first be received and interpreted by the appropriate areas in the cerebral hemispheres specialized to handle sights, sounds, and so on. *Therefore the amygdala passes judgment on stimuli that have first been filtered through the conscious parts of the mind,* where all inputs are registered; compared with past memories, beliefs and expectations; and interpreted. This simple anatomical fact serves to screen the midbrain from the world and is the built-in basis for cognitive regulation of anger reactions. (Deschner 1984)

Myth 2: Anger and Aggression Are Instinctual to Man

The idea that humans are endowed with a basic instinct for aggression received quasi-scientific support in the work of Raymond Dart. His analysis of the findings in the South African caves, particularly Makapansgat, led him to describe early hominid ancestors in vivid terms.

Man's predecessors differed from living apes in being confirmed killers: carnivorous creatures that seized living quarries by violence, battered them to death, tore apart their broken bodies, dismembered them limb from limb, slaking their ravenous thirst with the hot blood of [their] victims. (Quoted in Leakey 1981, 221)

When Dart continued his work by a detailed examination of the fossil remains of the australopithecines in the caves, he found that these also bore the unmistakable marks of violence. In a 1953 essay, he summarized his view of human origins by proclaiming that "the blood-bespattered, slaughter-gutted archives of human history from the earliest Sumerian records to the most recent atrocities of the Second World War accord with early universal cannibalism...this predacious habit, this mark of Cain separates man dietetically from his anthropoidal relatives and allies him rather with the deadliest of Carnivora" (ibid.).

Dart's conclusions were expanded upon by his disciple, Robert Ardrey, in such books as *African Genesis* and *The Territorial Imperative*. Ardrey's vivid portrayal of a prehistory rife with predatory, carnivorous, and cannibalistic scenarios was instrumental in furthering the idea that man cannot escape his aggressive instincts and that he is, in fact, "...a predator whose instinct is to kill with a weapon."

The result of modern scientific enquiry tends to refute the claims on which Dart and Ardrey based their descriptions of our bloody past. The principle investigator in this area is Bob Brain, working from the Transvaal Museum in Pretoria. Brain discovered that fossils buried close to the bottom of a deep cave may have as much as 100 feet of sediment resting over them. This weight has the effect of flattening and distorting the hominid fossils. If a hard pointed object lies close to the skull, the pressure can push the point into the bone, causing a localized compound fracture which can resemble the effects of a deadly blow to the head.

Brain capitalized on the results of a "natural experiment" when he discovered a large number of goat bone fragments in a Hottentot village. Goat was the primary source of meat in that region, and the leftovers were thrown to the dogs. When he collected and sorted the remains, he found that only the most tough and resistant part of the skeleton survived. This bone collection was remarkably similar to that found at the Makapansgat site. It now appears that the fossils Dart interpreted as weapons of a prehistoric culture are more likely the leftovers of many carnivore meals.

Perhaps the most popular proponent of the evolutionary basis for human aggression was Konrad Lorenz. Best known for his book *On Aggression*, he relates human aggressiveness to a universal territorial instinct in biology. Throughout the animal world, territories are established and maintained by ritualized displays of aggression. According to Lorenz, our ancestors acquired weapons and turned these rituals into bloody combat, which were heightened by a primal lust for killing.

The Lorenzian school suggests that aggression is a basic part of the territorial animal's survival mechanism and is fueled by a continuous pressure for expression. According to Lorenz, aggression may be released by an appropriate cue, such as the appearance of a threat from another animal. But if no such threat appears, the internal pressure will eventually reach a "critical point," and the aggressive behavior will burst out spontaneously. This theory could be used to explain anything from marital spats to nuclear war, as biological pressures push human beings past some built-in anger threshold.

Anthropologist Richard Leakey (1981) disagrees with the Lorenzian hypothesis. He suggests, to begin with, that animals are territorial for a reason, usually to protect resources or a reproductive area. The lunging behavior by sticklebacks and the morning cacophany of the gibbons both are displays announcing ownership of territory. Intruders are met with these ritualized confrontations in which the more biologically fit of the two inevitably wins without inflicting physical damage.

These forms of "aggression" are, in fact, an exercise in competitive display, as opposed to physical violence. The biological advantage of this behavior is obvious. A species which settles its disputes through violence will reduce its overall fitness and be less likely to survive in an environment that is difficult enough already. This law is deeply embedded in the nature of survival and evolutionary success depends on it. An animal that is unable to restrain its murderous lust puts itself and its species in a disadvantageous evolutionary position.

Our ancestors probably lived in small bands of closely related members. Nearby bands were also similarly related. Any act of murder would probably have involved someone who was kin to the murderer, and since evolutionary success requires the production of as many descendants as possible, an innate unrestrained aggressiveness would have doomed the human species.

The principal factor in successful evolution is cooperation rather than conflict. Even in primates, most fighting is a ritualized process which preserves the species. Thus the evolution of *Homo sapiens* would appear to stem from our ability to live in effective groups, unlike other protohominids who failed in this endeavor.

Leakey concludes that territoriality and aggression are not universal instincts. Territorial behavior is triggered, as required, by scarcity in food supplies or mating spaces. It is inevitable that some of the weakest individuals will fail to secure food or a mate. This is the harsh lesson of natural selection or "survival of the fittest."

In 1986, a remarkable group of twenty distinguished behavioral scientists gathered in Seville, Spain. This group included psychologists, neurophysiologists, and ethologists from twelve different nations. The conference concluded that there is no scientific evidence to support the belief that humans are innately aggressive and warlike. The "Seville Statement" that resulted from their deliberations has since been endorsed by the American Psychological Association and the American Anthropological Association, among others. The following excerpts from that document (*Psychology Today*, June 1988) served to summarize their position:

1. It is scientifically incorrect to say that we have inherited a tendency to make war from our animal ancestors. Warfare is a peculiarly human phenomenon and does not occur in other animals. War is biologically possible, but it is not inevitable.
2. It is scientifically incorrect to say that war or any other violent behavior is genetically programmed into our human nature. Except for rare pathologies the genes do not produce individuals necessarily predisposed to violence.
3. It is scientifically incorrect to say that in the course of human evolution there has been a selection for aggressive behavior. In all well-studied species, status within the group is achieved by the ability to cooperate.

4. It is scientifically incorrect to say that humans have a "violent brain." While we do have the neural apparatus to act violently, there is nothing in our neurophysiology that compels us to do so.

The group concluded that "biology does not condemn humanity to war, and that humanity can be freed from the bondage of biological pessimism. Violence is neither in our evolutionary legacy not in our genes."

Myth 3: Frustration Leads to Aggression

According to Freud, individuals are born with an innate aggressive instinct. He further argues that when this instinctual urge is blocked or "frustrated" it will lead to a hostile attack. When the real object of the anger is perceived as being too risky to attack, the anger is displaced. Thus a child displaces aggression toward its parents by fighting with a sibling or talking back to a teacher.

In 1939, Dollard et al. formulated the *frustration-aggression hypothesis*. They believed that "aggression is always a consequence of frustration. More specifically the proposition is that the occurrence of aggressive behavior always presupposes the existence of frustration and, contrawise, that the existence of frustration always leads to some form of aggression."

Although there is a great deal of evidence for the usefulness of the frustration-aggression hypothesis, it requires careful qualification. While frustration may lead to aggression, reports from many different cultures throughout the world indicate that this transfer is by no means inevitable. For example, the Kwoma of New Guinea may respond to frustration by submission, dependence, or avoidance, as well as anger (Whitting 1941). The Balinese are also unlikely to respond angrily to frustration (Bateson 1941). A more common response is for the Balinese man to withdraw from all contact and go without food or water for days. The Semai (a Senoi tribe) are renowned for their nonviolence (Dentan 1968). Semai children are taught to deal with frustration by using their dreams to work out alternatives.

Alternative responses to frustration may be found in our own culture as well. Losing money to a coffee machine may provoke some people to cursing and kicking behavior. Others will simply write down the name and address of the vending company and mail a request for their money back.

The second part of the hypothesis, that frustration invariably precedes aggression, has also been called into question. One need only think about hired mercenaries who kill in cold blood or children who imitate violence on TV to see the problems with this formulation.

Frustration is definitely related to anger arousal, but a cognitive factor is involved. Frustration can only occur when you have an expectation that is not fulfilled. Disappointment requires cognitions that include memory and imagination. In addition, a frustrated person will not act in an aggressive way unless the setting is perceived as appropriate for the expression of hostility. Whether on the battlefield or in a domestic argument, aggression only occurs if it is considered appropriate or acceptable for the situation at hand.

It must be noted that Neal Miller did modify the famous hypothesis in 1941. Miller's reformulation stated that frustration instigates many forms of behavior, and that only one of these is aggression. This clearly more realistic assessment lacks the dramatic flair of the original and hence has received much less attention.

Many people use the "frustration leads to aggression" myth to explain and excuse their anger. Since frustration is seen as invariably provoking anger and aggression, these individuals view anger as automatic and uncontrollable. When frustrated, they assume that anger is the only reponse possible. This myth leads to the belief that you have no choice. When things go wrong, anger is the natural response, the only response to frustrated drives. In truth, anger is only one response to frustration. This book will offer you a whole new range of choices and ways to cope when your needs are blocked.

Myth 4: It's Healthy To Ventilate

Much of current misunderstanding about anger can be traced back to the work of Sigmund Freud and his disciples. Freud used a number of metaphors to describe his view of psychological processes. He regarded these as useful aids to understanding, and cautioned his readers that these models should not be regarded as established scientific facts. He looked forward to the eventual discovery of the basic psychological mechanism that would validate his assumptions. Unfortunately, many of Freud's disciples took his metaphors to be reality, and these transitional notions took on a life of their own.

One of these concepts is the so-called "hydraulic model." Freud conceptualized the libido as the source of energy that fuels internal conflicts between id, ego, and superego. If the energy is blocked or dammed up, it will either find alternative routes of expression or eventually spill over the hypothetical "reservoir" and flood the system. Similarly, Freud described *repression* as the unconscious "damming" process that keeps dangerous material from coming into awareness, thereby producing a host of neurotic symptoms.

Although psychoanalysis was designed to alleviate neurotic symptoms by bringing to light this repressed material, Freud did not believe that suppression of aggressive instincts was undesirable. In fact, he believed that their suppression and sublimation were necessary for the survival of society as a whole. He would have been appalled to find his theories used as a justification for the modern injunction to "let it all hang out."

The *catharsis hypothesis* is perhaps the best known theory for the reduction of aggression. This idea also stems from Freud (in collaboration with J. Breuer). For Freud, this hypothesis explained why there are relatively few instances of violent acting out of aggressive instincts. Catharsis was a way of emptying emotional reservoirs (as in the hydraulic model) that could be accomplished in a variety of ways. The range of cathartic activities included fantasies, tears, angry words, and the destruction of objects.

The past twenty years have seen the rise of many new psychological schools and theories. The notion that it is unhealthy to bottle up feelings is common to many of these, ranging from the encounter group movement to Janov's "primal scream." Advocates of this point of view have been termed "ventilationists" by Leonard Berkowitz. Many therapists of this school would agree with Adelaide Bry:

I've seen how suppressed anger festers in the mind and body of the individual, creating both emotional and physical ailments; how it insinuates itself between husband and wife, and between friend and friend, dissolving all the good warm feelings that first brought them together; how it poisons relationships at work, at school, at play, in love, in all of life itself. (Bry 1976)

Further on, she enumerates the virtues of expressing anger. These include making you feel better about yourself, making your relationships more meaningful and *real*, relieving both physical and emotional stress, and finally, whetting your sexual appetite.

This point of view cannot be dismissed as a "far-out" fringe position in psychological circles. Well-known psychoanalyst Theodore Isaac Rubin proposes a similar point of view in *The Angry Book*. The "message" of the book includes a number of related points: (1) by expressing anger you are working in the service of healthier and happier communication, (2) expressing anger gives you a "good, clean feel" and increases self-esteem, and (3) the purpose of "warm, healthy anger" is to clear the air and make corrections and reparations if necessary.

Even outside the psychological community, the general belief is that expressing feelings or "blowing off steam" is beneficial. But after summarizing the major research on anger, Carol Tavris (1982) notes that people who are most prone to vent their rages get angrier, not less angry. And the recipients of this rage have hurt feelings. The typical stages of a "ventilating" marital argument involve a precipitating event, an angry outburst, shouted arguments, screaming or crying, a crescendo (perhaps including physical violence), and exhaustion, followed by withdrawal or apology. This cycle is replayed *ad nauseum*, and no decrease in anger is apparent.

Jack Hokanson (1970) has done extensive research in the area of catharsis theory for the past twenty years. His original finding was that aggression was cathartic (in that it lowered blood pressure), but only when directed against peers. Expressing anger to a superior was actually anxiety producing, adding a new dimension to the anger rather than reducing it. In a related series of experiments, Hokanson discovered that while aggression was cathartic for anger in men, friendliness was cathartic for women. Even when directed toward a peer, aggression was as upsetting for women as aggression toward authority was for men.

These findings led Hokanson to speculate that catharsis is not a natural consequence of anger, but a learned reaction. In a follow-up series of experiments, he paired students matched for gender and age in a situation where they could administer either shocks or rewards. Male subjects responded to shocks by giving back shocks and experienced cathartic relief. Women, on the other hand, responded to shocks by giving a friendly response, thereby also experiencing cathartic relief. "Cathartic relief" was measured by physiological monitors hooked up to the subjects.

The experiment continued. In stage two, men were rewarded every time they gave a friendly response to a shock. Women were rewarded every time they were aggressive in response to a shock. Rapid learning occurred and the traditional form of catharsis for each sex was reversed. Women showed a reduction in blood pressure when they responded aggressively, and men now showed a cathartic response to friendliness rather than belligerence.

Seymour Feshbach (1956) had a group of nonaggressive children play with violent toys and "run amok" during free playtime. These boys, rather than behaving in a less aggressive way (as catharsis theory would predict), in fact became more hostile and destructive than previously observed. The same principles of anger and aggression were observed in adults by Murray Straus (1974). He found that couples who yell at each other feel more angry afterwards, not less.

Yelling or even talking out an emotion doesn't reduce it. What actually happens is that you are rehearsing for more of the same. Ebbesen, Duncan, and Konecni (1975) conducted exit interviews with men who had been laid off from an aerospace project, comparing them to others who had voluntarily quit at the same time. The finding was that "ventilation" of anger during the interview did not act as catharsis in any way. In fact, men who had taken an angry stance became even more hostile toward the company.

Tavris (1982) found in study after study that ventilation could serve to "freeze" a hostile attitude or opinion. This was true even among children who were encouraged to express their anger toward a child who had frustrated them in an experimental situation (Mallick and McCandles 1966). These children later expressed less liking toward that child than the children who were not permitted to express their anger. Similarly, college students remained angrier with someone who had irritated them when they were allowed a catharsis of their feelings (Kahn 1966).

Experimental studies consistently point out that the popular remedy for anger, ventilation, is really worse than useless. In fact, the reverse seems to be true: expressing anger tends to make you even angrier and solidifies an angry attitude.

There are, of course, exceptional cases. The incest victim who confronts her tormentor may experience real satisfaction. Cathartic experiences of this kind do not feel good simply because a psychic reservoir has been "emptied." Rather, the depth of the individual's emotional response is an outgrowth of facing and conquering a real situation involving objective instances of conflict, injustice, coercion, and so on.

The belief that anger and violence is unavoidable is psychologically attractive for many people. It allows individuals to excuse and justify acts of aggression by suggesting that they have little choice in the matter. Belief in the four myths discussed above makes anger and violence seem natural and even healthy.

In fact, the opposite is the case. Anger is basically a matter of choice. It is determined by your thoughts and beliefs far more than your biochemistry or genetic heritage. Venting anger rarely leads to any real relief or any lasting catharsis. It leads instead to more anger, tension, and arousal.

3

The Physiological Costs of Anger

Stella is standing in line at the bank. It is 1:20, and she is due back at her office at 1:30. She could make it in time if she is lucky and the line moves along. But things don't go well. Two of the five tellers close their windows. "How dare they take a break when there are people waiting?" she thinks. One customer is buying travelers checks. "Why don't they have a special window for that kind of service?" she asks the person behind her in line. The customer slowly signs each check as she cheerfully discusses her planned vacation. "Who cares about Florida in April? Just sign the damned checks and get going, for Christ's sake," Stella muttered under her breath. By now Stella is impatiently opening and closing the snap on her purse. At another window an elderly woman is leafing through a huge, over-stuffed purse looking for something. "This could take all day!" she sighs in exasperation. Her lunch, which she bolted down half an hour ago, sits like a rock in her stomach. The noise of other people's conversations is annoying, and the two men standing behind her in line are too close. A young man is counting out the money he received from the teller and carefully tucking it into his wallet before he leaves the window. "Good grief! Just move it!" she thinks.

By the time it's her turn at the window, at 1:29, she's in a rage. Her heart is pounding, she is breathing heavily, her mouth is dry, her hands shake. She's mad at the stupid, slow patrons and the inconsiderate bank tellers. She's mad at her boss for making her feel guilty if she's even a minute late and resents her job for only allowing a one-hour lunch break. She's angry at the restaurant for its slow, inefficient service and the undigested food she can still taste.

Stella's anger is a physical experience. All strong emotions—anger, fear, excitement—trigger powerful hormonal responses that cause body changes. These responses occur automatically in man and other animals and are an important survival mechanism.

While the physiological experience of anger proceeds automatically once it is triggered, getting angry is by no means automatic. Stella's anger is triggered by things that she tells herself while standing in line: "Tellers shouldn't take breaks while people are waiting...They should have a special window...Who cares about Florida?...This could take all day...Damn rigid boss...Bad service...Hideous food..." and so on. It is Stella's thoughts that actually start the emotional ball rolling, signaling her body to prepare for battle. Later chapters will have much more to say about the role of thoughts. Right now it's important to understand what happens to you physically when you get angry.

Early research into the physiology of emotion indicated that all strong emotions grew out of the same physical reaction. This reaction was dubbed the *stress response*.

The Stress Response

Walter Cannon (1929) first documented the physiological reactions of different organs to stress of all kinds. In experiments with animals, he observed a similarity in their physical responses to pain, anxiety, heat, starvation, and so on. When he performed autopsies on these poor creatures, he saw the same characteristic organ abnormalities in all the animals, no matter what kind of stress they had been exposed to. Their adrenal glands were enlarged, they had stomach ulcers, their thymus glands were small, and their livers were pale. Hans Selye (1936), considered the father of stress theory, called this whole pattern of organ abnormalities a "stress syndrome." He believed that the stress syndrome was an alarm reaction—a general call to arms of the body's defensive forces. He believed that the body's attempt to deal with stress and the hormones released in response to stress affected all tissues and cells. Selye was convinced that stress accounted for the wide assortment of "diseases of adaptation" found in man and other animals, diseases such as peptic ulcers, high blood pressure, heart attacks, and nervous disorders.

Of course the stress response isn't all bad. It enables the threatened person to run faster, climb higher, shout louder, see more clearly, hit harder, endure more pain, and do what must be done to survive an attack. The same hormonal response helps (or hinders) athletes, dancers, actors, and speakers. And it is that response that gives a horrified mother the strength to lift a car off of her trapped child. The stress response is highly adaptive in an emergency. But Selye demonstrated that if the body's alarm system is turned on chronically, serious organic damage will inevitably occur.

In Selye's day, it wasn't possible to measure the levels of hormones in the body directly. New technologies have since made it possible to measure hormones and endocrine levels at the very moment a subject is reacting. These more exact measurements have made it clear that each strong emotion has a characteristic physiological reaction and that emotions are not just varients of a single stress response. Although the sympathetic nervous system is involved in all strong emotions, producing epinephrin and norepinephrin, it is the mixture of types, amounts, and balance of hormones that cause important differences in the body's reaction. For example, fear and distress cause an increased heart rate and blood pressure, constriction of blood vessels in the skin, and a shunting of blood to the skeletal muscles. The person looks ashen, cold, clammy, and tremorous. On the other hand, situations that are challenging and exciting result in vasoconstriction in the skeletal muscles, and less change in heart and respiration rates.

The Physiology of Anger

Many studies show that the stress of anger produces a unique and specific hormonal response that is particularly dangerous. Anger results in elevated levels of testosterone (for men), epinephran, norepinephran, and cortisol. Chronic high levels of testosterone and cortisol potentiate atherosclerosis, the most common cause of coronary artery disease. Cortisol also depresses the immune system and reduces the body's ability to fight infection. Epinephran and norepinephran stimulate the sympathetic nervous system to shunt blood from the skin, liver, and digestive tract to the heart, lungs, and skeletal muscles. Blood pressure is elevated, and glucose is dumped into the blood system to provide energy for confrontation or escape. When blood is shunted away from the liver, the liver is less efficient in clearing the blood of cholesterol, thus contributing to the fatty deposits in the arteries. Elevated blood pressure also damages the arteries and the heart. Hypertension forces the heart to work harder and creates a large and less efficient heart muscle. Turbulence caused by the high pressure of the blood flow also damages the arteries. Tiny tears develop on the artery wall. Fatty deposits cover the tears, but these can eventually grow to fill the artery and stop the flow of blood.

Occasional anger creates no lasting harm. But chronic, sustained anger keeps the body in a constant state of emergency, and the regular body functions, such as digestion, clearing the blood of cholesterol, and resisting infection, may be delayed, depressed, or bypassed. Chronic anger thus contributes to the development of a variety of diseases—digestive disorders, hypertension, heart disease, susceptibility to infections, rashes, headaches, and many more.

Anger and Hypertension

Doctors have always suspected that there was an association between anger and high blood pressure. To understand how anger elevates blood pressure, it's important to first examine how the vascular system works. Blood pressure is simply the pressure exerted by the blood on the walls of the blood vessels. It is really two different pressures and is expressed in two numbers such as 120/80 or 140/90. The higher number represents the *systolic pressure* of your blood as it surges through the arteries during each heartbeat. You feel that wave of pressure as you touch the pulse in your wrist. The lower number is a measurement of the *diastolic pressure* in the artery *between* heartbeats. A blood pressure of 120/80 means that the pressure in the arteries is 120 at the time of the heart's contraction and 80 between beats.

You can think of your blood system as a big pool of fluid enclosed in a limited but somewhat flexible amount of space—like water in a balloon. The two ways you can affect the pressure in that balloon are to increase the amount of water in it or to make the space smaller. The high levels of norepinephrin associated with anger have the effect of squeezing the balloon. Norepinephrin raises the diastolic blood pressure between beats by constricting the large peripheral blood vessels.

The association between anger and high blood pressure has been demonstrated by many studies on many different patient populations. Schwartz, Weinberger, and Singer (1981) compared changes in blood pressure as subjects experienced fear, happiness, anxiety, and anger. They found that anger caused the greatest response of heart and blood vessels and the greatest increase in blood pressure.

Anger-In and High Blood Pressure

As early as 1939, Franz Alexander proposed that hypertensives struggle against their feelings of anger and have difficulty expressing them. He suspected that angry feelings and the corresponding chronic activation of the sympathetic nervous system eventually led to high blood pressure.

Alexander's hypothesis that unexpressed anger (anger-in) was linked to elevated blood pressure has been confirmed again and again in studies of hypertensive young adults and middle-aged populations (Hamilton 1942; Harburg et al. 1964, 1973; Kahn et al. 1972; Esler et al. 1977; Miller and Grimm 1979; and Diamond 1982). Other studies have demonstrated that hypertensives lack basic assertiveness skills (Gressel et al. 1949; Wolff and Wolf 1951; Harris et al. 1953). It is clear that the inability or unwillingness to express anger and the consequent holding in of hostile feelings contribute to the development of hypertension for many susceptible people.

Anger-Out and High Blood Pressure

While the weight of evidence points to anger-in as a major culprit in hypertension, other studies have found that people with high blood pressure tend to show more hostility and behave more aggressively than people with normal blood pressure (Schacter 1957; Kaplan et al. 1961; Baer et al. 1969; Mann 1977;). Harburg, Blakelock, and Roper (1979) did an interesting study in which they asked people how they would deal with an angry and arbitrary boss. Some subjects reported that they would just walk away from the situation (anger-in). Others said that they would protest, confront the boss, and might even report him to the union (anger-out). Still another group stated that they would try to talk it over later, after the boss had cooled off. The researchers called this coping style "reflection." They found that subjects who chose to express their anger to the boss had the highest blood pressure. Anger-in subjects had somewhat lower pressure. Subjects who used reflection had the lowest blood pessure, prompting Harburg and his colleagues to suggest that reflection was a coping style that could be taught to hypertensives.

Anger and Heart Disease

What Is a Heart Attack?

Just like every other part of the body, the heart muscle needs oxygen and nutrients to keep its cells alive. These essentials are supplied by the coronary arteries. Between each heartbeat, the coronary arteries feed the heart cells with oxygen-rich blood.

Anything that interferes with coronary artery function is potentially life threatening. When cholesterol is desposited in the lining of the essential coronary arteries, the resulting plaques can irritate the artery and cause spasm (experienced as angina pain). But something more serious can also happen. The rough lining of the coronary arteries may cause the formation of a clot that completely occludes the artery. This condition is called a heart attack, or myocardial infarction. In a heart attack, all muscle tissue downstream from the clot dies. Whether or not a person survives a heart attack depends on how much of the muscle tissue has died, and if the remaining undamaged part of the heart can still continue to function.

The Discovery of Type A

In the 1950s, Friedman and Rosenman, two San Francisco cardiologists, were trying to determine what put individuals at risk for coronary heart disease. Who was likely to have blocked arteries, heart attacks, and angina pain? They found that people who had heart attacks had some things in common, such as high blood cholesterol levels, hypertension, and some bad habits like smoking or sedentary lifestyles. But Friedman and Rosenman hit the jackpot when they examined their patients' personality patterns. They found a cluster of personality traits that appeared to be linked to heart disease.

In their famous book, *Type A Behavior and Your Heart* (1974), Friedman and Rosenman made the revolutionary suggestion that the high-risk cardiac symptoms and habits were not diet or activity level or stress, but a personality style. They identified the Type A as having personality traits of time urgency, competitiveness, high ambition, hyperaggressiveness, and free-floating hostility. They saw that this form of hyperaggressiveness was a desire not just to win, but to dominate. It was as if the hostility was always present and took any opportunity to attach itself to a person or a situation. The Type A person was full of anger—anger looking for an excuse to get out.

Laboratory Evidence

Friedman and Rosenman did many experiments on lab animals to try to recreate the physical changes that occur during anger (Friedman and Ulmer, 1984). In an experiment on rats whose hypothalamuses were electrically stimulated in such a way as to create rage, they found something very reminiscent of Selye's early work. Autopsies showed that the rats had very pale liver tissue. Since anger diverts blood away from the digestive system, the pale livers of these raging rats show the effect of constant sympathetic nervous system stimuation. Friedman and Rosenman saw these liver changes as one of the major contributors to heart disease. Because the liver is the organ that removes cholesterol from the blood, a restricted supply of blood to the liver tends to elevate cholesterol levels.

Confirming Studies

Many studies have documented the association between Type A behavior and heart disease. Between 1960 and 1969, Friedman and Rosenman (1974) conducted the Western Collaborative Group Study on 3,500 healthy men. First, they found that 113 of the original group already had heart disease and that 80 percent of these men could be classified as Type A. Over the course of eight and a half years, Type A men were twice as likely to have heart attacks as Type B's. In the Framingham Heart Study (Haynes, Feinleish, and Kannel 1980), 5,500 men and women were tested. An analysis of data collected between 1950 and 1980 again revealed a significant link between Type A patterns and heart disease. A study supervised by Redford Williams at Duke University Medical Center (Blumenthal et al. 1978) showed that Type A patients undergoing diagnostic coronary angiography (x-rays of the heart's blood supply) had more severe atherosclerosis than Type B's. And over 90 percent of individuals with servere coronary artery disease were determined to have Type A personalities.

The Real Culprit: Hostility

Rosenman, working in recent years at the Stanford Research Institute, has concluded that of all the personality traits found in Type A, it is the potential for hostility that is the key predictor of coronary disease. Rosenman and others reanalyzed data from the Western Collaborative Group Study (Rosenman 1985) and found that the anger-hostility dimension proved to be "the dominent characteristic among the coronary prone Type A behaviors."

Corroborating evidence came from a study of 1,877 men at the Western Electric Company in Chicago (Shekelle et al. 1983). Men who scored high on a hostility scale were one and a half times more likely to have a heart attack than men who had lower hostility scores. Barefoot, Dahlstrom, and Williams (1983) did a follow-up study of 255 male physicians who had completed the Hostility Scale 25 years earlier while they were in medical school. Men who scored at the median or below in hostility had one sixth the incidence of coronary heart disease of men who had scored higher on the scale. Williams et al. (1980) tested 424 patients who were referred for coronary angiography. Forty-eight percent of patients with low hostility scores were found to have coronary atherosclerosis. But 70 percent of patients with higher scores had significant atherosclerosis.

The evidence seems clear. Chronic hostility and anger damage your heart and arteries.

Anger and Digestion

Anger has a dramatic impact on your stomach. Wolff and Wolf (1967) noticed that anger produces effects quite different from depression or fear. Angry subjects manifested red stomach linings with increased rhythmic contractions and increased secretion of hydrochloric acid. People who were depressed or frightened had pale stomach linings, and decreased contractions and acid secretion. Anger's role in increasing acid secretion is very significant. Because hyperacidity is associated with the development of gastritis and ulcers, chronic anger may increase your risk for these diseases.

Anger may also be implicated in the development of ulcerative colitis. Researchers Lewis and Lewis (1972) have argued that "predisposed persons" may show symptoms of colitis when they maintain and hold in chronic resentment and anger. The mucus membrane of the colon reacts sharply to suppressed anger. It becomes engorged with blood and peristaltic activity is increased.

Beyond the Anger Response

It seems that it doesn't matter whether anger is expressed or suppressed. It's just plain bad for you. Chronic anger that is expressed is bad for you because it feeds on itself. It prolongs and supercharges all the associated hormonal changes. Chronic suppressed anger is damaging because it mobilizes the sympathetic nervous system responses without providing any release of the tension. The effect is the same as flooring the accelerator of your car at the same time as you are slamming on the brakes.

While anger is an unhealthy habit, it's one that can change with awareness and effort. Remember Stella at the beginning of the chapter? If her distress in the bank is part of a chronic anger response, she may eventually be at risk for a serious illness. But Stella is not the helpless victim of an anger-triggering hormonal storm. She has a choice. The potential for anger resides far more in how she interprets and thinks about events than in the events themselves. Later chapters will show how your perceptions, assessments, and interpretations of the world are learned responses. Anger can be controlled by changing the habitual ways that you perceive, assess, and interpret what goes on around you. A traffic jam, a long line at the bank, or incompetent or stupid or even malicious people need not trigger the deadly physical reaction of the anger response. You can learn to live without anger. And learning to do so will be good for your health.

4

The Interpersonal Costs of Anger

While anger can sometimes feel enormously relieving, and while it can act as a powerful tool for influence or control, anger has a price. This chapter is about the toll anger takes on your relationships, what it costs you in the currency of support and satisfaction.

The price you pay for anger may seem obvious. A cooling friendship. Resistance or withdrawal at work. A marriage where you have each become vigilant, ready for another caustic round. Other costs may be more subtle. The decision of a friend not to give you vital feedback. A colleague who recommends your work, but without enthusiasm. A lover who keeps quiet rather than attempt some risky problem solving. It comes down to this: each angry episode cuts into the fabric of good will, care, and appreciation that's vital to your relationships. Angry people are experienced as dangerous. They are handled like a loaded gun—with caution or downright avoidance.

Anger stuns. It frightens. It makes people feel bad about themselves. And of course warns them to stop doing whatever is offending you. But people gradually become inured and resistant. As soon as they see you, they put on their emotional armor in preparation for the next upset. The more anger you express, the less effective your anger becomes, the less you are listened to, and the more cut off you may begin to feel from genuine closeness.

Anger has its place. There are times when it is healthy, even necessary (see Chapter 1). Yet those times are rare. In general, the more frequent and intense your anger, the more likely you are to sustain irremediable damage in your relationships.

Raising Defenses

With its penchant for the obvious, psychology has recently learned what most people already knew: anger leads to physiological and verbal aggression (Rule and Nesdale 1976). The angrier you feel, the more likely you are to act it out in the form of an attack. But here's the rub. Aggression begets anger and aggression. The more you behave aggressively, the angrier you become, and the more you want to keep up the assault. As Carol Tavris (1984) concluded after an exhaustive review of the anger literature, "the primary result of aggressive behavior seems to be to stimulate both parties to continued aggression."

That's what makes the aggressive expression of anger so damaging—it doesn't stop. Once you permit verbal or physical aggression to enter your relationships, you develop a tendency to return again and again to the aggressive response. Each episode contributes to an atmosphere of blame and resentment, each episode breeds new fuel to generate attacks. A relationship that started in hope and trust evolves into each partner's list of sins and violations.

Anger-fueled aggression cuts and scars the tissue of relationship. Scar tissue isn't healthy tissue. It's thick and hard and inelastic. It covers, but it can no longer feel.

Anger and Rigidity

As frequency of anger increases, there is a corresponding decrease in tolerance and flexibility (Biaggio 1980). That's because angry relationships spawn an atmosphere of vigilance and fear. Your energy gets channeled into erecting barriers, rather than into communication and problem solving. The barriers defend you against hurt, but they also create a maze of psychological mines and trenches that make it impossible for angry people to reach each other—even with genuine feelings of love or support.

Typical defenses against anger include numbness, judging, irritability, attack, withdrawal, revenge, and extreme restriction of response. Once laid down, the barriers make you rigid and trigger-happy. It's hard to switch from defense to appreciation, from vigilance to any kind of trust. You'll tend to stay in the bunker, rather than risk real openness. And your tolerance for mistakes and criticism can get so low that even the slightest flaw or hint of disapproval can make you blow up.

Anger and Resistance

Because anger is so often used to coerce change in others, people erect defenses not only to shield themselves from hurt, but also to keep from feeling controlled. They resist the angry person's demands by means of avoidance, discounting, counterblaming, derailing, passive-aggressive sabotage, and a host of other defensive maneuvers.

People fight to maintain their boundaries and limits. Losing the capacity to say no, to have choice, to make independent decisions is a kind of psychological death. You feel as if you were being engulfed or suffocated, as if the framework of the self were being crushed. No matter how frightening coercive anger becomes, it can never be as scary as the loss of self. So people resist anger that is used to pressure change.

When you use anger to influence the behavior of others, it often works extremely well—the first time, the second time. But soon enough people learn to push you and your anger away. It's simply too scary for them to surrender control of their own behavior.

Losing the Sense of Well-Being

Helplessness

Angry people often express a sense of helplessness. Nothing seems to go as they would like. Friends are selfish and insensitive, employers are cheap and uncaring, a lover is unappreciative or withholding. Underlying these complaints is a genuine despair of ever feeling good, of feeling nurtured in relationships.

Anger leads to helplessness in four simple steps.

1. You tell yourself, "I'm in pain, something is wrong or lacking."
2. You tell yourself, "Others should fix or provide it."
3. You express your anger with aggression.
4. Your anger is met by resistance and withdrawal.

After step 4, the angry person feels frustrated: something is wrong, something is lacking. And the whole cycle starts again. This process continues, cycle after cycle, until a deep hopelessness and cynicism begin to form. Each relationship seems to reach the inevitable stage where disappontments overtake the earlier enjoyment, and chronic upsets make it too aversive to go on.

In truth, the helplessness is self-induced, and the despair is unnecessary. A sense of entitlement really starts the cycle: "I should never feel pain, but if I do, you must fix it." The angry person puts responsibility on others to meet his basic needs (more on this in Chapter 6) and gives up his own power in the process. The problem is compounded when he or she uses anger as a preferred strategy to make others change. As they increasingly resist, the angry person feels his or her life slides out of control. Nothing seems to work. No one really cares. No one seems good enough.

Diminished Satisfaction

In a way, this price is obvious: anger takes the fun out of things. As relationships become more defensive and distant, they offer fewer and fewer opportunities for wamth and nourishment. Very simply, the more one demands, the less one gets. This was documented in a recent survey of over 1,000 patients referred for coronary angiography. Hostile people were shown to have the same number of social contacts as people who are not hostile. But hostile people experienced these contacts as being lower in quality and less satisfying (Tavris 1984).

Clearly, entitlement and anger diminish your ability to really feel good with others. The myriad discomforts and little losses you experience all seem to be "their fault." And efforts to solve these problems with anger often serve to make things worse.

Problems on the Job

Dr. Myer Friedman, the man who identified the Type A personality, has determined that hostile, hard-driving people fail far more than they succeed in the workplace. "Type A behavior, far from bringing about success in the factory, office, laboratory or marketplace, is actually responsible for repeated disasters—careers and lives wrecked, whole businesses and large enterprises threatened with ruin." All too common are the Type A's who have "simply burned themselves out in pointless struggle, impatience and anger" (Friedman and Ulmer 1984, 62-63).

Anger doesn't work any better at the office than it does with friends or family. The results are exactly the same: defensiveness, counterattack, and withdrawal. While anger can sometimes be used to motivate subordinates, it has the long-term effect of driving people away—to other departments or other jobs. Or they begin to drag their feet in subtle ways—nothing you can really point to, but just enough to make you a little less productive or your stress level a little higher.

People talk. They know who blames, who becomes upset at any imperfection. So angry individuals get less business, fewer referrals, less help from the typing pool, more noncompliance with requests. The list goes on. And so will your difficulties at work if you are frequently angry.

Isolation

For many people, the price of anger is isolation. Friendships are distant, love relationships severed. Tavris observes that hostile Type A's "freely ventilate their wrath at anyone who displeases them and...thereby block off an important route to close friendships" (Tavris 1984). A 1986 study by Susan Hazaleus and Jerry Deffenbacher revealed that 45 percent of angry male subjects had suffered a "terminated or damaged" relationship during the previous year.

Divorce statistics underscore the role of anger in marriage breakups. Fifty-two percent of U.S. divorces are granted on grounds of either physical or emotional cruelty (Pino 1982). A study by psychologist Debra Weaver and Darlene Shaw at the medical school of South Carolina found that hostile Type A women had significantly worse marriages than Type B's (Wood 1986). The same result would almost certainly have been found if Type A men had been studied. In his famous book, *Marital Separation*, Robert Weiss concluded that separations usually follow a "long and anguished process of mutual alienation from which both partners emerge bruised...their ability to function damaged by the varied assaults of a failing marriage" (Weiss 1985). Anger plays a major role not only in the breakup, but the gradual decline and disenchantment of a rocky marriage.

Loneliness

Anger has been associated with loneliness by a number of researchers. One study which reviewed much of the previous research on loneliness found that anger cuts people off from social support in two ways. First, cynical attitudes toward others can result in a failure to recognize that real support is available. Secondly, unrealistic and overly demanding expectations can make available support seem worthless and lacking. In either case, the angry person cannot *feel* the support that exists. No matter how sincerely interested others may be in him, the judging, angry person simply doesn't see or appreciate it (Hansson, Jones, and Carpenter 1984).

Jones, Freeman, and Gasewick (1981) found that hostility, alienation, and negativistic attitudes were linked to such factors as low self-esteem and loneliness. An angry, unaccepting view of humanity and a picture of the world as an unjust place are associated with greater isolation.

It's clear that angry people keep others at bay. But in so doing they experience less support, less enjoyment, and a greater feeling of loneliness than their nonhostile counterparts.

Isolation and Illness

Anger-induced isolation affects you physically as well as psychologically. While the hormonal changes associated with chronic anger have been directly linked to cardiovascular and gastric disease, these are by no means the only physiological effects of anger.

Anger affects your body indirectly because people who lose or have weakened social ties are far more susceptible to disease of all types. In their fine book, *The Healing Brain*, Ornstein and Sobel (1987) point out that the incidence of infections, cancer, tuberculosis, arthritis, and problems during pregnancy are all higher for people who have fewer social supports. Other researchers have added diabetes, hypertension, and asthma to the list (Hansson, Jones, and Carpenter 1984). People who are divorced, separated, or have few close friends have a death rate two to five times that of married peers (Berkman and Syme 1979).

The relationship between isolation and a broad range of illnesses may explain why *hostile people have higher death rates from all causes* (Barefoot, Dahlstrom, and Williams 1983). As social supports weaken due to chronic anger, so do the body's defenses against a host of diseases and infections.

Assessing the Cost of Your Anger

Now is the time to ask yourself some serious questions. How is anger affecting you? What toll is it taking on your body and your relationships? Fill out the following assessment as objectively as you can and see what you learn.

Anger Impact Inventory

0 = No Effect
1 = Minor Effect
2 = Moderate Effect
3 = Very Significant Effect
4 = Major Effect

Instructions: Using the five-point scale, rate the degree of impact your anger has on the following:

                                                                    Rating

1. Relationships to authorities (teachers, bosses,
   police, government employees, and so on)   ____
2. Relationships to peers and colleagues at work   ____
3. Relationships to subordinates at work   ____

4. Relationships to customers, clients, business _____
   associates, and so on
5. Relationships to children _____
6. Relationships to children's teachers, other _____
   parents
7. Relationships to spouse or lover _____
8. Relationships to previous spouse or lover _____
9. Relationships to in-laws _____
10. Relationships to parents _____
11. Relationships to other family members _____
12. Relationships to current friends _____
13. Relationships to former friends _____
14. Relationships to neighbors _____
15. The role of anger in lost relationships _____
16. Relationships to recreational groups or _____
    organizations
17. Relationships to religious groups or _____
    organizations
18. Relationships to political and other groups _____
19. Impact on your health of anger episodes _____
20. Effect of anger symptoms (rapid heart rate, _____
    tension, shoulder and neck pain, headache,
    irritability, feeling of pressure, restlessness,
    insomnia, brooding, and so on)
21. Time lost to angry feelings _____
22. Anger intrusion into relaxing or pleasurable _____
    activities (sex, sports, hobbies, day in the
    country, vacations, and so on)
23. Effect of anger on drinking or drug use _____
24. Effect of anger on creativity or productivity _____
25. Effect of anger on experience while driving _____
26. Accidents, errors, and mistakes _____

As you examine your inventory, see if any patterns emerge. Are you angrier at work or at home? With intimates or more distant relationships? Do you tend to feel angrier with authorities and parents or with peers? Are your sexual relationships major battlegrounds? Have a significant number of relationships been lost in anger? Now is the time to identify one or two areas where you really want to concentrate your efforts. As you learn basic anger management skills in succeeding chapters, you may wish to practice these new skills in the critical areas that you are now identifying.

5

Anger as a Choice: The Two-Step Model of Anger

It's early evening. The TV is on. The kitchen is hot and full of oven smells. James and his mother, Sarah, begin the opening round of a familiar conflict.

Sarah: Is your homework done yet?

James: It's only six o'clock. I have all night to do it.

Sarah: Everybody has a job to do. This is my job right here, making dinner. You think I like standing in this hot kitchen? Your job is your schoolwork, and I don't see you doing it.

James: Look, I'm cooling out from school. Leave me alone.

Sarah: I want you to turn off the television and do your schoolwork. I'm sick of telling you. Just do your job like everybody else.

James: You think your job is to be the field marshal around here. Leave me alone. Go hassle Dad when he comes in.

Sarah (starting to shout): I'm sick of your mouth. Turn off the television, I said. You're lazy, you let your work go to the end, and then it's slipshod crap.

James (shouting): Stuff it, just stuff it. And you know where. You can't stand it when I relax; you never let me relax for a second. I guess you want everybody to be as crazy and screwed up as you are.

At this point a key is heard turning in the front door. James's father, Leonard, walks the short way to the kitchen. He leans against the counter and begins speaking in a quiet, compressed voice.

Leonard: What's going on in here? What's the matter with you? I'm walking up thinking, "finally I can relax," and I hear you screaming like banshees in here. (*He grows louder.*) James, did I hear you calling your mother crazy? Is that a way to talk? Do you want to shout? Why don't you shout at me? (*He moves towards James.*) Why don't you shout at me, huh? Why don't you try it? See how it feels. (*He pushes James backward.*) Nothing? You don't want to shout? (*He turns to Sarah.*) What's the matter with the two of you? What's wrong in this house? (*He shouts.*) Why don't you learn to talk to each other? Bickering, bickering. This place is like a damn asylum!

None of the participants wanted this fight. In retrospect, James described it as "spontaneous combustion—like we're a pile of dry leaves waiting for a spark." But Sarah, James, and Leonard are caught in a pattern that is anything but spontaneous. Each of them brings to the conflict a unique and largely unacknowledged group of stresses. Stress is the fuel of anger, because it creates high levels of physiological arousal that must be discharged. But stress does not, by itself, create anger. Each combatant also must bring a set of "trigger thoughts" that act as psychological flint to ignite the anger and aggression.

You can see how this works by viewing a "cognitive replay" of Sarah, James, and Leonard's fight. A cognitive replay documents the internal processes of each participant as reconstructed during a family therapy session.

Sarah's most immediate stresses are heat and fatigue. Additional stress comes from her unspoken fear that James is using drugs, a fear that she uses to explain his decreasing interest in schoolwork. Sarah also lives with a chronic level of frustration and sadness that James is much less close these days and reveals little about himself. She is hurt, too, that her husband has been distant and sexually unresponsive for the past several months. The decision to get angry occurs as Sarah listens to the sound of television in the living room. She uses two kinds of trigger thoughts to start her anger: shoulds and blamers.

Shoulds:
"Everyone must do his job."
"No one should watch television in the afternoon, it's lazy."

Blamers:
"He lets his work go to the end."
"His work is slipshod crap."

Sarah says variations of these four statements to herself throughout the fight with James. Each statement is like pushing down the handle of an emotional whirling top; she feels more and more righteous and angry.

James's stresses include muscle tension from a school day in which he felt unprepared for several classes and pain from a chronic knee injury aggravated during soccer practice.

James is also experiencing moderate levels of guilt over recent inattentiveness to his schoolwork. At the moment that the fight begins, he is experiencing high anxiety over a decision to call an attractive girl for a date. His strong drive to relax this tension is frustrated by his mother when she asks about his homework.

James triggers his anger with three blamers:

Blamers:
"You're trying to control me."
"You're deliberately preventing me from relaxing so I'll feel
     as bad as you do."
"You're crazy and screwed up."

Leonard's stresses include chronic tension in his neck and shoulders and rising anxiety over a recent symptom of skipped heartbeats. He is physically aroused from a rushed day filled with anxiety over new high production quotas instituted three months earlier. Leonard has a strong fear of rejection; the raised voices he hears as he walks in sound like threats that he will be hurt or abandoned.

Leonard triggers his anger with three blamers and two shoulds:

Blamers:
"They deny me a chance to relax."
"This house is crazy with bickering, a damn asylum."
"James is turning into a sullen, withdrawn ingrate."

Shoulds:
"James should never attack his mother."
"They should learn to talk to each other."

Sarah, James, and Leonard were each in pain. They each made an independent decision to cope with that physical and emotional stress by using anger-triggering thoughts to ignite a hostile outpouring. For a few moments the anger felt very good, the stress was masked or discharged. There was a release. In a while, the stress would be back—this time in the form of guilt or hurt or frustration. But in those few moments of discharge and relief, the strategy of anger was reinforced. When in pain, they would return again to the attack.

The Function of Anger

The sole function of anger is to stop stress. It does this by discharging or blocking awareness of painful levels of emotional or physical arousal. There are four kinds of stress that anger serves to dissipate.

1. **Painful affect.** Anger can block off painful emotions so that they are literally pushed out of your awareness. It can also discharge high levels of arousal experienced during periods of anxiety, hurt, guilt, and so on.

2. **Painful sensation.** Stress is often experienced as a physical sensation. The most common form is muscle tension, but stressful arousal may also stem from physical pain or sympathetic nervous system activity.

3. **Frustrated drive.** Anger can discharge stress that develops when you are frustrated in the search for something you need or want. It functions to vent high arousal levels that inevitably grow as drive activities are blocked.

4. **Threat.** Any perceived threat, either to your physical or psychological well-being, creates immediate arousal. The arousal mobilizes you and generates a very strong push for some stress-reduction activity.

Each of the four types of stress sets off a psychological alarm mechanism that tells you something is not right. As the arousal builds, so too does your need to cope with it, to stop the pain. As you'll soon discover, anger is just one of many coping strategies available to you to discharge stressful arousal.

How Anger Stops Stress

To understand how anger stops stress, it will be helpful to return to the four types of stressful arousal.

Painful Affect

Anxiety and fear. Consider the mother who, seeing her child run into the street, shakes him and shouts about his carelessness. Anger blocks and discharges her surge of fear so that the enormous terror of losing a child is hardly experienced before the rush of angry words. In the fight that opened this chapter, Leonard is afraid of failing at work and worries that there is something wrong with his heart. The arousal generated by these concerns is discharged for a while by his outburst.

Loss and depression. The stress is quieter, more aching here. But sadness creates a tension that is every bit as painful as fear and a need to escape the pain every bit as great. Consider the man whose girlfriend has announced her desire to date other people. The loss of intimacy and of sharing consumes him. Finally he upbraids his secretary for excessive typos, and there is a brief tension release until he resumes his sad review of lovely moments in the relationship.

Hurt. The pain of hurt can be so acute that anger is employed as a blocking mechanism almost immediately. A woman is criticized by her husband for being careless with money. She feels humiliated and dismissed. But within a few seconds her arousal is so high and so painful that she explodes in order to block any further awareness of it. You may remember that Sarah had been hurt by her husband's distance and sexual withdrawal. Some of that pain was discharged in her battles with her son.

Guilt and shame. Anger erases guilt. It is not you who has done wrong, but the other person. A woman comes home at six o'clock to find her son already in bed, lights out, surrounded by all his stuffed animals. When she asks what he's doing, he tells her that he's lonely. A wave of guilt surges up. As the arousal reaches intolerable levels, she reminds herself that his father never visits, and that's the real source of the problem. Now she is righteous and angry, discharging the guilt in a string of silent condemnations. In the opening fight, James's guilt over inattentiveness to his schoolwork was nicely buried under anger at this mother.

Feelings of failure, badness, and unworthiness. Consider the young man who shows some of his poetry to an English teacher. The teacher shows him how the lines don't communicate. For the next 15 minutes the young man wanders the halls, clutching his meaningless garble, feeling a deep worthlessness. The pain accelerates until he seizes on the teacher's accent and mannerisms to condemn him as an "affected twit." Many people have at their core a sense of wrongness or badness that can be activated with the smallest criticism or remark. Anger is a popular strategy to block awareness of these feelings and discharge any consciously felt pain that they might trigger.

Painful Sensation

Rushing. Leonard comes home after rushing to meet production quotas all day. He discharges stress by going on the attack.

Physical pain. You have undoubtedly noticed that when you hurt, you become tense. And with little effort, you can find something to get angry at. Imagine the scene where a man is dozing on the beach. His sons are kicking and chasing a beachball. One of them trips and falls on him. The man sits bolt upright and cuffs his boy because he has learned to relieve pain with anger.

Overstimulation. Too much excitement, too intense a conversation, the success of a great presentation at the board meeting, or a lucky day in the casino can all take their toll. The arousal from the good times may reach stressful levels. When you come home from a day of drama and intensity, anger may be your way of cooling down, of discharging the energy.

Muscle tension. In the process of coping with the day, most people gather tension in zones of vulnerability. The forehead, jaw, shoulders, and abdomen are the most common of these zones. Anger can sometimes relieve muscle tension by discharging energy until, in the aftermath, you finally relax.

Tiredness and overwork. Fatigue creates stress. Lactic acid builds up in your muscles until your discomfort forces you into some arousal-reduction strategy.

Frustrated Drive

Arousal from blocked needs or desires. This is the human condition, the struggle to have what there isn't enough of. Waiting and wanting. Consider the woman whose vacation is again and again delayed because co-workers fall unexpectedly ill and she is needed to fill in during their absence. Finally she is aroused to such a pitch that she attacks her boss as "uncaring and incompetent." She feels good. There is a moment of discharge. Then she is given her two weeks notice. In the opening fight, James's drive for recreation was frustrated when his mother demanded that he stop watching television. Anger was his chosen strategy to cope.

Things are not as they should be. Here the frustration is to one's sense of order, oughtness, perfection. Your picture of a world in which people act in good and correct ways is often violated. A checker puts your groceries in a single, flimsy bag. Your silent condemnation of his "wrongness" and "stupidness" creates painful arousal. Your daughter arrives home with a man friend dressed in purple leather. There is something wrong with the picture. As your tension rises, you wonder where she found this cross between a hippie and a motorcycle punk.

The sense of being forced. Not only aren't you getting your way, but you are being made to do something that's opposed to your needs or values. A man's lover insists on discussing "the problem of commitment" in their relationship. He knows from experience that she will feel hurt and withdraw if the issue is not explored. As the discussion continues, his tension rises until he blurts out something quite uncomplimentary about her recent haircut.

Threat

Feeling attacked. Here arousal is immediate. Anger is used to push away the threat so you can return to a relaxed state. Your boss announces that you are among a group of people who will be laid off. Your reaction is shock and a sudden surge in stress level. "Wait a minute, this isn't fair." You start to raise your voice. The anger helps you block awareness of the fear and tightness in your stomach.

Feeling engulfed. The experience is one of being controlled, of not having the right to set limits or say no. A teenager who felt overwhelmed by his father's rules and strictures could not bring himself to insist on greater freedom. He dealt with these threats to his autonomy by secretly burning important papers belonging to his father. A woman whose husband insisted that she forego all male friendships experienced this threat as tension in her diaphragm. "I felt I had to go along with it, but sometimes I'd want to scream. I knew if I screamed, I would feel better, so I imagined screaming the most horrible things at him."

Feeling abandoned. For a child, this is a threat to survival. Many adults experience abandonment as threatening in the very same way—as if their very existence were in danger, as if abandonment were death. Anger helps block awareness of the fear of loss and aloneness while mobilizing you to end the threat: to leave them before they leave you, to shake some sense into them, to make them hear your pain.

Alternative Stress-Reduction Strategies

There are many ways to discharge high levels of stress besides anger. Some of them are healthy, some are destructive. Any one of these can be used *instead of anger* when you are stressed. The following list is by no means inclusive, but will give you some ideas.

Crying. This is the first strategy you learn to cope with pain. Crying helps you discharge tension and discomfort, it relaxes tight muscles, it helps you communicate your needs.

Exercising. Walking, dancing, tennis, swimming—literally any aerobic reduces stress. (See Chapter 8.)

Intense work activity. Chores like washing the dishes and vacuuming, cooking, painting, fixing, and building, all function to reduce stress by channeling your energy into a focused task.

Humor. Looking at the light side, the absurdity of a situation. Poking fun at things. Reframing the stress as something much less serious, even silly.

Writing. Poetry and journal writing are effective vehicles for expressing and discharging feelings.

Relaxation exercises. Among the most effective are meditation, progressive muscle relaxation, deep breathing, autogenics, and self-hypnosis. (See Chapter 8.)

Verbalizing pain. The act of saying out loud that you hurt reduces painful stress. Even if you're shouting in your car or on an empty beach, just saying it is calming and sometimes even healing.

Recreation. Reading, TV, games, and hobbies act as psychological sponges that sop up stress.

Sex. Sex works well in two ways. First, it blocks awareness of painful feelings. Second, an orgasm has an enormous capacity to reduce tension from any source.

Problem-solving activities. Directing your energy toward fixing what's wrong reduces stress because you're dealing with the root problem. You anticipate some relief, you feel less helpless. (See Chapter 8.)

Problem-solving communication. Letting the other person know your needs, feelings, and limits reduces stress born of frustration. (See Chapter 12.)

Pillow and bed beating. This is a great way to have a private blowout. Sometimes using a tennis racket can make the pummeling louder and more satisfying.

Music. Whatever your taste or preference in decibels, music can be profoundly calming. A little time alone with a favorite recording is a nearly sure-fire strategy for reducing stress from any source.

Resting. A period of no activity can be very helpful. Even brief rest periods, like counting or taking a deep sigh before making a response, can bring a moment of relative calm.

There are also many arousal reduction strategies that are effective, but self-destructive. Included here are alcohol and drugs, recklessness and danger seeking, compulsive sex, and taking the helpless position. All of these can block, numb, or reduce pain, but their effectiveness is outweighed by obvious negative consequences.

The number of alternative stress-reduction strategies should make it clear that anger is only one of many possible responses to painful levels of arousal. In fact, anger is among the least effective of the listed strategies. It costs too much because it takes such a huge toll on you physiologically and because it damages relationships. The truth is that anger is rarely necessary. There are better ways to cope with stress than to go on the attack. Anger is usually effective only in the short term as a stress-reduction strategy. In the long run, it harms your health and isolates you. This book will help you develop more effective strategies to cope with the stress that underlies your anger.

Why You Choose Anger To Reduce Stress

There are three factors influencing the choice of any stress-reduction strategy, whether it's crying, relaxing, problem solving, or anger. The first is *physiological predisposition.*

You are born with a set of constitutional tendencies that make some responses easier or more rewarding than others. Some people are neurologically wired in such a way that anger tends to work better for arousal reduction than certain other strategies they have tried. However, a predisposition is just that. It's a tendency, a response that may be a little easier than other responses. While anger may be constitutionally somewhat easier or more effective for you in temporary stress reduction, you *can* learn other strategies.

The second major influence on the choice of a stress-reduction strategy is *instrumental conditioning.* This is the process by which, as a child, certain behaviors were reinforced while others were discouraged. If you had a tantrum and were given what you wanted, the effect was to reinforce tantrum behavior. If you demanded your sister's block set and she refused and you then hit her and she acquiesced, you were reinforced for hitting. If your mother gave in when you shouted, you learned that shouting was rewarded. At the same time, as a child, you could have been rewarded for any of the other stress-reduction strategies.

Intense work activity or problem-solving communication or verbalizing your pain could have been reinforced. Everyone responds in ways that he or she has learned to be effective. Anger is nothing more than a learned response to certain kinds of stress. In your family, anger worked well enough for it to become part of your adult strategic arsenal.

The last major factor in determining your choice of stress-reduction strategies is *social learning*. Social learning involves the skills and behaviors that you acquired through *modeling*. This is the process by which you imitate how parents and significant peers act. You try to do it like they do. You strive to look and sound and behave like your role model. If you grew up in a family where people coped with their pain by getting angry, no doubt you modeled some of your behavior on what you observed. If your parents were loud and threatening or blaming when they felt bad, then you are likely to use the same strategies when you feel bad. The old cliche "like father like son" is unfortunately true in terms of anger responses. Children very quickly learn how their parents cope and begin making it part of their own behavior patterns.

You use anger to control stress because of a unique combination of physiological predisposition, reinforcement, and social learning. But you do have a choice. This book offers new tools and skills in coping with painful levels of arousal. It is a matter of trying them to see which ones work best for you.

How You Create Anger

Anger is a two-step process. It usually starts with stress and the subjective experience of arousal that stress of any kind generates. Stress motivates you to begin coping. You want to lower or block these uncomfortable feelings. The *first step* in anger production concludes when your awareness of stress leads to a coping decision. While coping could include tears, relaxation, exercise, music, verbalizing, or problem solving, too frequently you may find yourself choosing to block and discharge pain through anger.

As you've seen, stress is not a sufficient cause for anger. You need the psychological flint of anger-triggering thoughts to convert stress into hostile affect. *Step two* in anger production is the process by which you focus on either *blamers* or *shoulds*.

Blamers. Here the generic thought is "you deliberately did _____ to me." The key idea is that you have been intentionally harmed by the wrong behavior of another.

Shoulds. The generic thought here is "you should not have _____ but instead you should have _____." The implication is that the person knows or should know how to act correctly and has, out of stupidity or selfishness, broken the rules of reasonable conduct.

Both kinds of trigger thoughts have, as a core belief, a perception of the other person as bad, wrong, and deserving of punishment. When Leonard says to himself, "They deny me the chance to relax," the implication is that Sarah and James are deliberately harming him. They are bad and should be punished. When Sarah says to herself, "Everyone must do his job," she sees James as breaking a basic rule of life. He is doing wrong and should be punished. When James blames his mother for trying to control him, he sees her as the "field marshal" deliberately inflicting harm. His response is to want to hurt her back.

Stress (painful arousal) plus trigger thoughts equal anger. You cannot have anger without both components being present. Trigger thoughts without arousal produce a judgment without emotion. Arousal without trigger thoughts leaves you in a chronic state of pain until you choose an alternative stress-reduction strategy.

The Anger Cycles

The anger cycle can start in two ways.

1. Arousal/stress ⎯⎯⎯⎯→ Trigger Thoughts

Anger

This is the conventional cycle described throughout this chapter. Notice that stress begets trigger thoughts, which beget anger, more trigger thoughts, more anger, and so on. Your thoughts and angry feelings become a feedback loop which can be self-perpetuating. The feedback loop is what keeps your anger simmering for hours or even days without letup.

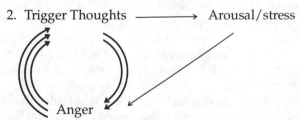

2. Trigger Thoughts ⟶ Arousal/stress

Anger

In cycle two, the trigger thoughts create a stress reaction (however brief), which then fuels anger. Some trigger thoughts are sufficiently provocative to create arousal where none previously existed. Arthur wonders if his wife will work long hours at her law office again tonight. The image of himself sitting through news shows and sitcoms waiting for her key in the door triggers a deep sense of abandonment. But he thinks that the pain is her fault. Almost instantly he converts the stressful feeling into anger. Now the anger stirs more trigger thoughts: "She doesn't care really about our marriage—there's that weekend where she decided to go away by herself, and the habit of reading in bed, and the fights about who was supposed to shop." Arthur is now caught in the feedback loop. Trigger thoughts breed more anger, which sets off more trigger thoughts, followed by more anger, and so on.

In cycle two, there is always an intervening moment of pain (loss, rejection, despair, fear, frustration, hurt, abandonment) between the trigger thought and the anger. But the perception that the pain is someone else's fault quickly ignites the anger and establishes the feedback loop.

Implications

As you come to understand the two-step process in anger production, it may affect some of your basic assumptions about the emotion. Consider the following implications of this model.

There Is Nothing Inherently Right or Legitimate About Anger

The only thing true and indisputable when you feel angry is that you are in pain and trying to do something about it. The trigger thoughts that you use to generate your anger may be false, or at best very debatable, and your anger may therefore have no legitimate basis. When Leonard tells himself that his son is a "sullen, withdrawn ingrate," these are global generalities that grossly exaggerate aspects of his son's behavior. This triggering thought is just plain wrong, and Leonard's feeling that James deserves punishment is equally wrong. His anger is not legitimate, it is not "right." When James decides that his mother is keeping him from relaxing because she wants him to feel as bad as she does, he is falsely assuming that his mother wishes him to feel pain. His decision to punish and attack her is based on an erroneous premise. Again, his anger has no legitimate basis.

The computer world uses the catch phrase "garbage in, garbage out." The same is true of your emotions. If you use triggering statements that are false or distorted versions of reality, the emotional storm that erupts is a response not to a real issue, but to an imagined violation. In the next chapter, you'll see that much of your anger may fall into this category.

Remember, your real motivation in getting angry is to reduce or discharge the arousal that comes from stress. The triggering statements you use may be quite arbitrary; they may even be total self-deceptions that you would deplore in a calmer moment. But at the time, you're not particularly concerned if your perceptions are true. What you want is to release or to block the pain.

Ventilationists claim that anger should be expressed because feelings have inherent legitimacy. As you've seen, a moment of anger can be fueled by many different, simultaneous experiences of stress. While the pain is important, and perhaps even the expression of pain is important, the anger is usually destructive. It is not the anger that needs to come out, but the pain (stress) that underlies the anger. It is not the anger that is legitimate and right, but the human suffering that must be acknowledged and explored.

The Dam of Anger

The ventilationists would have you believe that there is a great dam inside you, holding back a reservoir of anger and angry impulses. In this "hydraulic theory" of anger, unexpressed angry feelings build and build. Finally the accumulated weight bursts through, shattering your mask of calmness. The ventilationists are wrong. It is not anger that builds, but stress. Stress of all types and from all sources: emotional pain, physical pain, frustration, and threat. As long as stress persists without remedy, you will continue to feel tension and arousal. The stress grows. Anger, as you have seen, is merely one of many possible strategies you can use to cope. Failing to express your anger *does not build up more anger*. It does not, in itself, increase your stress. Choosing not to express anger merely means that the arousal will continue at painful levels until you find a way to reduce it.

If Sarah had decided not to express anger, she might have reduced the stress in other ways. She might have suggested eating out that night to escape the hot kitchen. She might have chosen to discuss her fears about drug use with James or to share with him her feeling of being excluded from his life. Or she might have done some problem solving around television and homework. Holding in her anger would not create more anger. In fact, her anger is keeping her from really doing something about the causes of her stress. It masks the pain without really changing anything.

The same is true for Leonard. He is tense and scared about failing at work and having a heart attack. Choosing not to express his anger won't have the effect of damming up his rage for some later, more destructive explosion. It would merely mean having to live with the stress for a while until he finds another way to cope: a medical exam, seeking feedback from his boss, relaxation exercises for his shoulder spasms, and so on. Leonard's anger masks the real problem and obscures the path to real solutions.

Forget Displacement

Displacement theory holds that there is an appropriate target for your anger. In healthy anger, you express your feelings to the appropriate person or in the appropriate setting. Displacement is seen as a less healthy alternative. Here you take anger that belongs with one target and direct it to another less threatening target. You can't shout at your boss, so you go home and scream at your wife. You can't say it to your girlfriend, so you take it out on your mother.

In the two-step model of anger, displacement is an irrelevant issue. Anger is a response to stress, and its function is to discharge or block awareness of that stress. It may feel somewhat more cathartic to express anger to the person you associate with your pain, but as you have seen with Sarah, James, and Leonard, the anger is rarely about the real issues anyway. All anger usually does is temporarily reduce tension. Whether you ventilate to the appropriate person or displace your feelings onto a less threatening object, the underlying stress is rarely addressed in a constructive way. Angry people become too defensive to engage in real problem solving. So don't ask yourself, "Did I get angry at the right person?" Ask yourself, "Did I express the pain in a way that may lead to a solution?"

You Choose To Be Angry

It may seem like a revolutionary thought, but you do *choose* to feel angry. Up to now, the choice has been largely unconscious. It's a habit, based on years of conditioning. Anger is a strategy you use to cope with many kinds of stress because to some degree and at some times it works for you. Now what was hidden can be observed. What was unconscious can be consciously experienced. When you feel stress, you can choose not to take the second step. You can begin consciously turning away from anger-triggering thoughts.

Developing the awareness that you choose trigger thoughts to cope with stress is easier said than done. Right now, this is an abstract idea. Interesting, perhaps. Maybe a little threatening. You can make this real for you by studying your own process and developing an intimate awareness of how your anger works. To accomplish this essential task you will need to do more work in your anger journal.

New Entries for Your Anger Journal

The anger journal is an important part of the work you'll do to change your anger. For the next two days at least, make an entry in your journal on each occasion that you feel angry. Sometimes you won't be able to take notes right away, but please go back and try to reconstruct the processes leading to your anger.

There are four questions you need to ask in your journal in order to more fully understand each occasion of anger.

1. What stresses preexisted my anger? Prior to the moment of anger, were you aware of any painful feelings such as hurt, anxiety, sadness, or guilt? Did you experience any sense of threat, frustration, or uncomfortable physical sensations?

2. What trigger thoughts did you use? Think back to exactly what was in your mind at the moment you became aware of the anger. What were the thoughts that ignited your feelings? Try to recall any shoulds. Remember, the generic should statement is "You should not have _____, but instead you should have _____." The should statement carries the implication that the other person is bad and must be made to admit his or her wrongdoing. Also, try to recall any blamers: "You deliberately did _____ to me." Note your asumption that the other person is culpable, that he or she has harmed you with intent. Can you identify the point where the trigger thoughts turn your stress into anger?

3. Were you angry or were you feeling some other kind of stress *before* the trigger statements? In some cases, this may seem very hard to answer. Anger has a strange halo effect, seeming to bathe the entire memory in a feeling of outrage and wrongness. The trigger thoughts lead you to the perception that you are a victim, that you have been "done to" by someone. It's hard to go back to the moment you decided that someone was "responsible" for your pain. However, it is that very moment where the anger began. Your stress was transformed then into hostile affect.

4. Was some of your preexisting stress blocked or discharged by the anger? Note in your journal whether you felt better, even for a few brief moments after you became angry.

The stress certainly may have come back, but did the anger give you even a few seconds of relief? Relief, no matter how short in duration, is highly reinforcing.

Do your journal work before reading the next chapter. It will help give you a foundation of awareness to build on as you learn more about the many specific cognitive triggers for anger and begin developing skills to resist them.

6

Who's Responsible

When you're in pain, you very often ask yourself, "Who did this to me, who's responsible?" The impulse to assign blame lies at the root of chronic anger. As soon as you decide that someone is responsible for your anxiety or hurt or physical tension, you feel justified in discharging your stress with anger. The perception that someone has caused your pain turns you into a victim. You see yourself as threatened, under seige by another's wrongdoing.

There is a pleasure in blaming. When someone else is responsible, you can turn your focus away from your pain and concentrate on listing the sins and the injustices that you have suffered. The stress is blocked or discharged and for a while you feel better.

But there's a problem with the habit of finding others responsible for your pain. It isn't true. You are solely responsible for the quality of your life. Whether you are in pain or not, whether your needs are met or not, whether your relationships feel good or not, is entirely determined by the choices you make. There are four reasons why you, and only you, are responsible for your experience.

1. **You are the only one who really knows and understands your own needs.** You are the expert on what feels good and what feels bad to you, your tastes and aversions, the subtle hurts, the hidden dreams, the slight but important difference between kinds of touching. Others can only guess about what rewards you and where you are vulnerable. They are hopelessly locked outside of your inner experience.

Much of what seems obvious to you about your needs is hidden from even your intimates. Consider the man who feels great resentment because his wife rarely touches his penis during foreplay. He has told her several times during the past year that "it would be nice" if she touched his genitals more often. But his wife has no way of knowing how deep his desire is or precisely what sort of touching feels most stimulating to him. Nonetheless, he blames her for not really caring about his pleasure.

2. It is appropriate for others to focus on meeting their own needs. Their first responsibility must be to take care of themselves, to minimize pain, to provide for their own emotional nourishment, and to pursue those experiences that they find most satisfying. It is NOT the responsibility of others to take care of you. If others place your needs above their own, then they must neglect their own first responsibility of preserving their own lives and well-being.

If you feel that others should be willing to endure pain so that you won't have to, or give up what is emotionally or physically nourishing so that you can be nourished, then you are expecting a degree of altruism that is rarely encountered. Even the Christian ethic of loving others as yourself assumes that you first provide for your own needs (by loving yourself) before you give to others. Consider the woman who wanted her husband to give up watching TV sports on the weekend so that they could take drives in the country. She was enraged that he wouldn't "do something I would enjoy." The fact was that he despised driving because he spent long hours on the road during his workweek. Only when she came to accept that her husband's responsibility was to take care of his needs and not hers was she able to generate real solutions to her problem. By organizing weekend trips to the Napa Valley (winetasting was one of his hobbies), she was finally able to entice him into a car.

3. Peoples' needs inevitably conflict. Everyone on the planet struggles to get basic needs met, and the struggle often leads to disagreement and competition. Every relationship must come to terms with this basic reality: the pursuit of one person's needs will frequently mean discomfort and frustration for the other. You may be tempted to ignore this reality by redefining your needs as "doing what's right" while dismissing the needs of others as a selfish indulgence. But this view belies the fact that your need to feel good and avoid pain is no more important than anyone else's.

The solution that usually works best for conflicting needs is compromise, giving something to get something. Helen, a 34-year-old mother of two, was angered because her ex-husband brought the children home late from visits. While she waited for her kids, anxiety rose as she imagined them being abducted. The fear was unnerving, so Helen pushed it away with her anger. When she reframed the problem as a collision of needs, steps toward a solution began to present themselves. In a discussion with her ex-husband, she learned that he tended to return late because he wanted to spend more time with the children. He told her that he especially enjoyed taking them on day-long outings, and so he often had a hard time meeting her three o'clock deadline. Her need was predictability; his need was more time. He proposed a seven o'clock deadline, and after some bargaining they agreed to a six o'clock limit with a phone call if he were going to be late.

4. Your overall life satisfaction depends on the effectiveness of your strategies for meeting needs and avoiding pain. By making others responsible for your needs, you are obscuring this basic law of human interaction. If you're unhappy, it means that the strategies that you typically use to get nourishment aren't working.

Consider the case of Al, whose girlfriend said he never listened. He reacted by expressing anger and withdrawing. Al's strategy wasn't effective because his girlfriend only became angry in turn and intensified her criticism. The problem doesn't lie with the criticism, but with the effectiveness of Al's strategy for dealing with it. Evenually he developed a better way of coping: he responded by expressing hurt rather than anger and then encouraged his girlfriend to express the specific needs underlying her global criticism. The same analysis can be made of his girlfriend's side in the exchange. She needed attention, but her strategy of blame and anger triggered Al's withdrawal. Only when she developed a more effective way of coping would there be any real chance for improvement in the relationship.

The Principle of Personal Responsibility

To understand how the principle of personal responsibility can change your anger, start with the assumption (whether you believe it or not) that (1) *you are responsible for your own pain*, and (2) *you are the one who must change your coping strategies to better meet your needs.* Applying this rule can revolutionize your attitude toward problematic situations as it allows you to shift from helpless anger to an awareness of the control that you have in each situation. Consider the following real cases.

Case 1.   Irene describes Ms. Late and Loquacious.

"Nora arrives half an hour to an hour late for everything. You sit in the restaurant, the waiter brings you endless cups of coffee while you twiddle your thumbs. Finally she blows in with a hundred apologies and you make your biggest mistake of the day: you ask her how she is. Thus begins the litany, the anecdotes, the meanderings. The next time you open your mouth it's to ask the waiter for a dessert menu. It's interesting, I'll grant you, but Nora's talked for 45 minutes nonstop without asking a single thing about me." Irene was so angry that she considered getting up and walking out on the luncheon. Let's use the two-step model of anger to examine her experience.

Stress: Irene is hurt and frustrated in her desire for attention and acknowledgment. "It's like I wasn't even there."

Trigger thoughts: "Nora's a self-centered motor-mouth... doesn't give a damn if she's late...doesn't care a bit about anybody but herself."

The trigger thoughts created a reality in which Irene felt victimized by the wrong and selfish behavior of her friend. When Irene learned the principle of personal responsibility, she began to accept that Nora was neither right nor wrong, but merely had very different needs. The activities that delayed Nora were simply a higher priority for her than being on time. And Nora's need to talk about her experience was considerably larger than her need to hear the experience of others. With the luncheon interaction reframed as a problem of conflicting needs, Irene was able to give up the expectation that Nora would take care of her and begin to develop new strategies to meet her own needs. Here's what she decided.

1. I'm really responsible here because I'm the one who chooses whether to see Nora or not. I have choices about how to structure the visit and how I act in the course of the conversation.
2. I can choose to have lunch with Nora only in a group so it doesn't matter if she's late. Or I can pick her up at her house. Or I can bring a good book so that I won't mind waiting. I know that she'll usually be late, so it's up to me to take care of myself.
3. Nora's conversational style isn't going to change, so I'll have to interrupt her to get my own stories in. I'll just barge in by saying "That reminds me of the time..." I can break in rather than politely waiting for her to finish or ask me a question.

Notice that the rule of personal responsibility creates new options for problem solving. None of these solutions could possibly come to mind while focusing on trigger thoughts and the feeling of being victimized. When you're a victim, the responsibility always seems to be on the *other* person to change and make things better.

Case 2. Arthur describes the Jungian work junkie. "Sylvia lives at the typewriter. They keep asking her to present papers and she keeps saying yes. Case studies, monographs, even something on Jung's garden. She's a slave to it and we find ourselves nodding in the hall on our way to our respective studies. Pleasing every Tom, Dick, and Harry who has a sand tray is more important to her than our relationship. Some pitifully irrelevant paper matters more than a nice weekend together or going dancing."

Stress: Arthur feels hurt and lonely; he has a frustrated need for recreation.

Trigger thoughts: "Sylvia doesn't care about me...she chooses to please others at the expense of our relationship...she prepares trivial lectures and papers rather than making time to enjoy each other."

The trigger statements turn Arthur into a victim. He is helpless, while Sylvia's behavior is labeled wrong and outrageous. The trigger statements are an absolution that relieves Arthur of any responsibility for an empty marriage. After exploring the principle of personal responsibility, Arthur was able to reframe the problem as a conflict between his need for emotional closeness and his wife's need for social approval. He began to recognize that no one was to blame, but if he wanted to change the situation he would have to use new coping strategies. By taking responsibility for his own wants he was able to make the following decisions:

1. I'll buy that book on bed and breakfast inns and make reservations far in advance for weekend trips.
2. The only way to get Sylvia away from the typewriter is to create something more attractive, so I'll whip together a romantic candlelit dinner once a week.
3. Racquetball is the one sport we share. With a family membership in a racquetball club, I'm sure she'd be willing to schedule one night a week to play.
4. We haven't done much with the massage class we took. I'll schedule time with her each week for mutual massage.
5. Sylvia's needs are such that I don't think she'll cut down on the academic work (unless she gets too busy having fun). But I'll ask that she travel to conferences and training seminars no more than once every three months. If she doesn't like that, I'll try the fallback position of travelling with her to weekend conferences.

Case 3. Dumping Marty. "I've known this guy since high school. We're close. Sean and I get together once or twice a week, play cards or backgammon, eat dinner, talk about his life, my life. But every damn time he gets interested in a woman the whole thing evaporates. It's like he's saying, 'Forget it guy, first things first,' I feel like he doesn't give a shit. Like it's OK hanging out with me until something better comes along. I saw him last week and he ran off to her right after dinner. And what gets me is I know when things don't work out it'll be like old times again."

Stress: Marty has feelings of loss and abandonment.

Trigger thoughts: "He doesn't give a shit...I'm a fill-in till something better comes along...I'm being used."

Marty made Sean responsible for his own feeling of loss. Like an animal in winter, he saw himself malnourished, living on scraps. He was helpless during the seasons of closeness and distance. The principle of personal responsibility made it possible for Marty to change his perspective and explore new ways to cope. It was important to face, without blame or judgment, that Sean had a very high need for sexual intimacy. Sean was merely taking care of himself, and Marty needed to do the same. After a good deal of thought, he made the following decisions.

1. I can't put all my eggs in one basket. I'm going to develop my friendships with John and Louise, schedule regular lunches, movies, and so on.
2. I'm responsible for getting my needs met, I'll have to create a situation where Sean will want to spend time with me. I know his new girlfriend is busy Saturday afternoon teaching piano. I'll suggest we get together at that time. Sean likes to play pool, and we can meet down at Town and Country for a few racks and some lunch.
3. I can also be frank with him and say I feel somewhat discarded with each new relationship. I can tell him that I would like to see him at least once a week and find out if he sees any way of doing that.

Case 4. Joan, the reluctant accountant. "Since I spend my life balancing books, Bob and I agreed that he'd pay our bills and handle the checkbook. But he's unbelievably lazy about it. The bills lie unpaid, we get late notices, we get collection notices! I can't believe it, he's willing to destroy our credit rating because he can't get off his ass and pay some bills. Bob doesn't even pay the mortgage, and I worry that some day I'll find a notice of intent to repossess buried in the pile. It's a nightmare, and he's such an irresponsible jerk about it."

Stress: Joan feels anxiety.

Trigger thoughts: "He's lazy...irresponsible...he's destroying our credit rating and could lose us the house."

Joan's anger was built on her assumption that she was a victim of Bob's irresponsibility. By learning to take 100 percent responsibility for her need to reduce financial anxiety, she began to consider the following options.

1. Do the bills myself.
2. Give my husband reinforcement for doing them. For example, we could set deadlines for the bills and take a nice weekend trip if he got them done.

3. I could pay someone I know to balance the accounts and write the checks. All we'd have to do is sign them.
4. I could negotiate. If Bob would do the bills by an agreed deadline, I could offer something in return.

Case 5. Julie's emptiness. "There are times I just feel lonely. Even though he's there I just feel it. It's worse when I have deadlines, and it's worse with the hideous PMS. It's funny, Richard always seems to choose those times to withdraw. Every time I say I need more support he gets angry and accuses me of demanding too much. So I tell him that he deliberately withholds support at the very time I need it most. Then Richard gets more upset and shouts that I'm a demanding bitch. I tell him he's a self-centered, vulgar asshole. Then we really start shouting and sometimes we even slap each other. It's the same thing over and over: I tell him I'm lonely or ask him why he's so far away; he gets very mean, very brutal."

Stress: Julie has feelings of emptiness, rushing, abdominal cramping.

Trigger thoughts: "He deliberately withholds...he's ungiving...doesn't care...selfish asshole...vulgar and brutal."

Julie believed that her husband was responsible for her pain. Her main strategy for getting support was to remind him that he was withholding in the hope that he'd be moved to change. Despite consistent failure with this strategy, Julie continued to use blaming-style attacks because she saw Richard having all the power to give or withhold what she needed.

The principle of personal responsibility changed Julie's perspective. She began to accept that her pain was her responsibility. She was the only one who really understood her needs and it was her job to develop strategies to meet them. She learned that the failure of one strategy only meant she would have to develop a more effective one. She decided on the following course of action.

1. Get medical help for the PMS.
2. My old way of asking for support is too vague. It always ends up sounding like a complaint. From now on I won't comment on how distant or unavailable Richard is. I'll

merely suggest doing different things that I know will feel good to me.

3. If he's unwilling to do anything that moment, I'll suggest scheduling something where we'll have a lot of contact, such as dinner out. In the meantime, I'll get support from a friend so I feel less focused on his withdrawal.

4. I'll give myself three months to work on better strategies to help me feel closer. If I still experience strong bouts of loneliness, I'll insist on therapy.

5. If he resists therapy, I'll need to consider the possibility of separating.

Case 6. Ariel, the good daughter. "He's got his beacon-red nose and this funny high step from losing feeling in his feet. And he's killing my mother with his demands, his screaming criticism if she makes a microscopic mistake. Drunk or sober, he's relentlessly cruel. I'm doing his laundry, taking him to the doctor, I'm running from store to store helping him find the right wingtips. But I can't not do it. If I tell him to stuff it, the whole burden of his selfish ass will fall on my mother. He's the kind of father who belongs in a Dickens novel. Always putting me down, always angry, and he gets meaner on booze. She'll never leave him because she feels she has no way of supporting herself. So I have to take care of that old disgusting man. I can't leave her to cope with him alone."

Stress: Ariel feels hurt, threatened, and forced.

Trigger thoughts: "He's a mean drunk...cruel...disgusting... selfish. He's trapped my mother and he's trapping me."

Ariel *is* trapped, but not by her father. She is held captive by the perception that her father is responsible for her pain. She sees her mother and herself as victims of a punishing and demanding monster. In blaming her father for her pain, she has handed control of her life to a very toxic person. When Ariel was introduced to the principle of personal responsibility, she resisted the concept. "How am I responsible for the pain this man causes me? I love my mother, and my love for her obligates me to protect her as best I can."

What Ariel didn't grasp was that the principle of personal responsibility applied to her mother as well as herself. Her mother, too, was responsible for the decision to stay in this painful relationship. She had not been willing to pay the financial and emotional price to free herself from this angry man. By seeing her mother as a victim (denying the real choices that her mother had made), Ariel maintained her own identity as victim.

If Ariel took responsibility for her pain, she would arrange private visits with her mother while curtailing contact with her father. Her mother would have to make the best decisions she could in dealing with the angry man she had married.

Six Steps to Responsibility

In the cases just discussed, taking responsibility resulted in making important decisions that changed the situation. There are six ways to exercise responsible decision making when you are unhappy with someone's behavior.

1. Develop more effective strategies for reinforcing others. In Case 2, Arthur decided to schedule pleasurable weekend trips and join a racquetball club with his wife. He knew that these activities were reinforcing to her and might be an enticement away from academic pursuits. Likewise, in Case 4, Joan considered the strategy of making fun weekend trips contingent on Bob finishing the bills.

2. Take care of the need yourself. Again in Case 4, Joan considered taking over responsibility for the bills, rather than waiting helplessly for Bob to send them out. In Case 1, Irene decided to bring a book, pick up her friend, or only meet her friend in groups so that the problem of lateness wouldn't bother her.

3. Develop new sources of support, nourishment, and appreciation. Here the emphasis is on going elsewhere for what you need, rather than continuing to make demands on someone who is unable or unwilling to give you what you want. In Case 3, Marty goes on to develop alternative relationships, rather than keep "all of his eggs in one basket." In Case 5, Julie decides to seek the company of friends while waiting to set up an intimate evening with her husband.

4. Set limits. This is the art of saying no. Anger so often comes from feeling pressure to do specific things for others.

Your trigger thoughts may include the notion that people have no right to ask certain things of you, or that they want too much. The problem is not the requests that people make of you— they're entitled to ask for anything they want—the problem is your unwillingness to set limits. It's *your* responsibility to say no to the things you prefer not to do. If you don't give yourself permission to say no, you'll often wind up using anger as protection from the wants and needs of others.

Some people are very demanding. They've learned to be that way because it gets results. Taking responsibility means that you rarely waste time blaming people for their obnoxious or manipulative styles. You focus instead on how to get across the message that you have limits and are willing to do only so much. Limits are like good fences. They act as strict boundary lines to keep others from crossing into your territory. But while fences are plain to see, only you know your own limits. Only you can make them clear by saying them out loud. Remember Case 6, Ariel's reluctance to set limits for her father results in being used and abused.

5. Negotiate assertively. This is the process of directly asking for what you want. Since your needs often conflict with the needs of others, simply making requests is often not enough. You may have to offer something in exchange or make compromises so that each party in the negotiation feels satisfied. In Case 5, Julie decides to request shared activities that would bring her closer to Richard. If he resists, her fallback suggestion is to schedule something fun for later.

6. Let go. There are two ways of letting to. The first is to accept that the situation is not going to change and you will have to live with it. Resisting it or railing against it will only add to your frustration and unhappiness. Again in Case 5, Julie may eventually have to accept that her husband is much less supportive than she would prefer him to be. This may be an unavoidable negative in a relationship that has many positives that make it worth keeping. If Julie can accept this unchanging aspect of Richard's personality, it may reduce her overall sense of pain and alienation.

The second kind of letting go involves recognition of those situations and relationships that are unrewarding or toxic for you. Letting go involves facing first that the situation will not change, and second that it is costing you more than the benefits are worth. Ariel in Case 6 needs to literally let go of the relationship to her father. To do that, she will also have to give up some of the care-taking aspects of her relationship to her mother. Letting go is usually the choice reserved for those times when other pathways to responsibility have not worked. Yet it is perhaps the most important of your options. It is your ultimate protection, your last response to a closing helplessness where nothing seems to change and you are in pain.

Like Ariel, many angry people are afraid to face this option. They survive unhappily in marriages and jobs. They rage to drive away the pain. Of course, they have reasons for staying: someone depends on them, someone would be hurt, they would be alone, it would be a big financial loss, they would be rejected and disapproved of, and so on. But all the reasons reduce to a common thread: the angry person is unwilling to pay the price of letting go. He or she does not want to feel the loss, the rejection, the disapproval, the money fears, the guilt, or the aloneness. And so they're left with the stuck feeling, the sense of being a victim. Taking care of yourself often exacts a high price. But if you are unwilling to pay it, you are nonetheless responsible for that choice.

Taking Responsibility: An Exercise

This is your chance to examine some of the situations in which you have responded with anger. Think back to a recent occasion, ideally one that you have written down in your anger journal and one which you recall well. Now, in your anger journal, write down your answers to the following questions. The first two help you identify the "cause" of your anger. The last six questions will help you take responsibility by changing the focus from others to yourself.

1. **What stress underlay my anger?** When thinking about this question, look at both your antecedent stresses (those that preceded and contributed to the anger situation) and your

immediate stresses (those that grew directly out of the anger situation). Keep in mind the general categories of painful feelings, painful sensations, threats, and frustrated needs. (Refer back to Chapter 5 for a more detailed list.)

2. What were my trigger thoughts? Here write down all the things you said to yourself that inflamed your anger.

3. Are there more effective strategies than anger for reinforcing others to meet my needs? Since anger is frequently met with defensiveness, avoidance, or yet more anger, are there ways that you can reward people for doing what you want rather than punishing or attacking them? What can you offer the other person to reinforce desired behavior in this situation?

4. What can I do to meet my own needs (or reduce my stress)? Is there independent action you can take without relying on someone else?

5. Can I find other sources of support, nourishment, or appreciation besides the person with whom I feel angry? Are there other people or other situations that will give you some of what you need (or help you reduce your stress level)?

6. What limits do I want to set but feel afraid to acknowledge or insist on? Do you need to say no or reduce your involvement?

7. How can I negotiate for what I want? Can you make a direct, nonblaming request of the other person? Are you prepared to compromise, make counter suggestions, or offer something in return for the desired behavior? Write out your request and some possible compromises.

8. How might I eventually let go? If other strategies fail, you will have to let go of either your expectations in the situation or the person with whom you're struggling. In this case, which one will you choose? How will you implement your choice?

You probably found some of these questions difficult to answer. They go against the grain, because when you're angry you want to change the other person, not yourself. You have been turning to others to meet your needs and take away your pain. It's hard to reclaim this task as solely your own. Now, using the format on the next page, try applying these eight questions to other anger-producing situations in your life.

Analyzing My Anger

1. *Stresses*

   A. *Antecedent stresses:*
      Painful emotions
      Painful sensations
      Frustrated needs
      Threats

   B. *Immediate stresses:*
      Painful emotions
      Painful sensations
      Frustrated needs
      Threats

2. *Trigger thoughts*
   Blamers
   Shoulds
   They did something to me

3. Are there more effective strategies than anger for reinforcing others to meet my needs?

4. What can I do to meet my own needs (or reduce stress)?

5. Can I find other sources of support, nourishment, and appreciation besides the person with whom I feel angry?

6. What limits do I want to set but feel afraid to acknowledge or insist on.

7. How can I negotiate for what I want?
   My request: _____

   _____

   Possible compromises: _____

   _____

8. How might I eventually let go in the situation (if other strategies fail)?

Why It's Preferable To Take Responsibility

The first reason for taking responsibility is that anger costs you too much. Physically, anger makes you prey to ulcers, high blood pressure, and cardiovascular diseases. As you read in Chapter 3, anger releases powerful hormones in your body that prepare you to act aggressively. This is perfectly adaptive if you live in a primitive community where you must fight off threatening animals or other aggressive tribes. Those events are time-limited and the anger hormones quickly dissipate. But chronic, simmering anger is another matter. Your body is always revving up to fight, and this continuous arousal can eventually create illness.

Anger not only causes damage to your body, but also damages your relationships. Chapter 4 shows how angry people find themselves increasingly isolated. Friends and family get fed up with the tension and hostility. At first they become defensive, then grow less and less accommodating. Finally, they withdraw altogether. Most people are simply not willing to be pushed around by anger for an extended period of time. It's too aversive. It makes them feel controlled and hypervigilant for the first signs of a flareup.

The second reason for taking responsibility is that anger is an ineffective long-term strategy for changing others. In the short run, anger often works. People are hurt or shocked and they may exhibit temporary changes to avoid your wrath. But eventually, if you continue to use anger to coerce, people become inured to your attacks. They will resist or avoid you.

Consider the case of Julia. Shortly after getting married, she discovered that her husband was a couch potato. He spent the weekend drinking beer and watching sports. Julia felt lonely and frustrated in the desire to share more activities with her husband. She triggered anger by thinking of her husband as lazy and uncaring. "I really let him have it to get him off that couch. There were projects to do around the house and I wanted to have picnics and go hiking together." Julia was using her anger as a coercive force to make her husband change. And for most of the first year it worked. He felt scared and rejected each time she went on the warpath and he'd make efforts to appease her. After a time, however, he began to resist. In therapy, he described his reaction: "I always felt I had to do what she wanted or she'd be angry. I got resentful, I guess, and I didn't enjoy being with her as much. I got to the point where she accused me of not caring and she was right, I didn't care. I'd stay away from the house, I'd leave my clothes on the floor to deliberately annoy her, I'd make comments about her clothes—that really got her." As long as Julia's husband enjoyed her and wanted to please her, the anger worked. But soon enough he became desensitized to the upsets and less concerned about her feelings. He began to enjoy small passive-aggressive revenges. Within a matter of months Julia's strategy had backfired and the new marriage was deteriorating.

Seth used anger to "make the children behave." He was a single parent during the summer months when his children travelled 3,000 miles to live with him. The initial camaraderie and good feeling changed for Seth as he realized that his daughters took no responsibility around the house. They spent the day on the phone or watching soap operas. The background white noise of the TV was literally painful to him, and Seth experienced fatigue from the extra cooking, cleaning, and supervision of two children. He triggered his anger by telling himself that they *should* help more. Instead they were filling their heads with "video crap." When Seth used anger as a motivator to push the children into taking more responsibility, the initial response was frenetic cleaning and a surprise spaghetti dinner after work one night. Very gratifying. But in a week his daughters slacked off and Seth was angry again. He told the girls that they were testing him and they wouldn't get away with it. After a dozen angry go-rounds, the following response pattern emerged: sullenness and shouting back, followed by grudging help. The bare minimum. Following a summer of fighting, the girls left early for their mother's house. A week later, Seth got a letter from his ex-wife. No stranger herself to anger, she wrote: "Nice going, Seth. You ruined their summer. You know as much about parenting as you did about marriage. The way you get kids to do chores is to praise them. Make allowances and TV watching something they get *after* the work is done."

Some people learn faster than others that anger doesn't succeed as a long-term change strategy. Sherry wanted her husband to fold the laundry. After a month of argument and nagging, he had folded the laundry exactly once. She decided to switch strategies and make something he wanted contingent on something she wanted. She told him she would do his laundry only if he would participate by folding it. Two days after running out of shirts he was on the job.

Implications of the Principle of Personal Responsibility

1. **You are responsible for the outcome of all interactions.** If you are dissatisfied with how people are treating you, only you can make the necessary modifications in your behavior for the outcome to change. You are the one who knows what you want. And it is in your interest, not the other person's, that things change.

2. **If one strategy doesn't work to meet your needs or solve a problem, there is absolutely no point in blaming.** It's your responsibility to keep trying new strategies until something does work.

3. **The appropriate question is not "Who's responsible for my pain?" but "What can I do about it?"**

4. **The amount of support, appreciation, and help you are getting is all you can get, given the current strategies you are using.** No one will willingly give you more than you now receive if you continue your current methods. Moreover, if you use coercive strategies such as anger on a long-term basis, you can expect the support and appreciation you receive to diminish over time.

5. **You can't expect other people to change or to be different.** They are using the best problem-solving strategies available to them at the moment. These strategies may be painful to you or they may frustrate your needs, but they represent the other person's best coping solution given his or her stresses, skills, and available resources. The other person will only change with the perception that new behavior is in his or her best interest. Don't fight this one. It's a law of nature. Accepting it will make you far more effective in taking care of your own needs.

6. All relationships come down to two basic choices: adapt or let go. If your needs remain unmet, if the painful aspects of the relationship are unremitting, letting go is your only healthy choice. The alternative is chronic anger or depression. You can let go of either your expectations or of the relationship itself. In a basically rewarding relationship, where you have tried and failed to meet an important need, you may decide to let go the expectation that things will change. On the other hand, if the pain and frustration in a relationship outweighs its rewards, letting go will involve a movement away from the other person.

7. You are never a victim. The only true victims are children because they have so little control over the shape of their lives. An adult chooses to be a victim because an adult has choice. Ariel, in Case 6, saw herself victimized by her father's alcoholism. As a child she was a victim. As an adult, however, she could *choose* the degree of involvement that she wanted with different members of her family.

Coping Mantras

A coping mantra is something you can say to yourself when you're beginning to feel angry that will calm you and help you look for more adaptive choices. Mantras are usually contained in single sentences that distill an important truth or awareness. Read the following mantras and choose one or more of them to memorize and use in situations where you are responding with anger. They will help you remember to take responsibility.

1. I am responsible for what happens between us.
2. No point in blaming, try a new strategy.
3. What can I do about this?
4. The amount of support, help, and nourishment I am now getting is all I can get, given the strategies I am using.
5. People won't change unless I make it in their interest.
6. How can I reinforce him or her to change in this situation?
7. I may not like it, but he or she is using the best problem-solving strategy available right now.
8. Everyone is responsible for taking care of his or her own needs.
9. My choice is to adapt or let go.
10. Only children are victims, I always have a choice.

II

Skill Building

7

Combating Trigger Thoughts

A young woman sank back into the clients' chair and began her story. "I can't control my anger at my children," she said. "I scream, I shake them sometimes. It's hurting our relationship, and down the line I think it will affect their self-esteem. With my eldest I'm the worst. Totally nuts at times. I feel like slapping and slapping him till he shuts up."

"What are you thinking when you get so angry at your son?" the therapist asked.

"What a brat, what a selfish brat. He's trying to get back at me because I want a little order in my life."

"Does it feel like he's doing something to you, something to hurt you?"

"In those moments I feel like he's trying to drive me to despair, like he wants to destroy me."

"So you're saying to yourself that he's a selfish brat, that he wants to get back at you, that he wants to destroy you and drive you to despair. Let me ask you a question. Suppose, after his misbehaving, you said something like this to yourself: 'He's unhappy and he's trying to get my attention. His behavior is unpleasant, but he's just trying to take care of his needs.' "

"But I don't believe that, I think he's trying to...."

"I understand that, but we are speaking hypothetically. Suppose you were to say to yourself what I suggested. Would you feel as angry?"

"No, I don't think I would. I think I'd feel differently."

"Here is something very important, then, that we have to talk about. You do have control over your anger. What you think, what you say to yourself triggers your anger. You can gain control of your anger by changing your thoughts, beliefs, and assumptions about your boy's behavior."

You have already learned that there is nothing automatic about getting angry. Pain does not make you angry. Thoughts make you angry; beliefs and assumptions make you angry. This chapter is an opportunity for you to examine the traditional beliefs and assumptions that are the cognitive foundations for anger and the necessary prerequisites for every angry outburst you have ever experienced.

You'll recall that the cognitive triggers for anger fall into one of two categories: shoulds and blamers. What follows is an exploration of how both shoulds and blamers create a distorted, anger-inciting picture of reality that leaves you feeling victimized and controlled by others. This chapter will help you to identify your trigger thoughts and replace them with new, more-forgiving awarenesses.

Shoulds

If you listened carefully to the inner monologue with which you analyze and interpret your experience, you would notice that many times each day you are judging the behavior of others. These judgments are based on a set of rules about how people should and should not act. People who behave according to the rules are right, and those who break the rules are wrong. You assume that people *know* and *accept* your rules. When they violate your shoulds, their behavior seems like a deliberate break with what is correct, intelligent, reasonable, or moral.

While waiting in line at the toll plaza, John deeply resents drivers who use the carpool lane to get ahead of the jam and then cut in front of him. He believes that people should wait their turn, and those who don't should be punished. Samantha has had a recent hysterectomy and is enormously angry that her husband rarely checks in about how she feels and even more rarely helps with any household jobs. Her should is that a spouse ought to show his concern by checking in and doing things to help. The problem with John's and Samantha's shoulds is that the other people don't agree with them. This is almost always the case. Others don't see reality as you do. Their perception of a situation is colored by their own needs, feelings, and history.

The drivers who cut in think it's perfectly fine to do so, and Samantha's husband feels very righteous because he's given up golf and poker to be home with her. It never occurs to him to be more helpful or inquiring.

So the first problem with shoulds is that the people with whom you feel angry rarely agree with you. Their perception of the situation leaves them blameless and justified. Their rules and beliefs always seem to exempt them from the judgments you think they deserve. And the more you try to convince them of their wrongness and their failure, the more indignant and defensive they become.

The second problem with shoulds is that people *never* do what they should do. They only do what is reinforcing and rewarding for them to do. Shoulds are your values and needs imposed on someone with different values and needs. The most complex human behavior can be looked at in terms of a very simple formula: strength of need minus strength of inhibition. If the strength of the inhibition is equal to or greater than the need, the person does not act. If the need surpasses the strength of the inhibition, some behavior will be emitted. Consider the drivers who keep cutting in front of John. Their need to get ahead and save time is greater than the sum of all inhibiting factors—fear of disapproval or reprisal, fear of a traffic ticket, guilt for not waiting their turn, and so on. The same is true for Samantha's husband. His need to watch television, sleep or read, or do whatever else he does instead of helping Samantha must be presumed greater than his inhibitions—fear of Samantha's disapproval, his self-rebuke for violating values of helpfulness and caring behavior, and so on.

When you demand that people behave according to your rules, you are violating reality in two ways. (1) In most cases others will not agree with your values and rules. Their unique history and needs shape their perception in a way that justifies their behavior. Since you can rarely get others to agree that they are wrong, applying your shoulds to their behavior is an exercise in futility. (2) Since behavior is shaped by the formula of needs minus inhibitions, shoulds have almost nothing to do with it. Judging behavior according to your own arbitrary standard of right and wrong really seems to miss the point. The real issue is how much does this person need to act this way and what inhibiting influences, if any, might stop him.

Exercise 1. Stand in their shoes. When you're angry at someone, answer these four questions.

1. "What needs influence him or her to act this way?"
2. "What beliefs or values influence him or her to act this way?"
3. "What aspects of his or her history (hurts, losses, successes, failures, rewards) influence this behavior?"
4. "What limitations (fears, health problems, lack of skills) influence this behavior?"

Answer each question as completely as possible. If you don't have all the information, make up something that seems likely. The purpose of this exercise is to explain the behavior you don't like *from the other person's point of view.*

Exercise 2. Accurate empathy. In his excellent book, *Feeling Good,* David Burns suggests an exercise to help you cope with shoulds. Imagine a dialogue between yourself and the person with whom you feel angry. Start out by accusing him or her of acting wrongly, of violating some basic rule of conduct. Really try to articulate your should. State it as clearly and persuasively as you can. Now imagine yourself as the other person, trying to answer your attack. Do your best to really become this individual, to see the world from his or her point of view. After you've answered as the other person, go back to your original feeling of anger and expand on your accusations. Keep up the attack. Now go back again and answer as the other person, really explaining his or her viewpoint. Shuttle back and forth between your accusing voice and the other person's defense at least three times. Notice how your feelings begin to change as you acknowledge the other person's unique experience.

While any kind of should can trigger anger, the five specific types of should statements covered below are extremely damaging in intimate relationships.

The Entitlement Fallacy

The entitlement fallacy is based on this simple belief: because I want something very much, I ought to have it. The basic idea is that the degree of your need justifies the demand that someone else provide it. The feeling is that there are certain things you are entitled to. Many people feel they are entitled to be sexually fulfilled, or feel emotionally and physically safe, or have a certain standard of living. Some people feel they are entitled to always rest when they are tired, or never be alone, or to have their work appreciated, or to have their needs known without asking. The list of possible entitlements is endless.

Sabrina was 38 and very much wanted a child. Her husband remained ambivalent and was extremely fearful about losing a sense of spontaneity and freedom if they had children. Sabrina harbored a belief that if she wanted something this much, he should help her have it. Her anger with his ambivalence was so great that each discussion of the issue soon developed into an escalating series of accusations.

Sam wants his son to go on a fishing trip. After all, he pays for the boy's college education, he's his father, the boy can jolly well give up a few days chasing girls to keep his old man company. Sam is in a rage when his son tells him that he'd rather make a demo tape with his band.

The entitlement fallacy confuses desire with obligation. It says, "When I want something this much, you have no right to say no." Strong feelings of entitlement deny others the freedom to choose. And this is how entitlement damages relationships. It demands that the other person give up his or her limits and boundaries for you. It says your need and your pain must come first, that the function of the relationship is to serve you.

Now, most of the time you would deny feeling that way and be quite offended if anyone were to accuse you of demanding that your needs come first. But the feeling of entitlement waxes and wanes. Sometimes you have no awareness of it. But when the needs are very strong, when the feeling of longing begins to engulf you, all you care about is getting what you want. And for a little while the other person may become only an instrument to provide for you. These painful feelings of need may periodically tempt you to forget the other person's equally important needs; his or her right to say no and set boundaries.

Exercise. Remember times you had to say no to another person's strong desire—a time when someone was in love with you, wanted to sleep with you, wanted your money, your support, your energy. His or her desire felt as real and vital and legitimate and necessary as yours does to you. Now try to remember why you said no. Remember the ways that your needs were different or conflicted. Remember how important it was for you to set your limits and clarify what you were and were not willing to do. You knew you had a right to your limits, you knew you had to say no because you needed something else.

Coping statements. These are things you can say to yourself when you find you are falling into the entitlement trap.

1. "I am free to want, but he or she is free to say no. "
2. "I have my limits, and you have your limits."
3. "I have the right to say no, and so do you."
4. "My desire doesn't obligate you to meet it."

The Fallacy of Fairness

This belief hinges on the application of legal and contractual rules to the vagaries of interpersonal relationships. The idea is that there is some absolute standard of correct and fair behavior which people should know and live up to. The conviction that relationships must be fair reduces the complex give and take of friendship or marriage to a set of entries in privately kept books. Your books tell you whether you are in the red or in the black, whether you are getting as much as you give, whether you are owed something for all the sacrifices you have made. The difficulty is that no two people agree on what fairness is and in personal relationships there is no court or arbiter to help them. The measurement of what is fair is totally subjective and depends entirely on what you expect, need, or hope for from the other person. Fairness can be so conveniently defined, so temptingly self-serving that people can literally call anything fair or unfair. And as the debate rages, each person gets locked into his or her fortress of conviction. Each person is the victim, the bearer of injustice.

Joan was convinced that she had been victimized. "I supported him through grad school, and that was his dream. Now I want to buy a house—that's my dream—and he won't do it. It isn't fair." Anthony complains, "Ninety percent of the time we go to her place, ten percent to mine. She doesn't care if it's fair or not."

Joan and Anthony no doubt heard their parents appeal to the concept of fairness when they were children. "Be fair to your brother, let him play with the toys.... That's not fair, let her have some of the ice cream too.... I played with you now be fair and let Daddy read for a while." Fairness is sometimes a useful concept for controlling the behavior of children (after all, there is an adult present to be the final judge of all such matters). But as an adult, the concept is just too dangerous to use. The word "fair" turns out to be nothing more than a disguise for personal preferences and wants. What you want is *fair*, what the other person wants or does is unfair.

When you say, "This is fair," what you're really saying is my needs are more legitimate than yours. No one wants to hear this. People resist and defend against such assertions. A better approach is to throw out the concept of fairness altogether. Reframe the situation as one of competing needs or preferences. Each person's need is of equal importance and value. Each person's need is equally legitimate.

When you finally put away the idea of fairness, you can begin to negotiate as peers who have competing wants and somehow must resolve the problem. Joan wants a house, her husband doesn't. Instead of arguing about what's fair, they can negotiate from a position that each need has equal weight. Maybe they will buy a smaller house than Joan had originally envisioned, maybe they will put off buying till a specific date, maybe they'll buy a country place, maybe they'll continue to rent but invest in real estate. Anthony and his girlfriend can adjust the percentage of time spent in each house, or they may work out special compensations or accommodations and keep the current lopsided percentage. Once fairness is thrown out, real negotiation can begin.

Exercise. If you are struggling with the issue of fairness, try reframing the problem as competing, but *equal* needs. Now attempt to make a clear, unbiased description of the other person's need. Don't try to evaluate whether it is more or less significant than yours. Now read Chapter 12 on problem-solving communication and apply those skills to working through the conflict.

Coping statements.

1. "Our needs are equally important."
2. "Each need is legitimate, we can negotiate as peers."

The Fallacy of Change

The fallacy of change is based on the assumption that you really can have control over the behavior of others. While sometimes people do change if you ask them, the fallacy of change reflects the belief that you can make people different if you just apply sufficient pressure. Richard expects that if he criticizes and belittles his wife enough, she will change into someone who is interested in discussing world affairs and political and social ideas. Leanne thinks that if she complains enough and gets angry enough she can change her husband's preoccupation with his job, his hobbies, and his personal experience (he keeps a detailed diary of his dreams and childhood memories).

The problem for both Richard and Leanne is that they are ignorant of one basic fact of human behavior: people change only when they are (1) reinforced to change and (2) capable of the change. In other words, people change when *they* want to, not when *you* want them to. Richard and Leanne find that their spouses are not changing, and the reason is that people do what is rewarding for them to do. Richard's wife finds it more rewarding to talk about the psychology of her friends than the relationship between the Druze and the Phalangists in Lebanon. Until Richard can make such discussions rewarding and fun for her, she will resist participating. Leanne has the same problem. Her husband is highly reinforced to keep doing the things he does. He won't change until she can make it more rewarding for him to spend time with her. Her current strategy of getting angry is having the opposite effect. He finds it more and more aversive to be with her and hence takes refuge in his hobbies and dream journal.

Expecting people to change leads to frustration and disil-lusion. If you can't find a way to make them *want* to change, you have undertaken a quixotic mission. You are tilting at wind-mills.

Exercise. Think about and answer the following questions:

1. How many times have you made a major change *and sustained* it because someone pressured you to do so?
2. What percentage of the people you have known have made a major metamorphosis to satisfy the needs of someone else?
3. How often have you succeeded in changing someone by pressuring him or her with anger?

Coping statements.

1. "The amount of support, help, and nourishment I am now getting is all I can get, given the strategies I am using."
2. "People will change only when they are reinforced to change and capable of change."
3. "People only change when *they* want to."

Conditional Assumptions

Conditional asumptions are based on a syllogism like this:

"If you loved me, you'd pick me up at the subway station after work (or do the dishes, or show more sexual interest, or get home earlier, or help me when I'm tired, or spell me with caring for the kids, or fix things in the house, or finish school so you could get a real job)."

Other variations include:

"If you were a real friend, you'd help me lay the bricks for my patio (or initiate more often, or just spend time with me rather than always having to do something, or take more inter-est in my problems)."

And a last one:

"If they valued my work here, they'd get me a nicer desk (or give me a raise, or give me a better secretary, or ask what happened when I was sick last week)."

It's possible to love or care for someone and still not meet his or her needs. Disappointing others doesn't make one uncaring, and caring doesn't obligate one never to disappoint. No matter how much someone loves you, that person is still responsible for taking care of his or her own basic needs. That person is still responsible for saying no, setting boundaries, and protecting his or her own limits. "If they cared, if they loved me," is a setup to make you feel righteous and make the other person feel bad. Truthfully, it's a strategy for manipulation. But the result is rarely what you might hope. In the long run, making others feel bad doesn't reinforce them to do what you want. It makes them want to run away, to avoid you.

Exercise 1. List the times you have disappointed someone you loved or cared for. Remember the times you have had to make difficult choices, when you decided to take care of your needs over someone else's. As you think back, notice how little your choice had to do with how much you loved, but rather with how much you needed, or how much you were afraid, or how much energy you had.

Exercise 2. As you did with the fallacy of fairness, reframe your conditional assumptions as a collision of equally legitimate needs. Define your need, and then carefully describe the needs, as you understand them, of the other person. See the problem as two peers, working to negotiate. Read Chapter 12 and apply the assertive communication skills discussed there to a process of compromise and accommodation so that each of you gets some of what he or she needs.

Coping statements.
1. "Disappointing someone doesn't mean you don't care."
2. "Our biggest task, no matter how much we love, is to take care of ourselves."
3. "His or her needs are as legitimate as mine, and we can negotiate."

The Letting It Out Fallacy

This fallacy rests on the belief that people who hurt you or cause you pain *should* be punished. It often feels very good to express anger when you're frustrated and hurting. It helps to discharge the pain. And it functions as a kind of revenge for any perceived injustice.

The underlying belief is that you are not responsible for your pain. Someone else is. That person must have done wrong in order for you to feel so badly. Therefore, he or she deserves every bit of anger you feel like expressing. Maybe he or she will learn to do better in the future.

The problem with this whole line of reasoning is that you *are* responsible for your pain. And taking care of yourself is *always* your first responsibility. Pain and pleasure are an essentially private experiences. You are the only one who really feels *your* hurt, you are the only one who experiences your joy. No one else can be held accountable or responsible for your private experience. You know it and you feel it. Therefore, you are the only one who can be responsible for it. If someone is frustrating or hurting you or causing you pain, your job is to either negotiate for your needs or let go of the relationship.

The second problem with letting it out is that anger destroys relationships. (This is particularly true for anger used as revenge.) When the object of your anger is to inflict the same degree of hurt that you are feeling on someone else, people begin to erect psychological barriers to protect themselves from you. The tissue of a relationship gets thickened and scarred. And finally you both become insensitive to pain and pleasure. This is how anger kills love: it makes you thick-skinned, untouchable. You no longer feel the warmth, the caress.

The last reason letting it out doesn't work is that anger rarely gets you what you want. What you want is to be listened to, appreciated, cared for. Anger gets you coldness, withdrawal, and anger in return. Letting it out feels good. But it's like smoking crack: a five-minute high, followed by depression, pain, and emotional bankruptcy.

Exercise 1. When you are tempted to let it out, first review the positive and negative consequences of using anger with this particular person in the past. Make four columns down a piece of paper. Over two of the columns write "short-term consequences" and over the other two write "long-term consequences." Label the two short-term consequences columns "positive" and "negative." Do the same with the long-term columns. Write down all the long- and short-term consequences of anger that you can think of, both positive and negative. At the end of the exercise, ask yourself this question: "Did anger get me what I wanted?"

Exercise 2. Using the "I think, I feel, I want" structure discussed in Chapter 12, make assertive statements to express the speaker's needs in the following situations.

1. "When she gets these stinking grades it makes me so depressed that I feel justified in letting her have it."
2. "I told him that I hate musicals, but off he goes to buy tickets to *Chorus Line*. I just blow up, it's so frustrating. He deserves it."

Coping statements.

1. "Anger won't get me what I want."
2. "I can protect my relationship by saying it assertively."

Blamers

They did it to you. You are lonely, hurt, frightened, and they did it. Blaming triggers anger by making your pain someone else's responsibility. In intimate relationships, blaming leads to the development of negative cognitive sets in which you begin to label, classify, and interpret a person's behavior in consistently negative ways. He is controlling or uncaring or selfish or insensitive. And as this negative cognitive set hardens, so do your assumptions about the other person. Even neutral or ambiguous behavior gets a negative label. More and more parts of the relationship are tainted by the consistently negative way that you interpret and evaluate the other person.

The probem with blaming is that it denies reality in two ways. First, blaming assumes that you are not responsible for your pain, someone else is. Chapter 6 on responsibility contains specific reasons why you should view yourself and only yourself as responsible for your experience. The second way that blaming denies reality is by constructing a world in which people are deliberately doing bad things. People do not do "bad" things. As Plato observed, people always choose the good. You and everyone else will always choose the action that seems most likely to meet your needs. The potential benefits of the action you choose, at least at the moment of choice, seem to outweigh the foreseeable disadvantages. Obviously, the action that seems best at the time depends on your awareness. Awareness is the degree of clarity with which you perceive and understand, consciously or unconsciously, all the factors relating to the need at hand. At any moment in time, your awareness is a product of your innate intelligence, your constitution, your physiological state, your emotional state, your beliefs, your needs, your total life experience and conditioning, and your skills and competencies. All of that goes into making a decision. And the decision you make is the very best one available *at that moment in time*. Good or bad is nothing more than a label you apply to decisions after you have observed their consequences for yourself and others. But at the moment the decision was made, those consequences were unknown. And it was therefore the best choice available.

Now you may be thinking that sometimes people know better but do the wrong thing anyway. "My son knows I'll be upset and that he diminishes his chances for college when he brings home C's and D's. He knows better, but he does it anyway." But "knowing better" is not sufficient to "do better" if the boy's awareness at the time is focused on stronger and opposing motivations. If his need to play football or go out with girls or rebel against the family rules is larger than his need to please you or his long-range concerns about college, then grades will be a low priority. It all comes down to what *is most important at the time*.

So blaming doesn't make sense. It labels people and behavior as bad when in fact each person makes the best choice available. By blaming, you end up punishing people for actions *they could not help performing*.

Exercise. The components of awareness. Think of someone you know well, someone you have at various times blamed. Think of a decision that person made that angered you. Now here's the hard part. Try to reconstruct the decision *from that person's point of view.* What do you know of his or her constitution or physiological state, emotional state, beliefs, needs, conditioning, competencies, or limitations? Try to see how these factors could combine so that his or her decision was the best choice available.

Good-Bad Dichotomizing

If you do a lot of blaming, you're beginning to repaint the world in black and white. People are good or bad, right or wrong. You don't see any shades of gray or any continuum between the polar opposites.

Once you start labeling people as bad, the problem with cognitive sets comes in. You develop a kind of tunnel vision that blocks out every behavior that doesn't fit your assumption of badness. You simply don't see the things that are kind or generous or loving. Jim very often sees Martha as selfish and uncaring. Even though she frequently gives him little hugs, does his laundry, and invites his friends to dinner, he fails to notice these as loving or generous acts. Jim is missing a big part of the relationship because his cognitive sets blind him to seeing the way Martha expresses her caring feelings.

Exercise. Finding shades of gray. Write a complete description of someone you know well, someone you care for but with whom you also feel angry. Read over your description. How many of the items are judgments, implying that some aspect of his or her personality is either good or bad? How much of your description is either pejorative or praising? Now try rewriting the description without any hint of judgment. As best you can, make the descriptions neutral. Instead of saying that he's fat, say that he weighs 250 pounds. Instead of saying that she has a beautiful face, say that she has even features and smooth skin. Stick to the facts. Don't embellish with your value judgments. How does it feel to think about people without judgment? Does the description feel more accurate or less accurate when it is nonpejorative?

Coping statements.

1. "I make no judgments."
2. "People are coping with pain and stress in the best way they can, given their level of awareness."
3. "It is merely a problem that our needs conflict; he is not wrong, and I am not right."

Assumed Intent

This is mind reading, the tendency to make inferences about how people feel and think. Assumed intent triggers anger when you conclude that your pain is a consequence of someone's deliberate effort to do you harm. Jill lost track of her nine-year-old son at the county fair. She assumed that he had deliberately disappeared to scare her. Joshua believed that the waitress was being deliberately slow and inattentive because he had asked for extra cream and wanted his eggs done a special way.

Notice that assumed intent must include two important concepts to make you angry. First, that you are in pain through the fault of someone else. Secondly, that you are being *deliberately* harmed. Few people would get angry if a pine cone fell and scratched their car. But a child throwing pine cones would be a different story. Now the two elements necessary for anger are present: harm and deliberate intent.

There are several problems with assuming intent. It is very difficult to accurately assess the true motives of another person. The word "assume" means that you think you know, but you never asked. Mind reading is so often dead wrong, yet it is probably the greatest source of anger. Claudette thought that a friend had deliberately excluded her from a luncheon "as a kind of slap." She was irate until she learned that the lunch had honored an unknown co-worker of her friend's. Reese thought that his girlfriend was trying to hurt him by deciding to spend fewer nights together. After first withdrawing, then picking several fights, he discovered that her very deep feelings of love and dependence were frightening her. The motive that he had assumed was quite the opposite from the facts. It was her positive feelings rather than any attempt to harm that lay behind her decision.

Exercise. Try this process for one day. Make a commitment to yourself that you will make absolutely no assumptions about the motivations of others unless you *check out* your assumption with the other person. In other words, you have to ask, "Is it true that you're being slow getting ready for the movie because I didn't wash the car today?" "I have a feeling you're being a little withdrawn because I spent the day with Rich. Is there anything to that?" "When you said the potatoes were over-cooked, I felt like you were mad at me or something, is that true?" "You're driving so fast, I wonder if you're trying to scare me?" Your rule for yourself for this day will be that you either avoid assumptions or find out if they're true.

If you succeeded in doing the exercise for a day, try extending it to a week. The more you avoid mind reading, the healthier your communications will be.

Coping statements.

1. "Assume nothing or check it out."
2. "I don't guess at the motives of others."
3. "No mind reading."

Magnifying

When you magnify, you make things worse than they are. You use words like *terrible, awful, disgusting, horrendous.* You overgeneralize by using words such as *always, all, every,* and *never.* Jill complains about her boss: "He's *always* handing me things at the last minute. He's *awful* with the whole support staff. *Never* a kind word, *never* a smile. He's just a *lousy* person to work for." Art complains about his neighbor: "He's *always* piling crap in my walkway. He *never* asks, he *never* even talks to me. It's *terrible* to live next to somebody who doesn't give a damn."

Both Jill and Art are magnifying. Jill's boss doesn't *always* give her things at the last minute. It isn't true that he *never* smiles. Art's neighbor isn't *always* piling things in the walkway. Nor does he *never* speak to Art. These magnifications crank up your sense of being victimized. By exaggerating the problematic behavior, you generate a feeling of being deeply wronged. They're bad and you're innocent.

Magnifying your trigger thoughts is like throwing gasoline on a fire. Your anger explodes because you feel so wronged, so righteous, so justified.

Exercise. For one day, eliminate these words from your vocabulary: *all, always, every, never, terrible, awful, disgusting, horrible, sickening,* and so on. Commit yourself to describing people and events without magnifying. Strive for accuracy rather than exaggeration. Give the exact frequency: "Three times in the last two weeks..." "The second time this quarter..." "Once a month we chat for five minutes." Avoid using generalized pejoratives like *terrible* and *awful.* Instead, stick to simple conclusions like "I don't like it..." "I'd prefer he didn't hand things to me after four o'clock."

Coping statements.

1. "No more always and never."
2. "Accuracy, nonexaggeration."
3. "Let the facts speak for themselves."

Global Labeling

Your office mate is an *imbecile.* Your roommate's *neurotic.* Your father's *stupid.* The grocery checker is a *jerk.* Your lover's a selfish *asshole.* Your landlord is a *ripoff artist.* Your cousin is a *blabbermouth.* Global labels fuel your anger by turning the other person into someone who is totally bad and worthless. Instead of disliking specific behavior, you indict the entire person. Global labels are always false because they focus on a single characteristic or behavior, but imply that it's the whole picture.

It's much easier to get angry at an ogre, a despicable person, than it is to rage at one specific behavior. It's hard to really work yourself into a true feeling of victimization if you're only responding to one unfortunate event. But if you decide you've been mistreated by a selfish jerk, you anger comes to a quicker boil.

Exercise. The antidote for global labeling is specificity. The next time you catch yourself using pejorative labels, shift into a specific description of the offensive behavior. Leave the person out of it. Describe what he does, not who he is.

Coping statement.

"No labels. Be specific."

Changing Your Trigger Thoughts

Changing a long-standing pattern of thinking is no easy task. But it's absolutely necessary. If you don't find ways to combat your trigger thoughts, your shoulds and blamers, they will continue to ignite anger.

It'll take hard work and discipline to change what seems second nature now. But there is a way. Aaron Beck, one of the founders of cognitive behavioral therapy, devised an extremely effective process for confronting your distorted thoughts. It's called the three-column technique. Divide a page in your anger journal into three columns. Whenever you feel angry, write down in Column A what you're saying to yourself. In Column B write down the kind of trigger thought you were using (some are listed below as a memory aid). In Column C, rewrite your original statement so that it no longer contains the distorted trigger thought.

Shoulds	Blamers
Entitlement fallacy	Good-bad dichotomizing
Fallacy of fairness	Assumed intent
Fallacy of change	Magnifying
Conditional assumptions	Global labeling
Letting it out fallacy	

Here's an example of how you can use the three-column technique.

Ann's Diary

That jerk's keeping me waiting	Assuming intention, Magnifying	I don't like waiting.
Yard duty again. The principal always does this to me.	Conditional assumptions	I assume he's doing the best he can, but it's quite inconvenient for me.
Why doesn't he learn to sit down and behave?	Fallacy of change	He'll learn to sit down when I figure out how to reinforce him to do so.
If she was any kind of a friend, she wouldn't stick me with the whole damn thing.	Conditional assumptions	It's a conflict of needs. I've got to negotiate this with her. Neither of us wants to do it.
Why do these people keep me waiting?	Shoulds	People never do what they should do, only what they're reinforced to do.
Why do I have to live in this closet when my ex-husband is still living in the house?	Entitlement fallacy	Just because I want that house doesn't mean I can afford it. He owns a plumbing business, I'm just a teacher. There is no reason why he should give up a house just because I want it.

As you can see, the third column is the most important. That's where you talk back to the trigger thoughts and begin to modify your anger. Here's another example.

Harold's Diary

Now she's off to yoga and aerobics. We'll lose the whole morning, God damn her, she's avoiding me.	Letting it out fallacy, Assuming intention	Blowing up won't get me what I want. I'll stop assuming and find out what her needs are.
She consented to have breakfast. Big deal. I work all week so she can go to school, and I have to talk her into breakfast.	Fallacy of fairness	OK, both our needs are important. She doesn't owe me anything. Her needs are as legitimate as mine.
Why do they always screw up my photos everytime I bring them here?	Good-bad dichotomizing, Magnifying, Global labeling	They're not that bad. They're doing the best they can. They don't always screw up. This is 4 out of 36 negatives.
Why can't she wear something sexy to bed?	Entitlement fallacy	Just because I want it doesn't mean she has to do it. She has her own needs and limits. If I want to work on this, I can find out what her needs and fears are and negotiate some compromise.

Now it's time for you to try some on your own. In Column A you'll find a list of trigger thoughts. Name the distortion in Column B. In column C, rewrite or refute the distortion so it no longer triggers anger.

Column A	Column B	Column C
1. Are you stupid? How can you forget your homework?		

2. He should stop the
   damned gambling.
   It's destroying our
   marriage.
3. If she cared about
   me, she'd come home
   earlier.
4. He never listens when
   I'm upset about some-
   thing.
5. He should have
   walked me to the car
   in this neighborhood.
6. I took care of her when
   she had a cold last
   week. Now I have
   atoothache and she
   doesn't even ask how I
   am.
7. He's walking this trail
   when he knows very
   well I'm afraid of
   heights.

Suggested Answers:

1. *Global labeling.* "I don't like you forgetting your homework. How can we help you remember it? Perhaps you can stay
up a half hour later if you remember your homework."

2. *Shoulds, fallacy of change.* "He'll only stop if he's reinforced
to change and capable of changing. Pressure from me isn't
working. I have to decide whether to live with this or let go."

3. *Conditional assumptions.* "Love has nothing to do with it.
This is a conflict of needs. I have to find out what needs or fears
keep her working late and negotiate some sort of compromise."

4. *Magnifying.* "Be specific. He listens maybe _____
percent of the time. How can I take responsibility to reinforce
him to listen more?"

5. *Shoulds.* "That's my value and need, not his. He doesn't
do what I think he should, only what his values and needs
dictate."

6. *Fallacy of fairness.* "She has her own needs at this moment. Both our needs are equally legitimate. It is my responsibility to ask her for what I want."

7. *Assumed intent.* "I'm assuming things. I don't really know why he's walking here. Better check it out. I have to negotiate for my own needs."

Here are the main points to remember when you are writing your refutations to the trigger thoughts:

1. Be specific, not global.
2. Be nonpejorative, nonjudging.
3. Punishment and revenge won't get you what you want.
4. Check out all assumptions.
5. You, and only you, are responsible for your needs.
6. Recognize that people do the best they can given their level of awareness *at the moment of choice.*
7. Recognize that people do what is reinforcing for them to do. You can only get them to change by negotiating for and reinforcing new behavior.

Whenever you feel anger, continue to use the three-column technique to confront your trigger thoughts in your anger journal. It's essential that you make a commitment to keep at this. It is difficult, arduous work to keep examining your thoughts, to keep questioning and rebutting what seemed so natural, so reasonable. But getting control of your anger requires that you become more and more aware of how trigger thoughts create upsetting feelings. It will take at least three months of consistent effort monitoring and confronting your angry cognitions before you begin to feel the tide turn. Gradually they will become less automatic. Gradually you will find yourself experiencing more and more *discomfort* when the old trigger thoughts pop up. They will no longer sound so right, so convincing. In fact, you will begin to recognize them for what they are—excuses to discharge pain, deceptions that trigger destructive aggression. As you keep talking back to the shoulds and blamers, you will find your new attitudes and beliefs beginning to take hold. As you accept more responsibility for your needs, you will move beyond anger to problem solving, negotiating, and exploring the needs of others.

8

Controlling Stress
Step by Step

Stress is the fuel of anger. If anger is a problem in your life, it's essential that you learn a method for reducing stress that works for you. Read through the suggestions in this chapter and choose the techniques that seem most useful. You will find that you can learn alternative coping strategies that will help you regain control. You *can* successfully deal with stress, instead of being angry.

Scanning Your Body for Stress

The first step in controlling stress is to recognize how and where tension is affecting your body. The following technique and many of the others described in this chapter have been adapted from *The Relaxation & Stress Reduction Workbook* (Davis, Eshelman, and McKay 1988).

1. Begin by paying attention to your feet and legs. Start by wiggling your toes, then rotate your feet and relax them. Note any tension in your calves. Let go of this tension.
2. Now focus on your lower torso. Become aware of any tension or pain in your lower back. Relax as fully as you can. Notice if you have tension in your hips, pelvic area, or buttocks. Relax these areas.

3. Move your focus to your diaphragm and stomach. Take a couple of deep breaths, breathing slowly in and out. Feel yourself relaxing, more and more deeply. Notice any tension that you are experiencing in this area.

4. Become aware of your lungs and chest cavity. Search for tension in this part of your body. Take a couple of slow, deep breaths and relax.

5. Next, pay attention to your shoulders, neck, and throat. Swallow a couple of times and notice any tension or soreness in your throat and neck. Roll your head around clockwise a few times. Now reverse and roll your head the other way. Shrug your shoulders and become aware of any tension in this area and then relax.

6. Begin at the top of your head and scan for tension. Look for pain in your forehead. Perhaps there is a band of pain around the top of your head. Maybe there is pain or tension behind your eyes. Notice any tightness in your jaw. Check for locking or grinding of teeth and taut lips. Be aware of your ears. Go back over your head and relax each part.

7. Now go back and scan your entire body for any remaining tension. Allow yourself to relax more and more deeply.

If you do this exercise every day for a week, you will have a much better understanding of where your body chronically holds tension. Write in your Anger Diary each day the location where the tension seems to concentrate.

The next step is to learn a relaxation strategy that works for you. Experiment with each of the techniques suggested below and find out for yourself what gets the best results.

Stress Reduction Skills

Breathing Away Stress

In order to live, you have to breathe; in order to live well, you have to breathe well. Proper breathing is a natural antidote to stress. The basic technique is called *deep breathing* and may be practiced in a variety of postures. Try the following:

1. Lie down on a blanket or rug on the floor. Bend your knees and place your feet about eight inches apart, with your toes turned slightly outward. Make sure that your spine is straight.
2. Scan your body for tension.
3. Place your left hand on your abdomen (belly) and your right hand on your chest.
4. Inhale slowly and deeply through your nose, filling your abdomen. Push the air way down to your belly. Notice your left hand being pushed up. Your chest should move only a little underneath your right hand and only with your abdomen.
5. Now inhale through your nose and exhale through your mouth, making a quiet, relaxing, "whooshing" sound as you gently blow out. Your mouth, tongue, and jaw will be relaxed. Take long, slow, deep breaths that raise and lower your abdomen. Focus on the sound and feeling of your breathing as you become more and more relaxed.
6. Continue this deep breathing exercise for about 5 or 10 minutes. Do this once or twice a day for a couple of weeks. Then, if you like, you may extend this period to 20 minutes a day.
7. At the end of each deep breathing session, take a little time to scan your body for tension. Compare the tension you feel at the conclusion of the exercise with what you experienced when you began.

When you have learned to breathe easily into your abdomen, you can practice this exericse whenever you feel stress during the day. It doesn't matter whether you are sitting or standing up. Just concentrate on your abdomen moving up and down, as the air moves in and out of your lungs. Notice the feeling of relaxation that deep breathing gives you.

The next technique for controlling stress is called the *relaxing sigh*. During the day you probably catch yourself sighing or yawning. This is generally a sign that you are not getting enough oxygen. Sighing and yawning are your body's way of remedying the situation. A sigh is often preceded by a sense that things are not quite as they should be and by a feeling of tension. Since sighing releases some of that tension, you can use this practice at will as a means of relaxing.

1. Sit or stand up straight.
2. Sigh deeply, letting out a sound of deep relief as the air rushes out of your lungs.
3. Don't think about inhaling—just let the air come in naturally.
4. Repeat this procedure 8 to 12 times and experience the feeling of relaxation it provides whenever you feel the need for it.

Progressive Muscle Relaxation

There is a reciprocal relationship between tension and anger. Physical tension creates stress, which predisposes you to anger. Anger then causes additional body tension, which escalates and exacerbates the anger response.

1. Get in a comfortable position and relax. Now clench your right fist, tighter and tighter, studying the tension as you do so. Keep it clenched and notice the tension in your fist, hand, and forearm. Now relax. Feel the looseness in your right hand and notice how it contrasts with the tension. Repeat this procedure with your right fist again. Tighten for about seven seconds. Always notice as you relax that this feeling is the opposite of tension. Relax and feel the difference. Repeat this entire procedure with your left fist, then both fists at the same time.
2. Now bend your elbows and tense your biceps (in a Charles Atlas pose). Tense your biceps as hard as you can for seven seconds and observe the feeling of tautness. Relax and straighten out your arms. Let the relaxation develop. Feel the difference. Repeat this and each of the following procedures at least once.
3. Turn your attention to your head. Wrinkle your forehead as tightly as you can for seven seconds. Now relax and smooth it out. Allow yourself to imagine your entire forehead and scalp becoming as smooth as silk. Now frown and notice the strain spreading throughout your forehead. Let go. Allow your brow to become smooth again. Close your eyes now. Squint them tighter. Look for tension. Relax your eyes. Let them remain gently and comfortably closed. Now clench your jaw, bite hard, and

notice the tension throughout your jaw. Relax your jaw. When your jaw is relaxed, your lips will be slightly parted. Let yourself really appreciate the contrast between tension and relaxation. Now press your tongue against the roof of your mouth. Feel the ache in the back of your mouth. Relax. Compress your lips now, pursing them into an O. Relax your lips and blow out forcefully, making a sound like a horse. Notice that your forehead, scalp, eyes, jaw, tongue, and lips are now all relaxed.

4. Press your head back as far as it can comfortably go and observe the tension in your neck. Roll your head to the right and feel the changing location of the stress. Roll your head to the left. Straighten your head and bring it forward, pressing your chin against your chest. Feel the tension in your throat and the back of your neck. Relax, allowing your head to return to a comfortable position. Let the relaxation deepen. Now shrug your shoulders. Keep the tension as you hunch your head down between your shoulders. Relax your shoulders. Drop them back and feel the relaxation spread through your neck, throat, and shoulders. Experience the pure relaxation, deeper and deeper.

5. Give your entire body a chance to relax. Feel the comfort and heaviness. Now breathe in and fill your lungs completely. Hold your breath and notice the tension. Now exhale, letting your chest become loose. Let the air hiss out. Continue relaxing, letting your breath move freely and gently. Repeat this several times, noticing the tension draining from your body as you exhale. Next, tighten your stomach and hold it. Note the tension, then relax. Now place your hand on your stomach. Breathe deeply into your stomach, pushing your hand up. Hold, and then relax. Feel the contrast of the relaxation as the air rushes out. Now arch your back, without straining. Keep the rest of your body as relaxed as possible. Focus on the tension in your lower back. Now relax, deeper and deeper.

6. Tighten your buttocks and thighs. Flex your thighs by pressing down on your heels as hard as you can. Relax and feel the difference. Now curl your toes downward, making your calves tense. Study the tension. Relax. Now

point your toes toward your face, creating tension in your shins. Relax again.

7. Feel the heaviness throughout your lower body as the relaxation deepens. Relax your feet, ankles, calves, shins, knees, thighs, and buttocks. Now let the relaxation spread to your stomach, lower back, and chest. Let go more and more. Experience the relaxation deepening in your shoulders, arms, and hands. Deeper and deeper. Notice the feeling of looseness and relaxation in your neck, jaw, and all your facial muscles.

Perhaps the best way to do this exercise is to make a tape recording of the instructions for yourself. You can then play it back anytime you want, while you are relaxing. When you have followed this procedure daily for two weeks, you'll be ready to go on to the advanced, shorthand form of relaxation.

The following "short form" procedure can be used to achieve deep muscle relaxation quickly. Whole muscle groups are simultaneously tensed and then relaxed. As before, repeat each procedure at least once, tensing each muscle group for about seven seconds. Then relax for 20 to 30 seconds. Remember to notice the contrast betwen the sensations of tension and relaxation.

1. Curl both fists, tightening your biceps and forearms in a Charles Atlas pose. Hold it. Relax.
2. Wrinkle up your forehead. At the same time, press your head as far back as possible. Roll it clockwise in a complete circle, then reverse. Now wrinkle up the muscles of your face like a walnut: frowning, eyes squinting, lips pursed, tongue pressing to the roof of your mouth, and shoulders hunched. Hold it. Relax.
3. Arch back as you take a deep breath into your chest. Hold it. Relax. Take a deep breath, pressing out the stomach. Hold it. Relax.
4. Point your feet and toes back toward your face, tightening your shins, Hold it. Relax. Curl your toes, simutaneously tightening your calves, thighs, and buttocks. Hold it. Relax.

After you've learned the shorthand procedure, try to use it at least three times a day. It's particularly helpful to use it *before* stressful situations.

Meditation

Four basic components make up a meditation. First, you should be in a *quiet place.* It's essential that all external distractions be kept at a minimum. Second, it's vital that you choose a *comfortable position* that you can maintain for about 20 minutes without causing stress to your body. (*Helpful hint:* Avoid meditating within two hours of a heavy meal. The digestion process will interfere with your ability to remain relaxed and alert.) Third, select a *focal object.* This can be a repeated word or sound (mantra), or even a real or imagined image (such as a candle flame) that will hold your attention. When distracting thoughts enter your mind, you can let them come and go, returning to your chosen object of focus. The last, and most difficult component, is maintaining a *passive attitude.* A passive attitude is characterized by a lack of concern about everything (including how well you are doing). It means feeling yourself, uncritically and completely, in the here and now.

The *breath-counting meditation* described below was popularized by Herbert Benson in his book *The Relaxation Response.* It is used throughout the world and is particularly useful for achieving deep relaxation and reducing stress.

1. Go to a quiet place and center yourself. Assume the posture of your choice. Scan your body for tension and relax. Either close your eyes or focus your attention on a spot that is about four feet in front of you on the floor.
2. Breathe through your nose. Inhale, exhale, then pause. Allow yourself to breathe in an easy and natural way. Become aware of your breathing.
3. As you exhale, say the word "one" to yourself. Continue to breathe in and out, saying "one" each time you exhale.
4. When thoughts or perceptions threaten to take your attention away from your breathing, let go of them quickly and return to saying "one." Do this for 10 to 20 minutes at a time.

5. Each time you complete this exercise, spend a few minutes sitting quietly with your eyes closed. Allow yourself to experience your thoughts and feelings, body and environment. Then continue for a few minutes with your eyes open. Take time to appreciate the calming effects of the meditation process.

Plan to do this exercise five to seven times a week for about a month. Then you can evaluate the results and decide to either continue or discard it.

An alternative form of counting is to number your breaths by repeating "One, two, three, four; one, two, three, four"; and so on. Or you can try counting your steps while walking in exactly the same way: count to four and then start over.

Self-Hypnosis for Relaxation

The induction described below is adapted from *Hypnosis for Change* (Hadely and Staudacher 1985). Your best approach to using it may be to make your own tape recording. To prepare for the recording, first read the induction aloud several times to become familiar and comfortable with the content. Say the words slowly. Keep your voice level, and monotonous, as flat and expressionless as possible. (*Helpful hint:* Make sure that the tape you are using is long enough to handle the entire induction on one side.) When you're ready to use the tape that you have made, prepare a special place, away from noise and distraction. Wear comfortable clothing and get in a comfortable position. You may want to lie down or sit in a rocking chair. Now allow yourself to experience the deep relaxation of a self-induced hypnotic procedure.

1. Take a nice deep breath, close your eyes, and begin to relax. Just think about relaxing every muscle in your body from the top of your head to the tips of your toes. Just begin to relax. And begin to notice how very comfortable your body is beginning to feel. You are supported, so you can just let go and relax. Inhale and exhale. Notice your breathing; notice the rhythm of your breathing and relax your breathing for a moment.

2. Be aware of the normal sounds around you. These sounds are unimportant. Discard them. Whatever you hear from now on will only help you to relax. And as you exhale, release any tension, any stress, from any part of your body, from your mind and your thoughts. Just let that stress go. Just feel any stressful thoughts rushing through your mind, feel them beginning to wind down, wind down, wind down, and relax.

3. And begin with letting all the muscles in your face relax, especially your jaw. Let your teeth part just a little bit and relax this area. This is a place where tension and stress gather, so be sure to relax your jaw, and feel that relaxation go into your temples, and relax the muscles in your temples and as you think about relaxing these muscles they will relax. Feel them relax, and as you relax you'll be able to just drift and float into a deeper and deeper level of total relaxation.

4. Continue to relax and now let all the muscles in your forehead relax. Feel those muscles smooth, smooth and relaxed, and rest your eyes. Just imagine your eyelids feeling so comfortable, so heavy, so relaxed, and how all of the muscles in the back of your neck and shoulders relax. Feel a heavy, heavy weight being lifted off your shoulders and you feel relieved, lighter, and more relaxed. And all of the muscles in the back of your neck and shoulders relax, and feel that soothing relaxation go down your back, down, down, down, to the lower part of your back.

5. And those muscles let go with every breath that you exhale, just feel your body drifting, floating, down deeper, down deeper, down deeper, into total relaxation. Let your muscles go, relaxing more and more. Let all of the muscles in your shoulders, running down your arms to your fingertips, relax. And let your arms feel so heavy so heavy, so heavy, so comfortable, so relaxed. You have tingling in your fingertips. That's perfectly fine. You may have warmth in the palms of your hands, and that's fine. And you may feel that you can barely lift your arms, they are so relaxed. They are so heavy, so heavy, so relaxed.

6. And now you inhale once again and relax your chest muscles. And now as you exhale, feel your stomach

muscles relax. As you exhale relax all of the muscles in your stomach, let them go and all of the muscles in your legs, feel them relax and all the muscles in your legs so completely relaxed right to the tips of your toes.

7. Notice how very comfortable your body feels, just drifting and floating, deeper, deeper, deeper relaxed. And just as you are relaxing deeper and deeper, imagine a beautiful staircase. There are ten steps, and the steps lead you to a special and peaceful and beautiful place.

8. In a moment you can begin to imagine taking a safe and gentle and easy step down, down, down, on the staircase, leading you to a very peaceful, a very special place for you. You can imagine any place you choose. Perhaps you would enjoy a beach or ocean with clean fresh air, or the mountains with a stream. Anyplace is perfectly fine.

9. In a moment you can begin to count backwards from ten to one and you can imagine taking the steps down, and as you take each step, feel your body relax more and more, feel it just drift down, down each step, and relax even deeper. Ten, relax even deeper, nine...eight...seven...six...five...four...three...two...one...deeper and deeper, more and more relaxed.

10. And now imagine a peaceful and special place. You can imagine this special place and perhaps you can even feel it. You are alone and there is no one to disturb you. This is the most peaceful place in the world for you. Imagine yourself there and feel that sense of peace flow through you and sense of well-being and enjoy these positive feelings. And you can keep these good feelings with you long after this exercise is completed, for the rest of the day and evening, even tomorrow. Allow these positive feelings to grow stronger and stronger, feeling at peace with a sense of well-being. (*Pause.*)

11. And each time and every time that you choose to do this kind of relaxation you will be able to relax deeper and deeper. Regardless of the stress and tension that may surround your life, you may now remain more at peace, more calm, more relaxed, and allow the tension and stress to bounce off and away from you. And these positive feelings will stay with you and grow stronger

and stronger throughout the day as you continue to relax deeper and deeper.

12. Enjoy your special place for another moment and then you can begin to count from one to ten and as you do count from one to ten you can begin coming back to full consciousness, and you will come back feeling refreshed as if you had a long rest. Come back feeling alert and relaxed. Begin to come back now. One...two...coming up, three...four...five...six...seven...eight...nine, begin to open your eyes, and ten, open your eyes and come all the way back feeling great. Very good.

When you've listened to your tape long enough to become familiar with it, you may wish to say the relaxing suggestions to yourself. You can hypnotize yourself and receive all the stress-reducing benefits by systematically relaxing your body, doing a countdown, repeating deepening suggestions ("I am drifting deeper and deeper.... I feel more and more drowsy, peaceful, and calm"), and visiting your special place. Then count back up to full alertness.

Brief Combination Techniques

These are techniques that literally combine two or more relaxation strategies. The net effect is multiplicative, which means that one and one equals three or four. (No, this is not the "new math.") Combination techniques capitalize on a "piggyback" effect where each technique builds progressively on the other. And as an extra bonus, they're designed to be *quickies*. You can easily do them during a coffee break. Many can be completed in two minutes or less.

1. Breathing with imagery. This technique combines slow breathing with *imagery*. A mental picture of sun and sand will work well with this exercise, but any image that you find relaxing will do.

A. Imagine that you're lying on a beach. A few clouds drift overhead, and an occasional seagull. You hear the sound of the waves as they crash on the shore and then retreat silently. They ebb and flow in a rhythm that has been going on since time began. You're covered with sand.

Your limbs feel warm and heavy. Really try to experience your body as warm and relaxed. Feel the weight of the sand.

B. Center your breathing in your abdomen, as described earlier, by putting your hand on your belly. Inhale slowly and deeply through your nose. Allow the air to escape easily through relaxed, pursed lips.

C. As you continue to visualize the beach and sand, breathe deeply and easily. Notice the warmth of the sand and repeat the word "warm" on the in-breath. Notice the weight of the sand, and repeat the word "heavy" on the out-breath. As you do this, switch off your muscles and allow the stress and tension to drain from your body. Continue for at least five minutes.

2. Being in control.

A. Close your eyes and get comfortable. Loosen your tie, belt, or any other constrictions. Notice your breathing. Focus on each breath, one at a time. Each time you exhale, say the word "one." Continue saying "one" with each exhalation.

B. When you begin to feel yourself relaxing, allow your attention to drift to a situation that has been a problem for you. Now you can begin to visualize yourself handling that situation in a new and different way. Where you once felt stressed and uncomfortable, you now can see yourself as confident. You are smiling, and your lips say the right words automatically. Others around you lean forward, they smile, you're being a success.

C. Now you see yourself hesitating. A small mistake, a faux pas. You're uncertain for a moment. But you recover your poise and continue, confidently. You feel satisfied. You've done a good job. You remind yourself, "I can handle this, I'm in control."

3. Stopping and breathing.

A. When unwelcome intruding thoughts make you feel anxious or disturbed, you can hear your voice shout "STOP!" inside your head. (This technique is described in greater detail in Chapter 13 in the section on image stopping) You can imagine hearing your voice saying "STOP!" with clarity and real authority. If you need additional emphasis, put a rubber band around your wrist and snap it as you shout "STOP!"

B. Now shift your attention to your breathing. Take slow, deep breaths into your belly. Put a hand on your abdomen to make sure you're breathing properly.

C. Begin to count your breaths. Counting each time that you exhale. One, two, three, four. Each time that you reach four, start over again. Empty your mind and stay focused on your breathing. Continue this exercise until you feel relaxed. Repeat this process each time disturbing thoughts come to your mind.

4. Grateful relaxation. This exercise is great for combating the sense of rising frustration and stress that accompanies a long, hard day.

A. Begin by using the short form of progressive relaxation outlined earlier in this chapter. Assume a Charles Atlas pose. Wrinkle your forehead and hunch your shoulders. Arch your back and take a deep breath. Point and curl your toes and tighten your calves and thighs.

B. Let your mind wander and remember some good things that happened today. Find at least three things that you can feel grateful for. These experiences don't have to be "biggies." Your good things may be something as simple as enjoying a sunset, getting a hug from your child, or a co-worker offering to get you a cup of coffee. Or an unexpected smile from your boss, or getting into the shortest line at the grocery store, or the soothing feeling of a warm shower. Life is full of small pleasures. Take a moment to relive and relish these experiences.

C. Continue to reflect on your day. Remember three things that *you* did that you feel good about. Again, don't look for Oscar-award level events. Simple, satisfying things like being supportive to a friend or giving your spouse a compliment are ideal. Having the courage to say no to something you really didn't want to do or completing a difficult task are other good examples. Take a moment to reexperience these positive moments of your day.

Ultra Quickies

If all else fails, use one of these sure-fire strategies for guaranteed immediate (temporary) relief.

1. Spend 10 seconds rubbing a tense part of your body.
2. Take 10 slow deep breaths.
3. Change your posture and stretch.
4. Talk more slowly.
5. Get up and get a cold (nonalcoholic) drink.
6. Sit down and lean back.

Stopping Anger Before It Starts

These brief techniques are just the ticket for dealing with specific, anger arousing situations. Return now to your Anger Diary. You should begin to track the physical signs and symptoms that you feel just *before* the anger hits. Early warning signals might include such physiological cues as an increased pulse rate or heavy or rapid breathing. Some people report feeling hot, some become sweaty. It is very important to pay attention to your body. Notice *where* and *when* you begin to feel tension. For some people it's a tightness in the gut that signals the beginning of frustration. For others the tension might be located in the neck and shoulders. "Hunching" the shoulders might be an attempt to protect the neck, or even to cover the ears from hearing painful messages. Tension in the legs, calves, and thighs is often associated with the "fight or flight" syndrome. Tension in the jaw indicates an effort to stifle some response. A particularly telling sign is tension in the hands resulting in a clenching of the fists.

The early warning signs of stress are your signal to cope. When you feel the first symptoms of anger arousal, you can decide which of the brief strategies will work best for your situation. Try different techniques and find the one that's most effective for you. Once you find the best solution for reducing stress, be sure to use it consistently.

You now have two different ways to combat stress. The techniques for general stress reduction, such as meditation, progressive muscle relaxation, or self-hypnosis, should be practiced daily. They will help you to reduce chronic states of tension and arousal. Remember, consistency is the key to mastery. The brief, focused techniques should be reserved for dealing with specific anger-evoking situations. They can be used as needed to successfully manage acute problems.

Problem Solving

Problems that elude solution result in chronic emotional pain, which is often expressed as anger. When your usual coping strategies fail, you may experience a growing sense of helplessness. Problems may begin to appear insoluble. Increased anxiety and despair can make the search for successful solution even more difficult. The following problem-solving technique is adapted from *Thoughts and Feelings* (McKay, Davis, and Fanning 1981).

1. *Identifying Problems That Cause Stress*

Everyday life offers a broad spectrum of opportunities for experiencing problematic situations. Problems are normal, and may appear in any area of your life. It is often useful to examine your life, category by category, and make a checklist to pinpoint where to concentrate your attention. While reviewing the following list, pay particular attention to problems that seem associated with tension, emotional distress, or episodes of anger.

Health problems may involve eating (disgestion, poor diet, weight), sleeping (insomnia, trouble getting up in the morning), or feeling chronically tired or run down.

Financial problems might include insufficient money for necessities or recreation, increasing debt or difficulty making ends meet, or unexpected or catastrophic expenses.

Work-related issues include unemployment or underemployment, work conditions, boring work, trouble with a boss or co-worker, fear of being fired, or desire for a career change.

Living situations that may be unsatisfying or a bad neighborhood, a home too small or too far from work or school, a messy house, things always breaking down, or landlord hassles.

Interpersonal relationships may be a problem if you feel lonely or left out, want more closeness but have few friends, feel vulnerable or shy or unable to get along with people or make conversation, are experiencing an ending or ended love affair, feel a lack of affection or contact with the opposite sex, or can't find the right partner.

Recreational problems include not having enough fun, an inability to think of anything good to do, needing a vacation, wanting to travel, not enough free time, or lack of skill at playing games.

Family troubles include fighting and arguing all the time, not getting along with parents or children, being worried or irritated with a family member, feeling rejected by the family, feeling trapped in an unhappy family situation or insecure about losing a mate, an inability to be open and honest with family members, different interests from your spouse, recurring hurt and criticism from your spouse, children having problems at school, interfering in-laws, a sick family member, or a marriage breaking up.

Psychological problems include feeling nervous or depressed, excessive worrying or trouble with bad habits, problems with authority, feeling blocked from attaining goals or obsessed with unobtainable goals, lack of motivation, or loss of faith.

2. *Clarifying Your Goals*

The next step in problem solving is to describe the problem and your usual response in minute detail. This will allow you to reassess your goals.

Begin by examining the situation. First, *who is involved* (the cast of characters); *what happens* (what is actually being done, or not done, that bothers you); *where it happens* (location); *when it happens* (time of day, duration, frequency); *how it happens* (does it seem to follow a definite "plot"); and last, *why it happens* (the reasons given by you or others for the problem).

Now examine your response by summarizing what you do or don't do. First, *where you do it* (location); next, *when you do it* (duration of response and reaction time); *how you do it* (style, degree of force, mood); *how you feel* (angry, depressed, confused); *why you do it* (your thoughts, theories, explanations, rationalizations); and last, and most important, *what you want* (what would make you feel that the problem is solved).

Now that you have outlined the problem in detail, you may find it helpful to try a new perspective. Frequently the real difficulty is not the problem situation itself, but your *response* to the situation. The real problem is actually the way you're trying to solve the problem. It is often useful to make a statement along these lines:

"In reality, the problem isn't _____, the real problem is _____."

Some examples of how this statement might read: "In reality, the problem isnt *what's being done to you,* the real problem is *how you respond.*" Or, "In reality, the problem isn't *how it happens,* the real problem is *why you respond.*" Or perhaps, "In reality the problem isn't *the situation,* the real problem is *when you respond.*"

Creating statements like this will help you to pinpoint what needs changing in a given situation. They may also help you to see that sometimes your attempted solution has really exacerbated or maintained the problem. When you have completed the above exercise, it's time to make a clear statement of your goal in the situation.

3. *Alternative Strategies*

This part of the problem-solving process involves "brainstorming." There are four basic rules to brainstorming.

1. Be uncritical. Save evaluation or judgment for the next step. Write down whatever idea comes to your head without consideration of whether it is good or bad.

2. Be wild and crazy. The more "far out" your idea is, the better. Following this rule can help you out of a mental rut and allow you to break free of old, limited views of the problem. Getting a new perspective will let you see the problem in an entirely different light.

3. Be prolific. The more the merrier. The more ideas you can generate, the better your chances of finding some really good solutions. Write them down, one after another, without thinking about them. Don't stop until you have a good long list.

4. Be creative. Go back over your list and see how you can combine and improve the ideas you have thought of. Sometimes two fairly good ideas can be put together to make on excellent idea. Brainstorming at this point should focus on general strategies. The nuts and bolts will come later.

4. *Analyze the Consequences*

At this point you have defined a goal and developed a list of strategies for achieving that goal. The next step is to identify the most promising approaches and consider the consequences of putting each one into action. Some people can do this evaluation automatically, while others need to take some time to figure it out step by step. Whichever way you do it, it really pays off to do this step thoroughly and conscientiously.

Go over your list of strategies and rule out any obviously bad ideas. Whenever possible, combine strategies into one plan.

On a separate piece of paper list the best remaining strategies and make two columns below your list. Each strategy will necessarily have both positive and negative consequences. In the column on the left, list all of the positive outcomes. Negative outcomes go in the column on the right. Start with personal consequences. How would putting this strategy into action affect what you feel, need, or want? Now think of social outcomes. What impact would it have on the other people in your life? In what ways would it affect their reaction to you? Next explore short-term consequences. How would it affect your life right now? And finally look at the long-term consequences— how you might be affected in a month or a year.

When you have listed the major consequences of each strategy, it's time to evaluate the likely outcomes. Cross out any obviously unlikely outcomes. These are the catastrophic or Pollyannaish fantasies that everyone indulges in, but that you will need to weed out before you can proceed.

You can now score the remaining consequences using the following system.

- If the consequence is mainly personal in nature, give it 2 points.
- If the consequence is mainly social in nature, score 1 point.
- If the consequence is mainly long range, award it 2 points.
- If the consequence is mainly short term, give it 1 point.

Note that consequences can be both personal and long range at the same time (for a score of 4 points) or social and short term (for a score of 2 points), and so on.

Now add up the scores for each strategy to see whether the positive consequences outweigh the negative ones. Obviously, it pays to avoid strategies that have mainly negative outcomes. Choose a strategy that is heavily weighted with positive outcomes to put into action.

5. *Taking the First Step*

This is the hardest part of the process and the most important one. You've set a goal and chosen the strategies that you believe have the greatest chance of getting you what you want. Now it's time to put your decision into action.

First, decide what steps you will have to take to actualize your plan. Think of concrete behavioral steps. If you get stuck, go back to brainstorming to develop a range of possibilities and then analyze the consequences as you've done before.

It helps to "think small." What is the smallest possible step you can take that will get you started on the road to achieving your goal? A small pebble tossed in a pond will inevitably cause a "ripple" effect.

Now take a deep breath, and DO IT!

Aerobic Exercise

One of the best methods for controlling stress is to exercise. Vigorous physical exertion provides a natural outlet for your body. Exercise releases special chemicals in your brain called endorphins. These act as natural tranquilizers and have tremendous stress-reducing properties. When you experience a state of arousal, exercising can return your body to normal equilibrium, leaving you feeling relaxed and refreshed.

Aerobic exercise uses up oxygen. Your body's increased demand for oxygen is matched by an increased heart rate, faster breathing, and a relaxation of the small blood vessels. This allows more oxygen-carrying blood to reach the muscles.

Cautionary Note: Do not start a strenuous program of aerobic exercise abruptly. Get a checkup from you doctor. If you are not used to physical exertion, start slowly by walking or doing easy calisthenics. Every year at least one New Yorker gets a fatal heart attack shoveling his car out of the snow, after a year of living a sedentary lifestyle. If you develop heart palpitations, dizziness, or chest pain after beginning an exercise program, see a doctor as soon as possible.

The simplest and easiest form of aerobic exercise is brisk walking or jogging. However, the principles discussed here are equally applicable to swimming, bicycling, cross-country skiing, or even jumping rope.

In order to benefit from aerobic exercise, your heart must beat at 70 percent of its maximum rate for at least 20 minutes. The exercise must be repeated at least three times per week. By following this procedure you will place a moderate stress on your heart which will gradually improve its efficiency. The table below shows the estimated heart rates for different age groups. (From *The Relaxation & Stress Reduction Workbook*.)

Estimated Heartbeats per Minute for Average Man or Woman by Age Group

Age	Maximum Rate	80% Maximum Rate	70% Maximum Rate	60% Maximum Rate	50% Maximum Rate
18-29	203-191	162-153	142-134	122-115	101-95
30-39	190-181	152-145	133-127	113-108	95-90
40-49	180-171	144-137	126-120	107-102	90-85
50-59	170-161	136-129	119-113	101-96	85-80
60-69	160-151	128-121	112-106	95-90	80-75
70-79	150-141	120-113	105-99	89-84	75-70

In order to determine your heart rate, simply take your pulse for 15 seconds. Now multiply this number by four to get your rate per minute. You can practice taking your pulse while sitting quietly. Wear a watch with a second hand (or a digital readout) on your left arm. Turn the palm of your right hand toward you. Put the fingerstips of your left hand on your right wrist and locate the bone that comes down from your thumb. Move about 1/8 inch from the bone and press firmly. The throbbing feeling is your pulse.

A normal resting pulse may vary from 40 to 100 beats per minute. Most healthy men have a resting pulse between 70 and

84 beats per minute. Most healthy women's resting pulses range between 75 and 85 beats per minute.

In order to determine how fast you should walk or jog to achieve the optimal 70 percent, follow these instructions.

1. Walk at a comfortable pace for five minutes. Take your pulse immediately (the rate falls off fast). If the rate is about 50 percent of the maximum heart rate for your age group (see the table above), go to the next test. If it is already above the 70 percent level, continue to walk at this pace every other day until your rate falls below that level. When you have achieved that rate, continue to the next test. If you have not had a recent physical exam, have one soon.

2. Walk at a vigorous pace for five minutes. Take your pulse immediately. If your rate is about 60 percent of the maximum, go on to the next test. If your pulse is over the 70 percent maximum, continue at this pace. Take five-minute walks every other day until your pulse falls below the 70 percent level. Then go on to the next test.

3. Alternate one minute of slow jogging with one minute of brisk walking for five minutes and then take your pulse. If your rate is above the 70 percent maximum heart rate for your age group, continue this regimen until your pulse falls below that level.

4. You are now ready to proceed on your own. A good rule of thumb is to continue to jog until you feel winded and then slow to a brisk walk for a minute. (You should be able to carry on a conversation while you are jogging. If you can't, you're going too fast!) Check your pulse frequently to find that pace which allows you to maintain the ideal 70 percent rate for at least 20 minutes.

5. When you're finished exercising, COOL DOWN. Always end your exercise sessions with five minutes of slow walking. Take long, stretching steps. Let your arms dangle loosely and shake your hands. Rotate your head around on your neck a few times in one direction and then in the other direction.

Journal Writing

A very useful technique for controlling stress is to keep a journal or diary. Buy a spiral notebook and keep it in a safe place. You will want to be able to write your most intimate thoughts without the fear of being discovered. You may also want to record your dreams, or use your notebook to make spontaneous drawings or sketches.

Whatever you do, focus on the ways in which you are feeling stressed. It is not helpful, however, to dwell on all the ways that you are being victimized. Be especially careful to avoid making blaming statements or repeating the "trigger thoughts" that fuel your anger.

R & R

R & R means rest and recreation. This may be the best everyday method for controlling stress in your life. It is vital that you allow some space in your life for doing things that are fun.

1. Hobbies. It doesn't really matter whether you collect stamps or samples of barbed wire. The important point is that you are focusing your attention on something that gives you satisfaction.

2. Music. "...has charms to sooth a savage breast." It doesn't matter what you prefer, just spend a little time each day listening to your favorite kind of music and your stress will decrease automatically. There's something about music which takes us away from our everyday troubles. Beatles or Bach, Miles or Mantovani, sit back and relax and feel your stress float away.

3. Nothing. This is the most difficult, yet most rewarding kind of time to take. In this world of hectic doing, working, being productive, accomplishing, achieving, we rarely allow ourselves the ultimate luxury of simply doing "nothing." Even if you only manage five minutes a day, this small pleasure will give you great rewards in terms of controlling stress and enriching your life.

4. Humor. A good laugh is probably worth as much (or more) than an hour of psychotherapy. Less expensive too! If you can learn to look at the funny side of life, stress will diminish automatically. Clip favorite cartoons from the Sunday paper and tack them on the fridge. Learn to hum refrains from old Tom Lehrer songs, or recite Abbott and Costello's "Who's on first" routine at inappropriate moments. Norman Cousins (author of *Anatomy of an Illness*) was able to cure himself by watching Marx Brothers movies.

Substances That Increase Stress (A Cautionary Note)

Abusing any substance is a guaranteed way to increase your stress level. Drug-abuse problems involving opiates (heroin, demerol, darvon) and the major stimulants (speed and cocaine, particularly "crack") are beyond the scope of this book. If these substances are having an adverse effect on your life (i.e., causing problems at work or with your relationships or affecting your health), then it is a good idea to see a therapist or drug-abuse counselor.

More common legal substances, such as alcohol, nicotine, caffeine, and even sugar, are also potential stress inducers. All of these substances are intially pleasant to consume but eventually lead to irritability.

Alcohol is the most dangerous legal drug available. It affects (adversely) every major body system. Drinking one or two drinks will bring on euphoria and general good feelings. This deceptive "come-on" often tempts people into drinking more, which initiates the second stage. This is characterized by depression, fatigue, nausea, and general bad feelings.

Alcoholic hangovers are the major source of irritability, which often leads to rage and wife battering. Recent studies indicate that 72 percent of male batterers are abusing alcohol (or drugs). Surprise attacks in the middle of the night by drunken partners make a kind of perverse sense in light of the irritation created by the second-stage alcoholic effect. Often, bad physical feelings may be combined with anxious self-talk about the other partner's negative reaction. This may set off an angry and violent reaction before the victim is even aware that a problem exists.

The body responds to sugar with a sense of fresh energy and well-being. All too soon (10 to 30 minutes at best) insulin is released to metabolize the candy (and all available blood sugars from previous meals). The overall blood sugar level therefore drops lower than before, and an uncomfortable feeling of tiredness results. Because the brain cannot function well without a relatively high level of blood sugar, irritability is the inevitable result.

Nicotine and caffeine are both mild stimulants that raise the heart rate and give a temporary "high" feeling. These substances also increase insulin secretion, which accentuates the swings in blood sugar levels, resulting in irritable moods. These drugs cause other side effects that can increase stress, notably respiratory problems (due to heavy smoking) and stomach problems (caused by the caffeine in coffee and soft drinks).

Be aware of the effect that various substances have on your life. Stress and anger cannot be controlled if your life is ruled by drugs. If alcohol or drugs are taking over more and more of your life, it is strongly suggested that you find a therapist or counselor to help resolve this problem.

9

Stopping Escalation

This chapter is designed to give you specific tools to help control the two major contributors to anger escalation: aversive chains and mind reading. You can stop escalation by understanding exactly how conflicts start and learning how to modify your behavior so that a simple discussion doesn't turn into a thermonuclear war.

Aversive Chains

Gerald Patterson of the Oregon Social Learning Center has pioneered the systematic examination and analysis of social interaction sequences. According to Patterson (1982), escalating anger depends on chains of aversive behavior in which two people attempt to influence each other through a rapid exchange of punishing communications. Escalating aversive chains are most likely to occur between two people with approximately equal power: husbands and wives, co-workers, and (remarkably) parents and children. Aversive chains build over time. They usually begin with a common innocuous event and develop along predictable lines. Patterns of reactions and counterreactions can grow to incredible complexity.

Irritable exchanges often appear to be relatively trivial in the early stages. In fact, the beginnings of an aversive chain are often overlooked because they seem so unimportant. They are, however, the basic building blocks of family anger and violence.

The vast majority of aversive chains never proceed past the first link. For example, someone in the family will tease or insult another and then stop. Since no one reacts aversively to the provocation, it lasts only a few seconds. Three- or four-step sequences last less than half a minute and occur even in "normal" families. But when aversive chains last longer than half a minute, yelling, threatening, or hitting may occur. Sequences like these are frequently observed in dysfunctional families. The longer the chain lasts, the more likely it is that violence will occur.

The last link in a chain is often called a "trigger behavior." These behaviors usually precede and precipitate a violent outburst. Triggers are often verbal or nonverbal behaviors that bring up feelings of abandonment or rejection. The following list offers a representative sample of possible "links" that may be used to build an aversive chain.

Verbal Behaviors

1. Giving advice ("Ask your boss for a raise, you know we need more money.")
2. Global labeling ("All you women are alike...")
3. Criticism ("That's not a good parking job, you almost hit that car.")
4. Blaming ("If it weren't for you, we'd be on easy street right now.")
5. Abrupt limit setting ("That's it, I've had it." "Forget it." "Stop this instant!")
6. Threatening ("If you don't shut up right now...")
7. Using expletives ("Dammit!" "Shit!")
8. Complaining ("My life is empty." "All I do is work." "You never help me with the laundry.")
9. Stonewalling ("There is nothing to talk about.")
10. Mind reading or assuming ("I know what you're really trying to do: drive me crazy.")
11. "Innocent" observations ("I notice that the dishes haven't been done for the past two days.")
12. Teasing ("Those slacks must have shrunk in the wash, you're having a hard time closing that zipper.")
13. Humiliating statements ("You used to look good, now I'm embarrassed to be seen with you.")

14. Dismissing comments ("Get out of my life." "I'm tired of looking at your ugly face.")
15. Put downs ("Is this what you call a meal? I've had better grub at the greasy spoon on Market Street.")
16. Profanity ("You son of a ...")
17. Sarcasm ("Sure you're going to fix it. Like last time when we had to call the plumber after you...")
18. Accusations ("You went out and did _____ again, didn't you?")
19. Guilt ("You should know better...")
20. Ultimatums ("This is your last chance. If you don't shape up, I'm leaving.")

Nonverbal Sounds
1. Groaning ("Oh no, not that again.")
2. Sighing ("I'm tired of this crap.")
3. Clucking sound ("Do you have to bring that up right now?")
4. "Tsk, tsk" ("You've done it again.")

Voice Quality, Tone, and Volume
1. Whining (trying to irritate)
2. Flatness (suggesting "I'm not here.")
3. Cold, frosty tone (suggesting "I'm here, but you'll never be able to reach me.")
4. Throaty, constricted (suggesting controlled fury)
5. Loud, harsh quality (attempting to intimidate)
6. Mocking, contemptuous tone (trying to get your goat)
7. Mumbling under your breath (making him guess what you said)
8. Snickering (demeaning, putting down)
9. Snarling ("Back off!")

Gestures Using Hands and Arms
1. Pointing a finger (accusation)
2. Shaking a fist (intimidation)
3. "Flipping the bird" (obscenity)
4. Folded arms ("You can't get to me.")
5. Waving away (dismissal)
6. Chopping motion (cutting off)

Facial Expressions

1. Looking away, looking at the floor (abandonment)
2. Rolling eyes ("Not that again.")
3. Narrowing eyes (threatening)
4. Eyes wide (incredulous disbelief)
5. Grimacing ("I don't like that.")
6. Sneering (disparaging)
7. Frowning (disapproving)
8. Tightening lips (suppressed anger)
9. Raising an eyebrow ("Watch it, buster.")
10. Scowling (annoyance)

Body Movements

1. Shaking head ("No, no, no!")
2. Shrugging shoulders ("I give up.")
3. Tapping a foot or a finger (annoyance)
4. Moving or leaning toward (intimidating)
5. Moving or turning away (abandonment)
6. Hands on hips (exasperation)
7. Quick movements or pacing (increased agitation)
8. Kicking or throwing objects (anger getting out of control)
9. Pushing or grabbing (angry physical contact)

Examples of Aversive Chains

Husband and Wife

1. *(Husband comes home, silent, eyes down.)*
2. *Wife (frowns, sighs):* "What's the matter now?"
3. *Husband (with folded arms, complaining, tightening lips):* "My boss is an asshole."
4. *Wife (In a cold tone, giving advice and using guilt):* "Well, you'll just have to stick it out. You should know we can't afford you quitting your job now."
5. *Husband (using an expletive and global labeling in a loud voice):* "Dammit, you give zilch support, you know that? I can't take much more of this!"
6. *Wife (abrupt limit setting, guilt, flatness):* "Stop shouting right now! The children will hear you."

7. *Husband (in a constricted voice, using global labeling, finger-pointing, and an expletive):* "Yeah, all you think of is the children. You don't give a damn about me."
8. *Wife (sneering, sarcasm, accusation):* "Oh yeah! I didn't know you had feelings. You haven't talked to me in weeks."
9. *Husband (with tight lips and narrowing eyes, complaining and using profanity):* "You never have time for me anyway. You're always on the phone to your goddamn mother. I wish she would keep the fuck out of our life."
10. *Wife (loudly and harshly) with narrowing eyes, using profanity and a dismissing comment, leaning toward):* "Shut up, asshole! You get out of my life." *(She throws her wedding ring.)*
11. *Husband (loudly and harshly, using profanity, threatening):* "All right, bitch, I've had it from you. I'll leave, but I'm going to shut you up first!" *(He makes a threatening gesture with his fist.)*

Co-Workers from a Repair Crew.

1. *(Matt comes to work five minutes late scowling.)*
2. *Jeff (frowning):* "Where you been? The truck's ready to leave."
3. *Matt (waving him away):* "Leave me alone. I've had a bad night."
4. *Jeff (accusing, using profanity):* "Hung over again! Fuck!"
5. *Matt (in a harsh voice, using profanity):* "Back off. What I drink is none of your fucking business."
6. *Jeff (turning away, in a cold tone):*"All right, buddy, let's get on the truck and get to work."

Later:

7. *Jeff (in a cold tone):* "Hand me a wrench."
8. *Matt (turning away):* "Get it yourself. I'm not your slave."
9. *Jeff (groaning, accusing):* "Come on, willya. We're supposed to be partners. And you haven't done a damn thing all morning."
10. *Matt (snarling, throwing tool, using profanity):* "Here's your goddamn wrench. And you know where to shove it!"

11. *Jeff (threatening, in a loud voice):* "Listen buster, I've had enough of this. Cut the shit or I'll get me another partner."
12. *Matt (sneering, moving away, using profanity):* "Big deal, who wants to work with a jerk like you anyway?"

After Lunch:

13. *Jeff (in a flat tone):* "All right, give me a hand with this cable, it's heavy."
14. *Matt (mumbling under his breath, sarcastic):* "Yes, master."
15. *Jeff (sniffing, rolling his eyes, using an expletive and global labeling, dismissing):* "Jee-sus! You smell like a brewery. You're a goddamn lush. Get out of here before you cause an accident."
16. *Matt (in a loud, harsh voice, using an expletive):* "Shit, you're as bad as my wife. Get the fuck off my back."
17. *Jeff (in a contemptuous tone, moving away, putting down):* "I feel sorry for her, having to put up with a bum like you. You used to be a man. But now you ain't worth shit, boy."
18. *Matt (moving forward, pushing, using a loud, harsh voice, threatening):* "You can't talk to me like that. I'll kick your ass."
19. *(Jeff moves to one side, Matt stumbles and falls.) Jeff (in a flat voice):* "Get out of here now."

Parent and Teenage Child

1. *(Child slams the door. Silence.)*
2. *Parent (frowning):* "Hi, darling. How was school?"
3. *Child (looking away):* "OK."
4. *Parent (sighing):* "What's the matter?"
5. *Child (rolling eyes):* "Nothing."
6. *Parent (hands on hips):* "Come on. Tell me what's going on."
7. *Child (groaning, turning away):* "Nothing, just leave me alone. OK?"
8. *Parent (moving toward, narrowing eyes):* "Listen, I have a right to know what's going on. You're not just a boarder here, you know."

9. *Child (moving away, scowling, mumbling):* "You're always hassling me."
10. *Parent (shrugging shoulders, sighing, making an "innocent" observation):* "I notice that the dishes weren't done last night, and there's a pile of your clothes in the living room."
11. *Child (rolling eyes, shaking head):* "I'll do 'em later, OK?"
12. *Parent (moving toward, setting an abrupt limit, threatening):* "No! You'll do it right now or you're grounded for a week."
13. *Child (grimacing, speaking in a loud, harsh voice, using an expletive):* "I'll do it later, now just leave me alone, dammit!"
14. *Parent (shaking head, constricted voice, dismissing comment, humiliating):* "I've had it with you. Go to your room right now. And clean it up, it looks like a pigsty in there."
15. *Child (turning away, "flipping the bird," using a loud voice and profanity):* "Fuck you. It's my room—and stay out of it!"
16. *Parent (shaking a fist, leaning forward, using a loud voice, dismissing, threatening):* "You can't talk to me like that. Get to your room right now. And no dinner until your room is clean!"
17. *Child (leaving, sneering, putting down):* "Big deal. You're not the world's greatest cook, you know."
18. *Parent (in a loud voice):* "You come back here!"
19. *(Child slams the door. Silence.)*

We will return to these examples several times in this chapter and give concrete suggestions for breaking the chains.

Anger Diary

It is now time to return to your Anger Diary and start a new section. In this part of the book, you can begin to jot down your observations about your own patterns of escalation. Make a point to spend some time each evening reviewing the events of the day. Fully explore each step in an aversive chain—particularly your verbal and nonverbal behavior. Over time you will be able to recognize repeating patterns.

Coping with Aversive Chains

What follows are four important methods for altering your aversive chains and beginning to set yourself free from a sequence of escalating attacks.

Time-Out

Perhaps the single most useful strategy in controlling the escalation of anger is the "time-out" technique. Part of its effectiveness undoubtedly stems from the fact that time-out is a familiar and acceptable metaphor in sports. It is also a guaranteed method for stopping violence. It has been used successfully by many men who have attended male "batterer" treatment programs.

Anger is not something that happens "in a flash." Even people who are "quick to anger," or have a "short fuse" go through progressive stages. Beginning with irritation, anger is "kindled" and the body begins to tense. Destructive self-statements "fan the flames," and trigger behaviors ignite the "explosive" rage. As you will see, this sequence is not inevitable.

"T" Time

When either person in an interaction notices the early warning signs, he or she may decide that a time-out is needed. This strategy could have been used effectively at any point in the husband and wife aversive chain scenario. Either person could have initiated the time-out, even as late in the chain as the "trigger event," which occurred when the wife threw the wedding ring.

The need for a time-out is communicated simply and efficiently by using the same gesture the referees use. The "T" sign is made with your hands. Nothing need or should be said at this point, except perhaps the announcement "Time-out!" The other person is then obligated to return the gesture and stop talking. It is permissible to say "OK, time-out."

DO NOT say "You are making me angry" or "You're getting out of control." These kinds of statements will inevitably lead to a defensive posture and escalation rather than the hoped-for cooling off and safety of temporary separation. Some people suggest using the statement "I'm beginning to feel angry and I need (or want) to take a time-out." This version has the advantage of being a nonblaming "I" statement that talks about how the person feels. However, there is some evidence that merely using the word "angry" will trigger an automatic aggression sequence. Therefore it is recommended that you stick with the neutral term, *time-out*.

Using this procedure has several benefits. First, the T sign makes it less likely that you will indulge in hostile or threatening gestures. Second, the T sign can provide a protective shield for a person feeling threatened if the sign is held directly in front of the face. Last, the procedure stops the tendency on both sides to try to "get in the last word."

Leaving and Returning

The T sign is a signal that it is time to separate for a while. (This works best if you have both discussed ahead of time what will happen next.) Ideally, the person who is "beginning to get angry" will take the cue and leave for an agreed period of time. Agreeing ahead of time will prevent any misconception that this necessary separation is a form of running away or a means of punishing the other person with abandonment.

A good rule of thumb is to separate for one hour (plus or minus five minutes). It is important to allow yourself an adequate amount of time to cool off. It is even more important to return when the time is up. This is hard to do. It takes real courage to return to a painful situation without the protective shield of anger. Similarly, it is of the utmost importance that the person who was left is there again when the leaver returns. Trust will grow as each partner becomes more experienced in this method.

While You're Gone

A few do's and don'ts are important to follow while you are away from the stressful situation.

DO something physically challenging that will help to reduce the tension in your body. Taking a long walk or going for a run are two of the best methods. If angry thoughts come to your mind, let them come. And then let them go. Use a relaxation or arousal-reduction technique that works for you. Picture a river that flows down to the sea. Put your angry thoughts on the river and allow them to float away from you.

DON'T hang on to angry thoughts or waste time building a case. The more you focus on proving how wrong and awful the offender is, the angrier you get. Resist getting stuck in rehearsing what you should say. If you do, you may return more upset than when you left. Don't drink or use drugs while you're away. Please don't drive. Angry drivers are a real danger to themselves and others.

When You Get Back

When you come back be sure to "check in." More than anything else, this will help to build trust in the relationship. The check-in involves a willingness on both sides to communicate. See if you're ready to talk about the issue. If not, set a specific time when you'll be ready to do so. Talking about what made you angry will help you both to reduce the possibility of escalating anger in the future.

Practice Time-Outs

The best way to get into the swing of taking time-outs is to practice when you are not angry. You might take a practice time-out at the first sign of mild irritation, or just for the hell of it. A practice time-out works just like a regular one, except that you say "Practice time out!" and the away time is cut in half. Go through all the steps, including the check-in. It is very important to do this. The more you practice taking time-outs, the easier it will be when the real thing happens.

Abuses of Time-Out

In order to build trust and reestablish a good relationship, it is critical that the time-out process not be abused. If time-out is called simply to avoid contact or to forestall any form of disagreeable discussion, it is bound to fail. Similarly, if time-out is used to hurt or punish the other person, it won't work.

Be particularly careful about scenarios like this one. An unpleasant scene is beginning to shape up. One person takes this as an opportunity to skip down to the bar or over to a friend's house. Watching football, drinking a couple of six-packs, and not calling or coming back for several hours makes matters worse. While it's understandable to seek support and solace, this kind of behavior undermines the trust you need to use the time-out as an effective strategy for anger control.

Making a Contract

When two people want to make a commitment to change patterns of anger that occur when they are together, a contract is in order. The following suggested outline (adapted from Deschner 1986) provides a framework for making the kind of changes that will benefit you both.

Time-Out Contract

When I realize that my (or my partner's) anger is rising, I will give a "T" signal for a time-out and leave at once. I will not hit or kick anything and I will not slam the door.

I will return no later than one hour. I will take a walk to use up the anger energy and will not drink or use drugs while I am away. I will try not to focus on resentments.

When I return I will start the conversation with "I know that I was partly wrong and partly right." I will then admit to a technical mistake I made.

If my partner gives a "T" signal and leaves, I will return the sign and let my partner go without a hassle, no matter what is going on. I will not drink or use drugs while my partner is away and will avoid focusing on resentments. When my partner returns, I will start the conversation with "I know that I was partly wrong and partly right."

Name _____ Date _____

Name _____ Date _____

Rechanneling

So far you've learned how an escalating pattern of behavior can be stopped dead in its tracks by using time-out. A more subtle approach is to *rechannel* or redirect the sequence at critical junctions. This is analogous to the shunting system used by railroads. When the engineer is warned of trouble ahead, he may avail himself of the opportunity to switch to another set of tracks.

The first step in this process is to identify a sequence of behaviors and then find the weak links in the chain. A "weak link" is that piece of behavior which is most easily changed and which will make a difference in the outcome. As a rule of thumb, earlier interventions are best. It's easier to stop a car that has just begun to roll than one that is speeding downhill, out of control.

A review of the husband and wife aversive chain, described earlier in this chapter, shows several opportunities for rechanneling. The earliest is response 4, when the wife is coldly unsympathetic to her husband's complaint about his boss. This chain is probably a familiar one, where behaviors like response 4 inevitably lead to escalation. A small behavioral change here can alter the whole course of the interaction. If the wife answers response 3 with understanding or compassion ("Is he giving you a bad time again?"), the aversive chain is stopped and a healthier pattern may emerge.

The next opportunity to rechannel occurs in response 7, where the husband discounts his wife's concern about the kids hearing their argument. The husband could instead reply by validating his wife's concern or by saying, "We're both getting upset; let's talk about it later when we're not so tired."

For another example, look back to the parent and teenage child aversive chain. In this familiar chain, the first opportunity occurs at response 8. In reply to response 7, when the teen wants to be left alone, the parent can say, "I know that you need your own space, but I really want to feel a part of your life. Maybe we can talk later?"

The child has a powerful opportunity to rechannel in reply to response 14, when the parent sends him to his room. Instead of response 15, he can say "OK, OK, I'll go. Let's both cool out for a few minutes. Can we talk in half an hour?"

If you want to successfully use the rechanneling technique, it is necessary to plan ahead. After laying out a typical sequence and locating the weak links, decide what you can do differently. What behavior can you substitute for that link in the chain? Whatever new behavior you decide on, it has to be something that you know from experience will relax and defuse the situation. Simple acknowledgment or murmuring a few sympathic words may be enough in some cases. Just keeping quiet may be the best thing in others. Remember that your verbal behavior is only part of the aversive sequence. You may also need to change threatening or accusatory gestures, expressions, tone of voice, and so on. Read Chapter 11 on response choice rehearsal and Chapter 12 on problem-solving communication to get more ideas.

When you've made your decision, you will have to wait for an opportunity to practice it. Usually this won't take too long. When you see your chance, say to yourself "Time to rechannel," and do it. The next day, review the sequence and notice the difference it has made. Or notice what didn't work about your new response and decide how to modify it. Continue practicing until your response becomes automatic.

Inquiry

Another subtle way to short-circuit an escalating pattern is to use the technique of inquiry. Remember, the basic assumption is that anger is a response to personal pain. It follows that when someone is beginning to get angry it makes sense to ask, "What hurts?" As with all of these intervention strategies, the sooner in the sequence this is done, the more effective it will be.

Let's return to Matt and Jeff, the repair crew. The first good opportunity to use inquiry in their aversive chain occurs in reply to response 3. Matt probably is hung over, but his drinking is an attempt to self-medicate his personal pain. Jeff can choose to respond to the "symptom" (being late for work and feeling ill) or to the underlying pain. If Jeff changes response 4 to "Having more trouble with your wife?" the whole rest of the day will go differently.

Another opportunity for Jeff occurs in reply to response 8, where Matt refuses to hand him the wrench. He can either escalate, as he does with his accusation (probably accurate), or choose the inquiry method. If Jeff changes response 9 to "You've been on a bummer all morning. Tell me what's really bugging you," this aversive chain can still be stopped before it gets worse.

Calling Process

This technique is probably most effective with people who have sophisticated verbal skills and tend to intellectualize. Instead of getting enmeshed in a hopelessly escalating argument about something (the *content*), you can choose to comment on how the discussion is progressing (the *process*).

Pat and Mike were having a pleasant conversation about football. As disagreements started to pile up, the discussion became more heated. When they got to arguing about the relative merits of Joe Montana and Steve Young, tempers began to flair. A potential disaster was neatly averted (they were already at the name-calling stage) when Mike said, "Hey Pat, we're both getting pretty excited." Instead of continuing with the *content* of the discussion (a losing cause), they could both agree about the *process*—how they are feeling or acting at that moment..

Other examples can be found in the husband and wife scenario. When the husband starts raising his voice in response 5, the wife can reply with "I can hear that you're getting angry, let's talk about this more quietly." Or later in the sequence at response 10, she could say, "I'm really getting upset. I don't even know what we're talking about anymore."

In the parent and teenage child chain, the first chance occurs at response 10. The parent can say, "I feel that you're always making distance between us, and I keep trying to get closer." The last opportunity for a process comment occurs at response 18. Here the parent can interject, "We seem to be caught up in more and more accusations. Let's stop now and talk some more when we've both cooled off."

Mind Reading

A major hidden factor in anger escalation is the tendency to mind-read. This process starts with an ambiguous interpersonal communication. Your lover looks up at the ceiling and sighs. Then she says that you got a call from work, they expect you to attend a conference Saturday morning. There's something incongruent about the communication. Her glance upward and the sigh indicate that something may be bothering her. But her voice is flat and expressionless.

You now have to figure out what's really going on. You start to mind-read. She's angry, you decide, because you'll be abandoning her on Saturday. So you get huffy: "Well, it's my job, what can I do about it?" (spoken in a loud voice, with a shrugging gesture). What you don't know is that her sigh had nothing to do with anger. She's just been assigned an overwhelming project at work and arrived home to find the toilet clogged.

Your assumption about her anger may trigger a process that Richard Bandler and John Grinder (founders of Neurolinguistic Programming) call *calibrated communication*. It works like this: An incongruent or ambiguous message creates uncertainty about the true meaning being conveyed. To deal with the uncertainty, you mind-read. You make assumptions about the feelings, intentions, motives, or attitudes of the other person. Since mind-reading is almost never totally accurate, your assumptions about the other person are always a little bit off.

Now the trouble starts. You respond as if your mind reading were accurate, as if your assumptions were absolutely true. You get defensive or critical. You withdraw or pout. However you express your negative reaction—by a shrug, a grimace, or a blaming attack—the other person is put on guard and begins to act defensively. Now you take their defensive reaction as a confirmation of your original assumption. They really were angry or judging or selfishly uncaring. Your anger grows. You step up the attack, and in turn you find yourself attacked.

With each exchange, you have gotten further and further from the original experience; further from the truth. Consider again your argument with your lover. You've interpreted her sigh as anger when in fact she felt overwhelmed. You've responded defensively. Now, in calibrated steps, the two of you will move away from the real experience. She hears your loud voice and notices your shrug. She reads the shrug as suppressed anger. (Her father did that when he was mad, and now her lover seems to do it also.) "You give too much to that job," she says coldly. You tell her that it pays the bills. "You're sucked dry at work," she says. "You're just a yes-man. You say yes to them, but no to me. You've shown zero commitment to making this relationship work." By the time the dust settles, the room will have a radiation half-life of 50 years.

Pathologically calibrated communication patterns are very similar to a well-choreographed ballet. Each member of the family moves in and out on cue, executing their steps with exquisite timing. As the ballet moves to an exciting crescendo, so too does the family's communication pattern lead to an inevitably tragic and painful finale.

Your Old Files

When you are confronted with ambiguous or incongruent messages, the uncertainty creates anxiety. One way to handle this situation is to go through your old memory files to see if you've ever experienced anything remotely similar before. Is the tone of the voice familiar? The gesture? The facial expression, the body posture? Who in your past looked or sounded this way? What were they conveying with that look or tone? Comparing the present situation to past experience is largely an unconscious process. Most of the time you'll have no idea you're doing it, or what it reminds you of.

Personality theorist Harry Stack Sullivan called this process *parataxic distortion:* the tendency to superimpose the experiences and meanings of an old relationship over a current one. It's as if you were no longer really seeing and reacting to the person in front of you. You are instead responding to your father or sister or your first boyfriend.

Mind reading is greatly influenced by parataxic distortion. Your assumptions about the thoughts, feelings, and motives of the person in front of you are very often based on repeated painful experiences during your earlier years.

Danny's childhood was full of angry exchanges with his father. At a certain point in their battles his father would always raise one eyebrow. Danny knew that meant his father was getting *really* angry, and was on the verge of "blowing it."

Now when he is interacting with someone who raises an eyebrow while giving ambiguous or incongruent messages, Danny assumes that that person is angry.

Sara's older brother was deeply involved in a fundamentalist church. She was an admitted hell-raiser during her late teens, and her brother frequently expressed disapproval. He'd stare at the floor or the wall behind her, but never make eye contact. His lips would pinch just before a lecture on her "affront to God." Now Sara finds herself inexplicably enraged when someone won't look her in the eye. Her husband tends to pinch his lips when his arthritic knee gets inflamed, and Sara's first reflex is to read disapproval in his expression. The residue from her painful sibling relationship still distorts her perceptions. And when Sara acts on assumptions pulled from her old files, she bewilders and then angers her husband.

Now consider Brenda's experience with her first lover. She was seventeen and very unsure of herself. He praised her, called her beautiful. He said she was the only girl worth knowing in the school. His mouth was always held in a broad, rather fixed smile. But the smile switched off instantly if Brenda disappointed him. Then, in a monotone, he'd describe with excruciating detail her physical and psychological flaws. Brenda spent her senior year slamming back and forth between total love and total rejection. Twenty years later, Brenda's new boyfriend tends to smile when he's embarrassed or threatened. If things are the least bit ambiguous, she reads this nervous reaction as a dangerous prelude to attack.

There are several examples of parataxic distortion in the aversive chains described earlier. Remember Matt and Jeff? Notice that Matt mumbles "Yes, master" in response 14. He does the same thing when his wife asks him to take out the garbage. As a boy, Matt used this very same phrase when his rather controlling mother told him to do his chores. He now responds to a simple request from his partner with feelings of annoyance that have their roots in his childhood and are echoed in his marriage.

In the parent and child scenario, response 8 seems like an overreaction. The child's turning away and unwillingness to talk has brought up old feelings of abandonment experienced in the mother's own childhood. In fact, the mom felt like a boarder in her own home, due to her parents emotional unavailability.

Coping with Mind Reading

The following two techniques will be helpful in the battle against calibrated communication and parataxic distortion. The more you practice them, the better control you will achieve.

Checking It Out

This technique is especially valuable to use in situations where mind reading is contributing to the escalation process. As noted earlier, mind reading occurs when someone makes assumptions about another person's thoughts or feelings, based on minimal or ambiguous cues. Remember Danny's mistaken assumption that a raised eyebrow means that someone is getting really angry.

The antidote for this poisonous problem is simply to "check it out." Couples can use a helpful exercise to undercut the problem. When something confusing is happening in an interaction, one person can say, "I observe _____ (*making an observation*), and I imagine _____ (*making an assumption or interpretation*)." It's now the other person's turn to give feedback. "Yes, I am doing _____, but I'm thinking (or feeling)."

To see the process spelled out more clearly, return for a moment to Matt and Jeff. Instead of response 4, Jeff could have said, "You look pretty bad this morning, are you hung over?" The reply to that might have been "Yeah I do look pretty bad. My son was sick and kept me up all night." Notice how that exchange would have changed the whole complexion of the situation.

Another example can be found in the parent and teenage child aversive chain. Instead of response 8, the parent might have said, "You seem kind of tired or unhappy or something. Am I guessing right?" To which the child might have responded, "Yeah, I just need to cool out." These two responses would undoubtedly have moved the interaction in an entirely different direction.

Hearing Voices from the Past

How do you know when you are using parataxic distortion? It's often difficult to tell, but there are four helpful cues. First, watch out for responses with a fast reaction time. Sudden anger or instant distrust suggests the presence of an habitual knee-jerk reflex. Ask yourself, "What past situation am I reminded of, what scene or relationship does it feel like I'm replaying?"

All-or-none, either-or, and black-or-white responses should also be suspected, since reality is rarely that clear cut. If someone seems all bad to you, if you're using global labels like *stupid*, *selfish, worthless, lazy,* and so on, check the old files to see who you're being reminded of.

A third thing to watch out for is a familiar physical feeling. Do you always feel a warm glow when someone with blonde hair smiles at you? Or a lump in your throat when the boss says something critical?

Finally, parataxic distortion is often present when a one-foot stimulus triggers a ten-foot response. If it feels like your reaction greatly exceeds the provocation, the situation may be charged with old pain and old conflict.

If you experience any of these four cues during an interaction, try the exercise of assuming that your present relationship is in some way being contaminated by a voice *from the past.* Start by writing down the salient elements of the current situation:

1. Describe the provoking person's physical characteristics.
2. Describe the tone of voice, gestures, body language, and facial expressions.
3. Describe the nature of the conflict. Is it a struggle for control? Do you feel devalued?
4. Describe your feelings in the conflict.

Do any of your descriptions ring a bell? What aspect of this experience have you lived through before? When you have an answer to these questions, you may choose to share what you've learned with the provoking person (especially if he or she is an intimate). Or you may privately use the knowledge to recognize the process and improve control over your responses.

This chapter has presented various ways of examining and understanding the process of escalation in angry interactions. More importantly, it has offered a variety of strategies and techniques that can be used to effectively stop escalation from occurring. The main thing to remember is that escalation is *not* inevitable. You can make choices all along the line that will enable you to prevent the escalation from reaching a tragic culmination.

10

Coping Through Healthy Self-Talk

Now it's time to begin practicing some of the basic skills of anger control. This chapter will help you select and develop coping thoughts that remind you how to respond effectively at the moment of provocation. Then you'll create a script that incorporates the best coping mantras you can find in a sequence which will enable you to stay cool when things get hot.

There are seven categories of anger-coping thoughts, and you will need all seven in your script. Read through the lists that follow and mark the coping thoughts in each category that you think might be effective for you. If you look ahead, you may think that the lists are too long to be useful and the authors should have their collective heads examined. Here's why there are so many items. For any given provocation, you'll only be using one or two coping thoughts from each category, but you'll need to change and modify coping mantras for different kinds of conflict. You'll also find that some coping thoughts prove more effective than others, so you will need to have a variety of examples to choose from as you experiment with cognitive control. Eventually you will be able to write your own coping thoughts. The thoughts that you develop yourself will probably be more effective for you than anything listed here.

Coping Thoughts

Reassurance

These are the things you say to yourself to prepare for a likely conflict or provocation. The basic message you give yourself is that you're in charge and you have the skills to manage the situation.

- "This may upset me, but I know how to deal with it."
- "I can make a plan to handle this."
- "I can find a way to say what I want."
- "I can manage the situation, I know how to handle my anger."
- "If I find myself getting upset, I'll know what to do."
- "There's no need for an argument. I can handle the conflict without escalating."
- "This could be a testy situation, but I trust my coping skills." *Or* "I believe in myself."

Stopping Trigger Thoughts

These coping mantras are divided according to the categories of trigger thoughts you learned in Chapter 7. After reading that chapter, you should have a good idea of the types of trigger thoughts that typically spark your anger. If you need to brush up, do a quick review before marking the coping mantras that seem best from this list.

Personal responsibility

- "I'm responsible for taking care of my own needs."
- "I'm responsible for what happens to me."
- "Only children are victims, I always have a choice."
- "I'm responsible for doing something about my pain."

Shoulds

- "People never do what I think they should, only what's rewarding and reinforcing for them."
- "Shoulds are my needs and values pushed on someone else."

- "People do what they need to do, not what they should do."
- "I can't expect people to act the way I want them to."
- "People don't do what I think they should, only what their values and needs dictate."

Entitlement fallacy

- "I am free to want, but he or she is free to say no."
- "I have my limits, and others have their limits. I have a right to say no, and so do they."
- "Others are not obliged to meet my expectations."

Fallacy of fairness

- "Our needs are equally important."
- "Each need is legitimate. We can negotiate as peers."

Fallacy of change

- "The amount of support, help, and nourishment I am now getting is all I can get, given the strategies I am now using."
- "People will change only when they are reinforced to change and capable of change."
- "People change only when they want to, not when I want them to."

Conditional assumptions

- "When they disappoint me, it doesn't mean they don't care."
- "Our biggest task, no matter how much we love, is to take care of ourselves."
- "His or her needs are as legitimate as mine. "
- "We can negotiate."

Letting it all out fallacy

- "Anger won't get me what I want."
- "I can protect myself by saying it assertively."

Blaming

- "Everyone chooses his or her highest good."
- "Everyone makes the best choice possible."

- "People do the best they can, given their level of awareness at the moment of choice."

Good-bad dichotomizing
- "I make no judgments."
- "People are coping with pain and stress in the best way they can, given their level of awareness."
- "It is merely a problem that our needs conflict; he or she is not wrong, and I am not right."
- "Forget right and wrong."

Assumed intent
- "Assume nothing, check it out."
- "I don't guess at the motives of others."
- "No mind reading."

Magnifying
- "No more always and never."
- "Accuracy, nonexaggeration."
- "Let the facts speak for themselves."

Global labeling
- "No labels, be specific."

Physiological Coping

In anger control, it's extremely important that you learn to monitor and release body tension. You need to do this throughout the entire provocative episode. By now you have had a chance to learn which relaxation procedures are most effective for you.

Choose statements from the following that will best cue your relaxation response.

- "Take a deep breath and relax (feel comfortable and at ease)."
- "When my muscles get tight, it's time to relax and slow things down."
- "Stay clam and relaxed."

- "It's time to check my body for tension and relax what's tight."
- "Relax the hot spots."
- "It's time to stretch my jaw."
- "It's time to shrug and relax the shoulders."
- "It's time to roll my neck."
- "It's time to stretch my arms."
- "Take a deep breath and visualize my special place."

Add any other brief relaxation procedure for your unique anger hot spots. See Chapter 8 on relaxation.

Sticking to the Task

This is one of the most essential components of anger control. Provocation is a cue to start coping, not exploding. In every conflict situation you have a task to do—to communicate your needs, understand the other person's point of view, and work toward solution. The following coping statements are designed to keep you task oriented. Mark the ones that you think will work best for you.

- "I'll state my needs clearly and simply. What do I want here?"
- "Try to understand his or her needs and concerns here."
- "Acknowledge his or her point of view."
- "Ask him or her for a solution. Work for compromise."
- "How can I negotiate for what I want?"
- "Try to reason it out. Treat each other with respect."
- "No point in blaming. Try a new strategy."
- "Stick to the facts, no putdowns or attacks."
- "Use 'I' statements only."
- "Let's try a cooperative approach. Maybe we're both right."
- "Conflict is escalating. Time to try another strategy."
- "What do I want to get out of this?"
- "Let's take the issue point by point."
- "Negatives lead to more negatives. Look for solutions."
- "I have the commitment and power to take care of myself."

- "How can I take care of myself, meet my own needs in this situation (regardless of what the other person does)?"
- "How can I reinforce him or her to change in the future?"

Coping with Arousal

As things heat up, it becomes very tempting to get out the psychological baseball bat and try to beat the offender into submission. The following are reminders of how and why you should stay cool. Choose the ones that are most helpful and convincing to you.

- "No one is right, no one is wrong. We just have different needs."
- "No matter what is said, I know I'm a good person."
- "Just as long as I keep my cool I'm in control."
- "Just roll with the punches. Don't get bent out of shape."
- "Stay away from blaming and judgments."
- "Neutral words only."
- "Voice calm and flat."
- "No sarcasm, no attacks."
- "Getting mad will cost me _____." (Insert the negative consequences of anger in this situation.)
- "If I start to get mad, I'll just be banging my head against the wall, so I might as well relax."
- "Getting upset won't help."
- "It's just not worth it to get so angry."
- "I'm annoyed, but I can keep a lid on it."
- "I'll stay rational. Anger won't solve anything."
- "Anger is a signal of what I need to do. It's time to cope."
- "Don't escalate. Cool it."
- "There's nothing gained in getting mad."
- "Easy does it, remember to keep a sense of humor."
- "If I'm stuck in a bad situation, I'll think about how to handle this in the future."

Coping with the Angry Person

Anger is frightening to be around. You get the message that you're bad, wrong. And suddenly your self-esteem is under seige, your worth in question, your relationship in danger. The only way to cope without resorting to defensive anger of your own is *distancing*. You have to psychologically push the person and his or her anger far enough away that the barbs and arrows fall just short of you. Distancing helps you see the other person as fallible and momentarily out of control. His opinions and judgments are distorted by anger. You don't have to fall into the same trap he or she is in. You can stay emotionally insulated, and if necessary set limits.

- "I'll let him make a fool of himself."
- "He'd probably like me to get real angry. Well, I'm going to disappoint him."
- "I don't need to prove myself to him."
- "I'm not going to let him get to me."
- "It's really a shame that he has to act like this."
- "For someone to be that irritable, he must be awfully unhappy."
- "There is no need to doubt myself. What he says doesn't matter."
- "I can't change him with anger. I'll just upset myself."
- "I don't like it, but he's using the best problem-solving strategy available to him right now."
- "Who cares what _____ thinks."
- "This person doesn't know me. His opinion means nothing."
- "I've acted this way in the past myself. I can give him some slack."
- "Stay cool. Make no judgments about this person."
- "I don't have to take shit, I'll simply withdraw from the conversation."
- "I won't be manipulated into blowing up or losing my cool."
- "Blowing up only gives them what they want."
- "If this goes on, I'll withdraw." Or "Say what I'll do to take care of myself if he doesn't cooperate." Or "Insist that he suggest a solution."
- "What needs or beliefs or values influence him to act this way?"

Coping in Retrospect

When it's all over and the conflict has been tabled or resolved, you still keep thinking about it. You remember what was said and what you should have said. You judge and grade yourself. Sometimes you get angry all over again. An important part of coping is knowing how to handle the aftermath; how to cool off and leave it alone. The following two lists include coping thoughts for when the conflict isn't satisfactorily resolved, and celebration statements for when a provocation ends well. Don't forget to celebrate. It's an important way to reinforce your new behavior.

When the problem is unresolved

- "Forget about the aggravation. Thinking about it only makes me more upset."
- "These are difficult situations, and they take time to straighten out."
- "Try to shake it off. Don't let it interfere."
- "I'll get better at this as I get more practice."
- "Remember relaxation. It's a lot better than anger."
- "Can I laugh about it? It's probably not so serious."
- "Don't take it personally."

When the conflict is resolved or coping is successful

- "I handled that one pretty well. It worked!"
- "That wasn't as hard as I thought."
- "It could have been a lot worse."
- "I could have gotten more upset than it was worth."
- "I actually got through that without getting angry."
- "My pride can sure get me in trouble, but when I don't take things too seriously, I'm better off."
- "I can get my needs met without anger."
- "I'm doing better at this all the time."

(Many of the above coping statements are taken from Novaco 1975.)

Writing Your Coping Script

This is where you begin pulling things together. Your coping script has three parts: (1) preparing, (2) coping with confrontation, and (3) coping in retrospect.

Preparing

When preparing for confrontation, you need to do several important things. First, you have to reassure yourself that you have the skills to handle it. Second, you need to neutralize any potential anger-triggering thoughts. Third, you need to release any buildup of physiological tension. And, finally, you should focus on the task ahead.

Select one coping statement from the list for each of the following categories and write it in the space provided. Make sure that it's a statement that appeals to you and feels like it will help.

Reassurance

_____

Stopping Trigger Thoughts

_____

Physiological Coping

_____

Sticking to the Task

_____

In the future, as you begin practicing your script, you'll want to change or modify some of these coping mantras. In particular, you may need to prepare a number of coping statements to neutralize the trigger thoughts that different provocations may set off in you. And you may end up writing entirely different scripts for different situations. For now, however, one coping statement is enough in each category.

Coping with Confrontation

When the provocation actually begins, when you start to feel the first physiological signs of anger, it's again time to remind yourself to relax and focus on the task. You'll also need coping thoughts to help as you get more aroused and the offender gets more angry. Write in one coping statement from the list for each of the following categories. Notice that *physiological coping* and *sticking to the task* appear for a second time, so you'll need new coping statements from those lists.

Physiological Coping (something to help when you're starting to get steamed)

_____

Sticking to the Task (something to get you back on track when things seem to be escalating)

_____

Coping with Arousal

_____

Coping with an Angry Person

_____

Again, this is a first draft. You'll probably experiment with many different coping mantras as you practice your script.

Coping in Retrospect

Choose one coping mantra from each of the following lists:

When the Problem Is Unresolved

_____

When the Conflict Is Resolved and Coping Is Successful

_____

Putting It Together

Get a 3 by 5 card or similar size piece of paper and type or write your script in its entirety. This will be an important part of your cognitive control training. You can refer to the card during practice sessions, and gradually you'll memorize the coping statements that work best for you. Carry the card with you so that you can review it when preparing for a possible confrontation. Try to "overlearn" your script so that the statements become almost automatic.

Example

Julie worked for a large utility where she acted as a union representative. She was also a board member for a conservationist political action group. In both capacities, Julie was forced to deal with conflict. She had strong beliefs about the right and just course of action. Often enough, people violated these convictions, and Julie found herself embroiled in escalating arguments. Here are the coping statements she selected for her script.

Preparing

Reassurance
There's no need for an argument, I can handle this without escalating.

Stopping Trigger Thoughts
People do what they need to do, not what they should do. Because I want something doesn't mean they have to give it to me.

Physiological Coping
Take a deep breath and relax.

Sticking to the Task
Try to understand their needs and concerns here.

Coping with Confrontation

Physiological Coping
Check for tension and relax what's tight. Deep breathe.

Sticking to the Task
Acknowledge their point of view. State your needs clearly and simply.

Coping with Arousal
As long as I keep my cool, I'm in control.

Coping with an Angry Person
I'm not going to let them get to me.

Coping in Retrospect

Problem Unresolved
Don't take it personally. Try to shake it off.

Conflict Resolved, Coping Successful
I handled that one pretty well.

Julie chose to combine and modify some of the coping statements so that they had more impact or sounded closer to her verbal style. She saw her main problems in a conflict situation as (1) failing to elicit the needs and concerns of others and (2) attacking rather than clearly stating her own needs. She found coping statements that reminded her to stick to both these tasks. Julie didn't use a file card. Instead, she put her script on tape (without the coping in retrospect segment) and played it nightly.

Practicing Your Script

You'll need to get used to this. At first it will seem awkward and forced. It won't sound like you. Right now, commit yourself to really working with it for a while. All you have to do is remember eight sentences (or peek at your card if you forget) and focus on the task of coping with the provocation. The key is to see it as a task—something you can coach yourself through, something that requires attention and effort, something that you can do successfully.

Practicing with Imagery

It's best to begin practicing your new script through visualized conflict situations. The idea here is that it's a lot easier to start with an imagined scene than to put your new skills immediately to the test in real life situations. To this end, Raymond Novaco, building on the work of Donald Meichenbaum, pioneered an anger treatment called stress inoculation. His approach involves developing a hierarchy of anger-provoking situations that you've encountered in your life. The hierarchy is really nothing more than a list that starts with the least upsetting provocations and goes all the way up to the angriest you can get.

To construct your own hierarchy, you need to explore some of the major areas of your life—work, family, sexual relationships, friends, recreation, daily responsibilities, creative endeavors, your relationship with your kids. Think of the specific settings and people involved in situations where you typically become angry. Try to include at least 20 items on your list, making certain that they are spread along the continuum from mild upset to your most extreme rage response.

Your list of anger situations can be converted into a hierarchy by ranking them in order, from the least to the most upsetting. To accomplish this, rate each of the items from 0 (no anger) to 100 (the angriest you get).

Ideally, each item on the list should be slightly higher on your anger scale than the item that preceded it. With a 20-item hierarchy, the items should increase by approximately five points on your anger scale—5, 10, 15, 20, and so on. If all your items seem bunched at the high or the low end, try to think of some anger situations that could be ranked near the middle of your scale. Whenever there are holes or gaps, try to brainstorm some anger situations that seem to fit at that point on the hierarchy. For example, if you have nothing between the item *Susan tracking mud on the floor* (30 points) and *Jim complaining about how I organize the house* (55 points), you need to generate some items in the 35 to 50 range so that your hierarchy will have a smooth progression.

At this point, you may find it helpful to see how a typical hierarchy is set up. Armand is a restaurant manager who has three children ranging in age from three to seven. His wife is a professional photographer who works many weekend hours at weddings, bar mitzvahs, and so forth. Here is Armand's hierarchy.

Rank	Item	Anger Score
1	Toys strewn on the floor when I get home.	5
2	Salespeople ignore me in a store.	10
3	Brother and his girlfriend drop over unannounced. He's slightly loaded.	15
4	Susan tells me a list of things I should do as soon as I get home.	20
5	A waiter complains about his table assignments.	25
6	Susan works late on the weekend and doesn't call to let me know.	30
7	Marta starts whining and demanding constant satisfaction—she wants this and this and this right now.	35
8	The cashier screws up the balance in the cash register again. But suggests, as always, that someone's stealing from the till.	40

9	Susan doesn't tell me about a wedding she's doing, and suddenly I've got all the kids. She makes this annoying, offhand announcement on her way out the door.	45
10	My father calls and just starts talking about this and that, all building up to some advice I didn't ask for.	50
11	The side work isn't right, the floors aren't clean, the food's sitting too long before being served—stuff like that.	55
12	Marta talks back to me when I'm correcting her.	60
13	I'm late getting Marta to school because she fools around and doesn't get dressed.	65
14	My boss is late with my paycheck. I confront him, and he starts criticizing how I run the restaurant.	70
15	The kids are screaming and off the wall, and Susan shrugs and says, "What are you going to do about it?"	75
16	Susan calls me lazy for not doing more (dishes, vacuuming, driving the kids around, picking up around the house).	80
17	Somebody charges me a helluva lot more than I expected to pay (mechanic, appliance repair, home improvement, babysitter).	85
18	Susan says I'm not a good father because I "never talk to Marta" or I don't "play games with the kids." You do "zilch childcare," she says.	90
19	Susan uses that sarcastic voice to talk about how my father can't stop running my life, how he's always calling, etc.	95
20	My father criticizes me in front of Susan, like about stuff that isn't fixed around the house, or why aren't I working in a better place, etc.	100

The Situational Analysis

Review the scenes in your hierarchy. Notice what you're saying to yourself to turn on the anger. Now write down the main trigger thoughts. Armand found three generic trigger thoughts for his anger, at least one of which was present in every scene.

1. "They shouldn't act this way."
2. "I have to get angry to stop them."
3. "They're wrong, and I'm right."

He recognized that each trigger corresponded to a style of negative thinking which he frequently used:

1. Focusing on shoulds.
2. Letting it all out fallacy.
3. Good-bad dichotomizing.

After you have noted your trigger thoughts, try, as Armand did, to identify which category each represents. Then you can find coping thoughts in the list appropriate for combating that particular trigger.

Now it's time to ask an important question. As you look over your hierarchy, what are the main behavioral changes you have to make so that things won't escalate? Do you need to acknowledge the other person's point of view more? Do you need to state your own needs more directly? Do you need to open the door for negotiation? Do you need to avoid judgments and blaming? Find coping thoughts in the section on sticking to the task (or write your own) that will help you handle the situation without a blowup. Armand saw that he failed to state his needs clearly, in a nonblaming way. He also realized that he needed to look for solutions rather than flaws. He found four mantras, one or more of which was appropriate for each anger scene.

After completing your situational analysis, go ahead and modify your script to include some of the additional coping statements that you found. You won't use them all for each situation, but they'll all help sooner or later. Armand's script sounded like this:

Reassurance: I can handle this without anger.

Trigger Thoughts:
1. "People do what they need to do, not what I think they should do. They do the best they can."
2. "I can protect myself by saying it assertively."
3. "Forget judging right and wrong—myself or anybody else."

Physiological: "Take a deep breath and relax."

Task:
1. "Stick to the facts, no putdowns or attacks."
2. "Ask for her solution. Work for compromise."

Physiological: "Relax the gut, take a breath."

Task:
1. "State your needs clearly and simply."
2. "Negatives lead to negatives. Look for solutions."

Arousal: "Don't escalate, cool it."

Angry People: "I don't have to take shit, I can withdraw if I need to."

Using Your Hierarchy

Start with your first scene (the lowest score), and construct it in your imagination. Conjure a clear picture of the situation—where you are and what you're dong. See who is with you and try to hear the sound of his or her voice. Try to recreate anything else that's important about the scene—smells, temperature, textures, and so on. Hold onto the image for 30 to 40 seconds. Notice how your body reacts. Changes in heart rate and respiration, and particularly the beginning of any muscle tension, are early signals of anger. Now bring on your script. Use the coping thoughts that seem appropriate for this scene.

During the scene, it's extremely important that you follow your own instructions to relax. If you tell yourself to take a deep breath, do it. If you tell yourself to relax your jaw, do it. And keep doing your relaxation procedures throughout the scene.

Take all your self-instruction seriously. Really try to believe what you are telling yourself. If a coping thought instructs you to "take the issue point by point," imagine yourself speaking clearly and logically. If you tell yourself to keep your "voice calm and flat," hear your voice slowing down and the pitch flattening out.

After holding the clear image of a scene for 30 to 40 seconds, shut it off. Take a brief rest before getting back to it. Keep repeating your first scene and your coping script until you have twice imagined the scene without tension or anger. As you did with scene one, continue up the hierarchy, from the lowest to the highest anger provocations. Expect to take several days as you slowly move through the entire list.

Some items may be more problematic than others. If this is the case, it may be an indication that you need to modify your coping statements to make them more appropriate for the scene. Or you may need to place greater emphasis on your relaxation procedures. Another problem may be that your old anger-evoking self-talk is still leaking through. Try to notice if any trigger thoughts are present while you visualize a scene. If you notice the lingering presence of trigger thoughts, you'll need to address them directly. Armand found that items having to do with his wife triggered the thought "She doesn't care about me." He was able to counter this by thinking, "She's just overwhelmed and hurting too." Should you continue to have problems with a scene, defer the item till later in your hierarchy. You may need more practice with anger-evoking scenes before tackling this particular situation.

Working with the hierarchy will give you much practice with your coping script. Gradually your chosen responses will become second nature. In the next chapter, another piece will be added to your coping repertoire—*response choice rehearsal*. This is a series of ready-made behavioral strategies for dealing with virtually any provocation. After you've practiced those in imagination, you'll be ready to tackle real-life situations.

11

Response Choice Rehearsal

So far you've been working on changing how you think during provocations. That's half the battle. In this chapter you will learn a way to structure your behavior in confrontive situations so that you get better results. What you're about to learn is a series of specific responses to provocation that will (1) keep the conversation focused on resolving the problem, or (2) cut off a discussion that's starting to escalate.

The Key Attitude

Behavior is enormously influenced by attitude. How you act when you're angry has a lot to do with your attitude toward conflict. Some people respond to conflict by becoming *avengers*. They want to injure and punish the offending party to the same degree that they've been hurt. Pain must be paid back. They believe in retribution; an eye for an eye. Avengers make their point. They're loud. They're cutting. But relationships are damaged, and very often the conflict continues.

The key attitude for successful conflict resolution is *problem solving*. You're not trying to get the other person to feel bad. You're not trying to prove them wrong. You're trying to *fix* what's wrong. The problem-solving attitude assumes that conflict has no moral dimensions. Instead, conflict is a matter of opposing needs. Disagreements are more easily resolved when each person's needs are assumed to be legitimate and important. That way you don't have to argue about whose needs are bigger, whose are more justified. Since everyone has an equal right to want it their way, problem solving becomes a matter of acknowledging and factoring these needs into an agreement.

Response Choice Rehearsal

This method for handling conflict has the advantage of requiring very little thought or preparation. You can do it when you're stressed, when you don't have time to plan a response. You can do it when your buttons have been pushed and the automatic rage starts to well in you. Even when all your instincts say "Smash the bastard," you can still use response choice rehearsal (or RCR) to keep things from exploding.

RCR consists of six prelearned responses to provocation. Each one is designed to de-escalate conflict *while making room for real problem solving.* When one response doesn't work (because you're feeling too angry or the exchange heats up), you simply choose another one. Eventually you will find a response that breaks the tension and gives you the emotional safety to start searching for agreement.

RCR is divided into active and passive responses. Either one may be effective, depending on the situation. The key to understanding and using RCR is to remember that no single response is likely to be the answer. The first thing you try may not have much impact on your anger or the anger of the provoking person. Your second response may still not be effective. Or the third. But taken together, a series of adaptive responses is very likely to both cool you down and de-escalate the conflict.

In RCR, you use your anger as a red flag that signals you to switch to a new coping response. Rather than fueling aggression, anger is a sign to change tack, to shift strategies. Anger lets you know that you're stuck. Your current method of coping isn't solving the problem. Something still hurts, and you need to try a new response.

Active Responses

1. Express a specific need. Anger starts with pain. You need to do something about it. One of the healthiest responses you can make is to ask for what you need to reduce the pain.

Opening line: "I'm feeling (what's bothering me is) _____
_____. And what I think I need (want, would like) in
this situation is _____."

Try to memorize this opening line. The less you have to think
when you're angry, the better. The first sentence, where you
describe your feeling or what's bothering you, is optional.
Include this if you think it's important information, if you think
it would help the other person be more responsive, or if the
other person is an intimate who deserves to know your reactions. Don't include it if you're going to end up sounding
judgmental and blaming. Don't include it if there's no need on
either side for your feelings to be part of the discussion. Telling
your garage mechanic that you feel betrayed by the size of his
bill probably isn't appropriate. A sales clerk doesn't need to
know that you're hurt by her brusqueness.

When stating your need, make sure you're asking for something that's behavioral, not attitudinal. Asking for someone to
be more sensitive, more loving, or more responsible sets you up
for a lot of disappointment. Research shows that people don't
know how to respond to nonbehavioral requests. First of all,
asking someone to be more caring or more responsible is pejorative. It implies that he or she is generally uncaring or irresponsible. Secondly, it's hard to know what is meant by value-laden
words such as "caring" or "responsible." What kind of responsibility are you requesting? Do you want your partner to do the
dishes more often? Or be more active in birth-control decisions?

Your requests should be specific, preferably limited to one
thing. The more you ask for, the less likely you are to get it. If
you stick to one specific behavioral request, you're much more
likely to reach agreement or negotiate a compromise.

While clarifying your request in your own mind, its extremely helpful to develop a fallback position. This is the minimum
change that would be acceptable to you. For example, if your
husband is unwilling to help with the kids immediately after
work, you might suggest a half-hour decompression time, after
which he'll do some child care.

John was angry because his girlfriend kept arranging that
they visit certain friends of hers he didn't like. He decided to
ask her to check with him *before* making any dates. As a fallback
position, he was willing for her to make dates as long as she told

people that he might not be able to come. Here's how John phrased his request: "What bothers me is you're making dates with people I'm not sure I want to see. What I'd like is for you to check with me first before making any arrangements."

2. Negotiate. Here your effort is to engage the other person in problem solving. You're both feeling stuck; the battle lines are drawn. Getting the other person to propose a solution, no matter how inadequate or self-serving, is the first step toward a negotiated agreement.

Opening Line: "What would you propose to solve this problem?"

If you get resistance or a worthless proposal in return, you can offer your fallback position at this point. On the other hand, if the proposal has possibilities, you can start to negotiate.

The section on negotiation in Chapter 12, "Problem-Solving Communication," has some specific suggestions.

- "My way this time, your way next time."
- "Part of what I want with part of what you want."
- "If you do_____ for me, I'll do _____ for you."
- "Meeting halfway or splitting the difference."
- "Try it my way for a week and see. If you don't like it, we'll go back to the old way."
- "We'll do this one my way, but we'll do _____ your way."
- "My way when I'm doing it, your way when you're doing it."

When working toward compromise, remember that each person's needs must be taken into account. Don't expect to reach agreement unless the solution in some way addresses the conflicting needs you both feel.

Audrey wants her brother to participate more in the care of their invalided mother. She's angry because he contributes nothing to the day-to-day work but gets a lot of strokes from Mom for his occasional visits. Here's how their dialogue went:

Audrey: I'm feeling overwhelmed by the responsibility and upset that you don't help more. What I think I'd like is for you to visit Mom twice a week, bring her a meal, straighten the place up, and stay long enough so that she feels she really got to talk to you.

Edward: I've got a full life, Audrey. A law practice, two kids, I can't do that!

Audrey: OK. What would you propose to solve this problem?

Edward: Audrey, I just don't have time. You're asking too damned much of me.

Audrey (presenting her fallback proposal): How about at least visiting twice a week, forget bringing dinner?

Edward: It adds more than an hour to my commute coming home. Plus it'll take at least an hour to get out the door once I show up. I don't see my kids enough as it is.

Audrey: Come on, Ed. Let's put our heads together on this thing. Do you have some ideas?

Edward: OK, OK. If you can find somebody, I'll pay for them to come in and cook and help her out three evenings a week. How's that?

Audrey (looking for compromise): That's a big help. But, Ed, she needs to see you. How about you pay for someone two nights a week, and you visit once a week?

Edward: You're relentless, Audrey. All right, I'll do it.

3. Self-care. This is where you deliver an ultimatum. You let the other person know your plan to take care of your own needs if he or she fails to cooperate with problem solving.

Opening line: "If (the problem) goes on, I'll have to (your self-care solution) in order to take care of myself."

It's important to say it exactly as it's written above. By framing it as taking care of yourself, the ultimatum doesn't sound so much like punishment or revenge. What you're really doing is letting the other person know the sanctions for ignoring you. But you're doing it in a nonattacking way, so that you're less likely to trigger an angry response.

Self-care is not something you're going to do *to* the other person. It is something you do *for* yourself. It emphasizes your commitment to meeting your own needs and finding alternative solutions to your problem if the other person won't help. Typical self-care solutions include paying someone else to do it (good if you have a penny-pinching spouse), doing it yourself (but using time that otherwise would have been devoted to the needs of the other person), getting the help of an authority (police, lawyer, principal, theatre manager), withdrawing from the relationship, (temporarily or permanently) or getting your need met elsewhere.

Jarret's friend won't take no for an answer. All through dinner Jim badgers him about a fishing trip Jarrett's already declined. Jarret tries several other responses, but now he feels pushed to make a clear self-care statement. "Jim, if you press me again about the fishing trip, I'm going to just pay the bill and leave. We'll go bowling like we planned tomorrow, but I'll pack it in for tonight." Jim got the message and gave it up.

Passive Responses

1. Get information. Many conflicts stay unresolved because one or both parties harbor unexpressed feelings or needs. If things feel stuck, one of the best things you can do is probe to understand more about the feelings and needs of the other person. Salesmen know this. When a customer says no, they immediately begin a line of questions to uncover the feelings and needs that lie behind the resistance.

Opening line:
1. "What do you need in this situation?"
2. "What concerns (worries) you in this situation?"
3. "What's hurting (bothering) you in this situation?"

Choose whichever of the three lines seems most appropriate. If your husband won't talk about his needs, perhaps he'll talk about his feelings, or vice versa. Camille was a nurse. One of her co-workers in the hospital repeatedly criticized her for various forms of inefficiency. After the fifth or sixth such encounter, Camille was in a froth. Here's how she handled the problem:

Camille: I understand your point, but what bothers you about my being slow?
Sandra: It's just not right, these people should have been bathed three hours ago.
Camille: I understand, but what bothers you about that?
Sandra: Well, whenever we get late admissions you can't take them. You're too behind. And then when you have special

problems, you don't have time to solve them. The admissions and the problems often end up in my lap.

Sandra's tone is hard-edged, but at least Camille understands her concern. From here, they can begin negotiating what to do about it.

2. Acknowledge. This is important for de-escalating conflict. People want to know that you understand what's bugging them. They need to feel heard. All you have to do is say in your own words what you understand their feelings or needs to be.

Opening line:
1. "So what you want is _____."
2. "So what concerns (worries) you is _____."
3. "So what hurts (bothers) you is _____."

Be certain that you describe the other person's position in a neutral, nonpejorative way. Your statement doesn't have to be sympathetic, just accurate. If there's any hint of sarcasm, exasperation, or judgment in your voice, the effort you made to acknowledge will be wasted.

Lennie's been taking a lot of flack from his father about his lousy computer science grades.

Father: I'm afraid you're not going to be able to compete. It's a technological world. A lot of jobs will depend on knowing this stuff. You're going to be stuck at the low end of the pay scale because you didn't learn it while you had a chance.
Lennie: What's worrying you about my grades is that I'll be stuck in a pretty low-level job. I won't be able to compete.

Lennie almost said, "You think a C makes me a computer nitwit." But he realized that this interpretation would sound mocking and derisive. The point was to let his father know that he heard him, not stir up more conflict with sarcasm.

3. Withdrawal. This is basically time out. If things are continuing to escalate despite a series of adaptive responses, it's time for damage control.

Opening line: "It feels like we're starting to get upset. I want to stop and cool off for a while."

Just keep repeating this statement like a broken record until you can get disengaged. With intimates, give a specific time when you'll return. Or set a time when you'll be willing to resume discussion of the issue. Don't get caught in any further discussion; don't get suckered by another provocation. The key is to say the line verbatim and then physically exit the situation as soon as possible.

Rules for RCR

The rules for RCR are very simple:

1. Memorize all six opening lines. This is a must. These opening sentences have to be so well learned that you can say them without effort, without thinking. See the chart of opening sentences at the end of the chapter. Test yourself daily for a week to verify your retention.

2. Whenever possible, rehearse in advance active responses 1 and 3. Decide if you wish to include your feelings about the situation. Then formulate your request and your fallback position. Make sure that your request is behavioral and specific. Also try to generate a self-care response. Ask yourself how you can take care of the problem *without* the other person's cooperation.

3. Continued anger or escalation are your signals to switch responses. Don't get stuck if a response isn't working. Move on to what you feel intuitively is the next best option.

4. Don't be afraid to repeat responses. You may wish to return several times to questions that get more information. You may wish to acknowledge what you're learning about the other person's experience. And as the discussion progresses you may wish to invite another round of negotiation.

5. If you don't know what to do next, try shifting from active to passive responses (or vice versa). If you've been focusing on getting information, try expressing your own needs now. If you're stuck in fruitless negotiation, consider asking for information.

6. Keep shifting among responses until the problem feels resolved or further communication appears pointless. If you're still angry and stuck, go to one of the exit responses (either self-care or withdrawal). Stop talking and physically leave the situation.

Practicing with Imagery

In 1971, Joseph Catella suggested that you can practice new, desirable behaviors by *imagining* yourself successfully performing the new behavioral sequence. He named his technique covert modeling. Here's how you can practice response choice rehearsal using imagery.

1. Go back to the hierarchy you developed in Chapter 10. Select a scene from the midrange of the hierarchy. Make sure it's one that you can visualize well and that it contains a considerable amount of angry dialogue. You'll probably find it easier if the scene is something that happens frequently and involves someone you know fairly well.

2. Choose several (two to four) of the coping statements that you used to reduce anger while visualizing your hierarchy. Make sure that at least one of the coping statements helps you relax your physiological arousal, and that another deals with trigger thoughts that occur during the scene.

3. Plan your RCR responses. Identify your feeling in the situation, if you wish to express it. Identify your need and your fallback position. Create a self-care option.

4. Now visualize the provocative scene. At the point where you are starting to get angry, imagine yourself using your coping statements to relax and neutralize your trigger thoughts. Now imagine yourself choosing the first response from RCR. Imagine the other person resisting this first effort. Hear him or her escalating and provoking you. Use your coping instructions again: remind yourself to relax, deal with the arousal. Feel yourself struggling to keep control and stay focused on the task. Remind yourself that the goal is problem solving, not revenge. Use your anger as a signal to switch to your next RCR response. Imagine that your second response is poorly received. See yourself starting to lash out, then hold back. Again instruct yourself to relax, to stay focused on the task. Use your continued anger as a signal to shift to yet another response.

5. For your first scene, imagine a negotiated compromise. Hear yourself suggesting your fallback position, and imagine the final agreement. Be sure not to give the resolution a Pollyannaish flavor. Imagine reluctance on the part of the other person. See yourself starting to attack, then pushing back the anger to work toward a compromise.

6. Continue the covert modeling process with at least five scenes from the upper end of your hierarchy. Note that you may need to change your coping statements to make them more appropriate with new scenes. You will also need to plan different need and self-care responses with each new scene. Let some scenes resolve in agreement and imagine that others require exit responses. You may even wish to rehearse the same scene with various endings.

Example of Covert Modeling

Jill was a law student who'd had several blowups with a colleague in a summer internship. The scene from her hierarchy went like this:

> Rebecca drops a case on my desk. It hits with a loud bang. She says it's almost past the statute for filing, and the paperwork has got to be done like yesterday. Otherwise the statute's blown, and the firm can be sued. She uses sort of a blaming "shame on you" kind of voice. I've never even seen the case before, but I feel put down because I didn't know about it. I'm starting to get steamed. "Leave it over there," I say coldly. "Well, it's your case," she says. "Blow it if you want to." I'm out of my mind. That prim, goodie two-shoes face. Then I start getting loud— "Leave me the fuck alone," etc.

Jill chose four coping thoughts to help her deal with the anger generated by the scene.

1. "Take a deep breath and relax."
2. "Look for the right response."
3. "I won't give her the satisfaction of upsetting me."
4. "That's how she copes with her anxiety."

Now Jill prepared her need and self-care responses. She decided that she didn't want to express her feelings to Rebecca. She wanted to stick with a simple request.

"Rebecca, what I'd like is if you wouldn't bring any cases to my attention. To not warn me about anything."

Jill also decided on a fallback request. She'd ask Rebecca to leave cases in her box with a statute date written on them.

For her self-care ultimatum, she decided she would have to appeal to authority.

"If you keep warning me about cases, I'm going to ask the head paralegal to clarify for both of us that we have separate duties and don't need to be involved in each other's cases."

Jill scripted the scene like this. First, she'd express her need. Rebecca would stay very prim, keeping an "I know better than you" tone in her voice. Jill would control her anger with coping thoughts. She'd use the anger as a cue to try another response. Moving from active to passive responses, she'd next try to get information. She'd ask Rebecca what bothered her about the situation with Jill's cases. She imagined Rebecca saying, "If you blow it, it'll look bad for me." Jill imagined her anger surging again and saw herself having to take a deep breath and remind herself to look for the right response. She'd try shifting to negotiation: "Rebecca, what would you propose to solve this problem?" "I guess for you to keep on top of your cases," Rebecca says primly. Jill pushes the anger down, reminding herself not to give Rebecca the satisfaction of upsetting her. "That's how she copes with *her* anxiety." Jill sticks with negotiation and offers her fallback suggestion. She imagines Rebecca awkwardly accepting it and leaving her office. She congratulates herself for getting what she wanted without blowing up.

Jill ran the scene through several more times, with different endings. She imagined the negotiations breaking down and pictured herself having to announce her self-care solution. She imagined her anger escalating so quickly that she had to withdraw before exploding. Each time Jill went through the scene, she found it easier to remember the opening lines of her responses. She was able to use anger as her cue to shift responses and a signal to use her coping statements.

Jill practiced with four additional scenes from her hierarchy. Before visualizing each scene, she prepared coping reminders, as well as need and self-care statements. She scripted the scene, deciding in advance which responses she would try and establishing how the provoking person would act at each point in the scene.

Role-Playing RCR

The ultimate goal is to use RCR in real-life situations. But you may need additional practice as you make the transition between visualized scenes and provocative encounters. There are three ways you can role-play RCR. First, you can rehearse in front of a mirror while imagining the other person's part in the dialogue. Second, you can act out both parts of a dialogue by saying your lines while sitting in one chair and moving to another chair to take the part of the provocative person. You keep shifting chairs as you alternately play the role of each person in the dialogue. A third method is to role-play with a close friend. Have your friend play the provocative role. Describe the scene and how he or she should generally respond. As always, you need to prepare for the scene by deciding on your coping reminders and your need and self-care statements. Then go ahead and play the scene, using your anger as a cue for shifting to a new response.

Doing It

You've practiced RCR, visualized scenes, and perhaps done some role-playing. Now it's time to incorporate the six response choices into your real-life repertoire of anger-coping strategies.

1. Choose a provocative situation that occurs with some frequency or predictability (ideally, one you've already practiced in imagination). Make sure it's a situation where you tend to *act* angry, not just *feel* angry. If it's a scene from your hierarchy, make sure that it falls in the midrange. Don't select a scene where your buttons are pushed so badly that you flash into instantaneous rage.

2. Prepare your coping statements, including ones that remind you to relax and neutralize trigger thoughts.

3. Plan your need, fallback, and self-care statements.

4. Commit yourself to using RCR. Remind yourself that anger is a signal to make your first RCR response or to shift responses.

5. If the first situation doesn't occur within a few days, prepare for a second situation that you're certain to encounter soon. When you're in the presence of a provocative person from one of your target situations, mentally rehearse the opening line of an RCR response.

6. When the target situation occurs, congratulate yourself if you were able to make even one RCR response. If you are dissatisfied with the outcome (either because you forgot RCR or got derailed very early in the process), rehearse the scene again in imagination. See yourself struggling for control, but finally switching to an RCR response that either helps you reach agreement or disengages you without a major blowup.

Don't be discouraged when you have trouble implementing RCR at first. Remember that your old way of reacting is a well-learned, habitual response. It takes time to change habits, particularly ones that help you cope with pain. The key is to keep rehearsing RCR in imagination each time you get derailed in a real-life scene. It takes time. It takes patience. But gradually you'll find yourself using RCR more and more naturally. The responses will come without thinking. You'll get better at remembering your coping thoughts as anger starts to rise.

Motivating Yourself

You need a lot of motivation to change deeply ingrained habits. The best way to do it is to use both a carrot and a stick.

The Carrot

1. Plan specific rewards in advance. Reward yourself both for practicing RCR through imagery and for using your new coping responses during real provocations. Set it up so that you'll go to that movie you've wanted to see or treat yourself to

a terrific dinner out. Arrange things so that you'll play tennis or call your friend or pick up your book *after* doing your covert modeling rehearsal.

2. Celebrate your success. Let people know that you've been working toward anger control in new ways. Tell them about situations where you're now able to stay cool and really focus on problem solving.

3. Put up signs. Stick reminders on your bathroom mirror, inside your front door, or in your briefcase. Remind yourself: "Use RCR with Nancy...express your need, negotiate...anger is a sign to cope," and so on.

The Stick

1. On your way to work each day, spend five minutes reviewing what your anger costs. Explore its toll on you emotionally and physically and reflect on how it has affected your relationships. Think about how your anger is affecting your career, your children, and your marriage.

2. Review in detail the consequences of your last anger episode.

3. Make a contract to use RCR with a friend or a support person or even with the provocateur him- or herself. Specify in your contract the target person with whom you plan to use RCR. Include in your contract the understanding that you will report the outcome of any interaction with the target person.

RCR is hard work. It costs you time and energy to learn these new ways of coping. Sometimes the process feels foreign, artificial. Sometimes you want to chuck it all and go back to handling things "naturally." But the natural way is the angry way. And the anger, as good as it makes you feel at the moment, has torn and damaged some of your important relationships. There is no other way to change except the hard way. You already know that. RCR and other techniques in this book will help you change the way you cope with pain. It is your decision now whether you are ready to implement them.

RCR Opening Lines

ACTIVE

PASSIVE

1. *Express specific need*

"I'm feeling (what's bothering me is) _____."

"And what I think I need (want/would like) in this situation is _____."

1. *Get information*

"What do you need in this situation?"

"What concerns (worries) you in this situation?"

"What's hurting (bothering) you in this situation?"

2. *Negotiate*

"What would *you* propose to solve this problem?"

2. *Acknowledge*

"So what *you* want is _____."

"So what concerns (worries) *you* is _____."

"So what hurts (bothers) *you* is _____."

3. *Self-Care*

"If (the problem) goes on, I'll have to (your self-care solution) in order to take care of myself."

3. *Withdraw*

"It feels like we're starting to get upset. I want to stop and cool off for a while."

12

Problem-Solving Communication

Your parents probably never sat you down and explained how to get your needs met. You learned those skills from observing them and other adults in your life. You saw how they settled the inevitable problems that arose when people had differing needs. You heard how they expressed their disapproval and how they set limits. You learned through example the tone of voice and body language that they used when they were on the warpath. If they used violence, tantrums, intimidation, or withdrawal, you learned that too. You saw the results when one person was unable to ask for what he or she wanted. You saw the results when people failed to set limits or couldn't say no to expectations or demands. You saw long-standing bitterness that set in when problems were not resolved but pushed under the rug.

You also learned what it felt like to have someone angry at you. To a child, anger is terrifying. Adults are all-powerful, and children depend on them for every aspect of their lives. Children cannot feel safe without adult acceptance and approval. It's vital, therefore, to find some way to cope with anger from your parents.

Some children learn to avoid anger by being compliant. Then, as adults, they deny their feelings and needs in order to feel safe. Other children find that the best defense is a good offense. As adults, they tend to act aggressively, using threats of violence or other means of intimidation to avoid conflict and escape criticism.

Neither the passive nor the aggressive styles of coping work for meeting your needs in the long run. While they may have helped you survive as a child, adult relationships are seldom improved by these strategies.

The Passive Coping Style

The essence of the passive style is to say nothing that would offend. At best, your needs are expressed indirectly. It feels too frightening to push for what you want if it conflicts in any way with the needs of others. And it's hard to say no. You set limits by going along begrudgingly, by dragging your feet, or by being less than competent.

Outwardly you're good, you're sweet, you're compliant. Inside you feel the pain of helplessness and unmet needs. The pain builds. Sometimes you feel suffocated by the demands of others. Sometimes you blame them for not seeing or acknowledging what's important to you.

The passive style leaves you invisible. Others are forced to guess about your feelings and wants. Usually they end up guessing wrong. Ralph's sister has asked him to help her move three times in the past year. Lugging boxes isn't his favorite recreation (particularly since she rarely has things packed when he arrives). But what really burns him is that his sister never initiates contact other than to ask for his help. She never calls to say hello, never invites him to dinner. Ralph misses her and he resents her. Never direct, he expresses his feelings by being curt and complaining about his back. His sister told him he was a sweetie to move her when he was in pain and gave him the name of her chiropractor.

The Aggressive Coping Style

The aggressive style lets people know how bad and wrong they are for not giving you what you want. The impulse is to punish, to climb into a tank and blow away the opposition. But as you've learned, this strategy costs a lot. When you're loud, others get loud. When you blame, others go on the attack. When you psychologically punch someone, that person punches back. People resist you. What is achieved through anger must be defended that way as well. The intimidated, frightened people you push around will find other ways of defeating and getting back at you. You are never sure if even those close to you are cooperating out of love or fear.

You pay for anger in the coin of guilt. Angry people often regret their outbursts. And they feel compelled to make it up in other ways—favors, gifts, concessions. Then in the process of compensating for the recent outburst, new resentments grow. You sit on all your needs and feelings for a week so that the pain can subside from the last explosion. But the nice-guy act wears thin, and soon enough you're attacking and blaming again.

Cheryl was chronically annoyed by some of her boyfriend's habits. He always left the milk out, he wore his stinky under-shirts to bed, he never made any salad when it was his turn to cook, and he often cooked pork (her least favorite meat). Cheryl periodically triggered her anger with the thought: "He never listens to me about my needs." Then the donnybrook. Cheryl's boyfriend would get so defensive that he simply stopped listening. Afterwards, Cheryl felt guilty and resolved to keep her mouth shut about "such petty stuff." Until the next time.

Passive Then Aggressive

When you're afraid to ask directly for what you want, the pain builds. Your passive response leaves you feeling stuck and helpless. And the helplessness adds to already high levels of stress. When the pain reaches a critical threshold, you seize on a convenient trigger thought to ignite rage. Usually the angry outburst is still not direct, still not about the real issue that bothers you.

Coming home after a long day and an hour's commute, Jim needs time to decompress before addressing the problems and pleasures of a noisy household. A half hour of peace and quiet with the paper would significantly reduce his stress. But he has trouble asking for what he wants. He picks up the living room, he sets the table, he reads a story to the kids. He sighs, he smiles weakly to his wife. During dinner, his four-year-old chatters with her mouth full. Jim blows up.

The Assertive Style

Assertive communication allows you to express feelings, thoughts, and wishes, and to stand up for your rights and limits without violating the rights of others. Assertiveness is the antidote for anger. You can say "I want more attention" instead of accusing your husband of being a "cold fish." You can say "I want help with the shopping" instead of complaining that your children are "hopeless, lazy bums like their father." You can write a proposal requesting a raise instead of complaining that you are not valued at work.

The most important thing to remember about assertiveness is that you have every right to express your needs. Other people have that same right, and their needs are every bit as important to them as yours are to you. By using assertiveness, you can work toward a settlement without anger and seek a solution where both parties get at least some of what they want. You can protect yourself without blame. You can set limits without turning other people off. Assertive communication works for nearly every interpersonal problem: sex, money, power struggles, conflicts at work or in school. The key is being direct, clear, and nonattacking.

How To Make an Assertive Statement

An assertive statement has three parts: I think, I feel, I want. The "I think" component is an objective description of what you see, hear, or notice. "The facts, and nothing but the facts," as you perceive them. An assertive statement presents the facts without judgment, blaming, or guessing the intentions of the other person. "The clothes are still on the floor." "When I called the office, the secretary said you had been out all afternoon." "When I got into the car this morning, there was no gas."

Sometimes it's hard to separate the facts from the feelings, but it is the first step in reducing the anger spiral. Stating the facts lays the issue on the table for discussion. You'll be more likely to get the other person's cooperation if you start with an objective statement than if you start with an insult ("What a lazy slob you are. Don't think that I'm going to pick up after you!") or a challenge ("Where the hell were you when I called this afternoon?") or sarcasm ("Thanks a lot for all the gas you left me this morning.") Statements like these fuel your own anger and make the other person defensive and angry as well. Nothing is solved, nothing changes.

The "I feel" statement acknowledges your honest reaction. It lets the other person become aware of how his or her behavior affects you without using tactics that blame, scare, or intimidate—and without making the other person defensive. At first, you may want to use a structure like this to state your feelings: "When _____happens, I feel." "When I come home and find dishes in the sink, I feel angry." "When you promise me a dinner out and then cancel it because you have to work late, I feel resentful." "When you ignore me at a party and talk to other men, I feel abandoned and humiliated."

It's important to look for and acknowledge other feelings that may underlie your anger. Often anger is the *overriding* emotion and the only one of which you are aware. Worry, fear, disappointment, guilt, and embarrassment are some emotions that can lead to anger. Bobby couldn't understand why he felt angry every time Ralph discussed his new girlfriend, Judy. When he really thought about it, he realized that his anger was made up of two other feelings. When Ralph and Judy started seeing so much of each other, Bobby was *worried* that he'd lose a friendship and *jealous* of the time they spent together. The pain of worry and jealousy made him angry.

When Meg got drunk at the company party, Paul realized that his anger at her was caused by his feeling *discouraged* that she would ever be able to stay on the wagon and *disappointed* that she had broken her promise not to drink. He was also *embarrassed* by her loud, inappropriate laughter.

Anyone with teenagers knows how often fear and worry will trigger anger. One teenager candidly said, "My parents were so mad when I got home late that I almost wish I had been in an accident and could call them from the hospital. At least they'd feel sorry for me." When you acknowledge the different feelings that make up your anger, the other person gets to understand you better. And they are more likely to cooperate with you in problem solving.

Notice that the emphasis is on the "I." "I think, I feel." Take responsibility for your own experience. She doesn't "make you jealous." He doesn't "make you feel stupid." When you blame others for how you are feeling, you end up feeling helpless. When you take responsibility for what you feel, you give yourself the power to change the situation.

Sometimes people think they are using "I" messages when they are really using "you" messages, and blaming the other person. For instance, "*I* think *you* are being controlling," or "*I* feel *you* are taking advantage of this situation." The "facts" should be as objective and fair as a photograph—a statement or a picture of what is there. The "feelings" are a statement of your emotional reaction, not a judgment or attack. Compare the blaming "you" message above with assertive statements. "When you make decisions without consulting me, I feel discounted and frustrated that I don't have any input about important issues." The *facts* are there, the *feelings* are there, and the other person knows what's bothering you without feeling accused of being "controlling." You say, "When you bring the children for me to watch them without calling or giving me notice, I feel a bit resentful." The *facts* are there, the *feelings* are there, and the other person gets to understand your limits without being accused of being "inconsiderate or selfish."

The "I want" part of an assertive statement is the most important. Here are the guidelines for making a request: (1) Be sure to deal with only one area at a time. (2) Make your request specific. (3) Make your request behavorial.

Deal with one area at a time. You're bound to overwhelm your wife if you ask her to be more supportive of your job, spend less money on the kids, give you a hand with the yard work, and wear sexy nighties! All of these issues might be important to you, but if you bring them all up at the same time the other person may feel attacked and overwhelmed.

Be specific. Instead of saying "I want you to help out more with the child care," describe exactly what you want. "I'd like you to get the girls ready for school while I fix lunches and make breakfast." Instead of saying "I want you to do more around the house," specify your needs. "I want you to clean the downstairs bathroom and vacuum the rugs." And you can be even *more* specific. Try describing when, how often, in what way you want things done. Instead of saying "I'll need the budget finished by the end of the week," try "I need four copies of the budget by 2:00 p.m. Friday." If you want your child home at 10:00, don't say "Be back soon, remember you have school tomorrow." You're likely to have a long night of worry ahead when the request is vague. Say the exact time limit and there's a good chance you'll avert a crisis.

Ask for behavior change. You can't demand that people change their attitudes, values, priorities, or feelings. You can only ask that they change behavior. For example, you can ask your husband to accompany you to your office party, but you can't ask him to *want* to go to the office party. Requesting that your partner be "more loving" or "more considerate" results in frustration and disappointment. At the particular moment when it's most important to you, he may not feel loving or considerate. Moreover, he may have only the haziest idea of what you mean by these words. Your best strategy is first to define for yourself and then for him exactly what loving *behavior* you're looking for. Does it mean making the tea after dinner, helping sort the bills, giving you a shoulder rub, cuddling with you in front of the TV, taking a shower together? It may not be romantic to define love behaviorally, but it is effective.

Even though you can't demand a change in attitude, when behavioral changes do occur, attitudes and feelings often change as well. John was a near-fanatical baseball fan. His family could simply forget any activity that included him during the season (six months of the year). Marilyn could put up with the daily radio broadcasts and the occasional TV games, but she really wanted him to be a part of their weekend plans during the summer. She tried sarcasm: "I see it's going to be another exciting weekend of beer and pretzels." And she threatened him: "One of these days you'll look up from that TV and find us gone." She wanted him to *want* to spend the weekend with them—a change in attitude. But she decided to settle for a change in his behavior. They worked out this agreement. He would spend every Saturday from the hours of 10:00 to 2:00 with their eight-year-old twins so that she could take an art class. They would arrange a daylong family outing one Sunday each month. He could pick which Sunday, but no baseball that day. At first, John agreed because he hated the nagging and complaining. At least she would be off his back about baseball during the other times. Later, John was surprised to learn that he tremendously enjoyed time spent with the twins. He taught them how to play ball. He made friends with the other dads at the park and started a little neighborhood softball team on Saturdays. The kids learned to enjoy the sport and looked forward to going to the games together on Saturdays. They loved being included in their father's favorite activity and were developing into precocious little ball players. By pushing to change behavior rather than attitude, Marilyn got much of what she wanted.

Saying what you think (the facts), feel, and want adds up to a complete assertive statement. Using this format will make it easier to organize your thoughts, avoid anger-evoking attacks, and get attention for your needs.

Anna May's best friend is always borrowing money. Fifty cents for the bus. Two dollars for burgers and fries at Mac-Donalds. A quarter for a package of gum. Half the time she forgets to pay it back. Using the I think, I feel, I want protocol, Anna May developed this assertive response.

> *I think:* "Two or three times a week you borrow money for the bus or to buy a snack. Some of the time you forget to pay it back."

> *I feel:* "I feel angry sometimes, and frustrated when I don't get the money back."

> *I want:* "Would you keep track of the tab in your civics notebook or somewhere and try to pay me back by the end of each week?"

Kate's first year teaching second grade was tough. There were times when she felt that she was doing creative and exciting work with her students. But there were times when she had a hard time keeping control of the noise and energy in her class. The teacher who worked next door would make sarcastic comments in front of the other teachers in the teacher's lounge. Kate felt critized and embarrassed. Finally she stopped the teacher in the hall and was assertive.

> *I think:* "You've been making comments in the lounge about how I manage my class."

I feel: "When you do that in front of the other teachers, it's embarrassing."

I want: "I'd like to talk to you privately sometime about what I am trying to do in my classroom and hear some of your suggestions. Maybe we can have lunch together next Monday."

Joanna provided afterschool child care for six children. She was constantly frustrated by the fact that some parents would come to pick their child up late and would never call to let her know. One parent in particular was often between 30 and 60 minutes late because she would stop to shop or do errands. Then she would casually say, "Oops, I guess I'm running a little behind. You don't mind do you? You're home anyway."

Joanna worked on an assertive response using the *I think, I feel, I want* structure.

I think: "In the last two weeks, you have been over 30 minutes late four times without calling and letting me know you would be late. When you're late, it means that I can't start my own evening activities. My work day isn't over until all the children are picked up."

I feel: "I feel a bit taken advantage of."

I want: "I would like you to be here at 6:00 promptly, and if you must be late please call and let me know."

Jeff and Bill were partners in a small design business. They operated on a very tight budget and tried to get along without hiring a secretary or office manager. That meant that there were many little tasks that needed to be done, and they tried to share the work. Jeff would ask Bill to buy stamps, make airline reservations, or call to check on the status of the loan that they had applied for. Bill would agree to do it, but when he got busy he would forget or put it off. When Jeff later found out that it wasn't done, he got really steamed. Jeff was finally able to put out what he wanted in an assertive way.

I think: "There are a lot of time-consuming tasks that just have to get done in order to run this business. Often when I ask you to take care of something, you don't get to it or forget. Meanwhile I've put it out of my mind because I assumed it had been done."

I feel: "I feel really frustrated when I look for a stamp and there are none. I felt angry when I found out that we had no plane reservations for that trip last month."

I want: "I want us to keep a list of all the tasks that need doing and put our initials on the ones that we agree to do. If you can't get to it, I want you to tell me. You can cross them off the list once it has been done."

Paul hired his friend's nephew to paint the front of his house. They had agreed in writing what the cost would be. When the job was done, the nephew added $150 in labor to the price, claiming that the wood was cracked and needed filling and sealing. Paul felt like he was being manipulated, but was able to put together an assertive statement.

I think: "We had an agreement in writing of what this painting job would cost. You did extra filling and sealing without asking me."

I feel: "I feel very unhappy about the price change."

I want: "I'm willing to pay you the amount that we agreed upon, plus the cost of the wood putty and sealer."

Cassie loaned a friend her suede suit. When she returned it, it was soiled. Cassie was shocked. She had just assumed that her friend would return the suit in good condition, although they had never discussed it. Instead of supressing her resentment, she expressed what she wanted assertively.

I think: "When I loaned you the suit, it was clean and pressed. Now it's soiled."

I feel: "I feel a bit hurt and taken advantage of."

I want: "I want you to pay me the amount it costs to have it cleaned."

Being assertive means that you get your needs met because other people know about them. Being assertive means that others listen to you because they are not afraid of your anger. Being assertive establishes you as a person who can take care of yourself, who can be cooperative, but who is honest and open about what you want and what you expect from others.

Sanctions

Some people are already motivated to go along with what you want. They might value your friendship or want a favor from you in the future. They might see the fairness of your position or just want to make you happy. But when people aren't motivated to meet your needs, you'll need to provide some form of reinforcement. Whenever possible, use positive reinforcement to motivate people to cooperate. It generally works better than punishment (if they don't go along with you, something bad will happen). Punishment creates resistance and resentment. Typical positive reinforcers include:

"If you'll do the dishes, I'll hang out with you and dry."
"If you handle the checkbook, I'll give you a foot massage."

"If you take Bill to school, I'll be able to start on the painting earlier. I'd really appreciate it."

"If we meet at the restaurant near my house, I could spend more time with you at lunch."

There are times, alas, when positive rewards don't work. No amount of praise or promised benefits gets you anywhere. One solution is to develop sanctions. Sanctions are the consequences or costs of not going along with what you want. "If _____ _____ happens, then I will do_____." Their purpose is to motivate the other person to cooperate with you or respect your limits. Used appropriately, sanctions can help you get your needs met without anger. In using sanctions, remember these four rules.

1. Sanctions should be specific. Be precise about what behavior will trigger the sanction and what specifically will happen. Vague threats like, "If I can't reach you, we'll have a real problem," don't give the other person enough information. Say instead, "If you refuse to accept my calls, I will find another lawyer."

2. Sanctions should be reasonable. There's no sense going after a mosquito with a shotgun. You'll probably blow a hole in the wall and miss the mosquito anyway. Reasonable sanctions help you feel in control. Reasonable sanctions are respectful of other people and their right to make their own decisions. Using public humiliation, betraying a confidence, threats of violence, or other unreasonable sanctions make people angry and less likely to cooperate with what you want. Sanctions such as, "If you are not here on time, I'll leave without you," or, "If you bring up that subject again, I'll leave the room," are appropriate for minor irritating behavior. Bring out the big guns only for the big battles, not the little skirmishes.

3. **Be sure you can live with the results.** The sanctions you impose shouldn't hurt you more than the other person. Peggy, a Catholic, was marrying a Jewish man. Peggy's mother said she wouldn't attend the wedding unless it was in a church with a priest. Peggy and her fiance chose to have a nonsectarian wedding officiated by both a priest and a rabbi and including traditions from both religions. Just as she threatened, Peggy's mother skipped the ceremony. Peggy felt hurt, but it was her mother who was the real loser. She missed seeing her daughter marry, she was in none of the wedding pictures, and her relationship with her daughter and their family was damaged. Be careful when you threaten to divorce, quit, call the FBI, or kill yourself. Dramatic ultimatums might seem appropriate in the heat of battle, but usually end up hurting you more. When you create sanctions that you can live with, you make it possible to follow the next rule.

4. **Sanctions should be consistent.** Be prepared to carry out what you said you would do. If you said that under certain circumstances you would hang up the phone, call the manager, or refuse to pay, then do it. Do it every time the situation arises. If you don't, you are *training* the other person not to take you seriously. Being consistent makes the other person respect you and your limits, and lets them know where you stand. Being consistent means that others will be less likely to take advantage of you in the future.

Negotiation

Negotiation doesn't only take place between labor and management or between super powers. You can use negotiation any time you have a conflict of needs and want to work out a solution for mutual benefit. "I give you what you need, you give me what I need." "I give you a pound of apples, you give me a dozen eggs." "I give you several hundred dollars, and you give me a ride on your airplane."

People often hesitate to negotiate when they have conflicting needs because it requires that they listen and understand the other person's position. They have an easier time being assertive if they see the other person as wrong, stupid, selfish, inconsiderate, or unfair. Instead of negotiating, they try to convince the other person of the rightness and fairness of their own position. They expect others to do all the changing.

Negotiation requires a different attitude. It starts with the premise that the other person's needs are just as important to him or her as your needs are to you. Nagging, shouting, or being angry or coldly rational usually won't get others to change their view. If you have a conflict of needs, negotiation allows you to find a middle ground where you both can get some of what you want. Here's how it works.

1. Know exactly what it is that you want. State it in behavioral terms—what you want the other person to do or not do.

"I want you to return the children by 6:30 Sunday night."

"I want to be in charge when you go on vacation."

"I don't want you to use our driveway."

2. Listen to the other person's objections. The purpose of this step is to understand his position; not to argue or try to convince him to give up his needs. Be an active listener by asking questions, clarifying, and paraphrasing what you understand the other position to be. Don't be afraid to hear or even empathize with the other person's view. Just because you understand it doesn't mean that you have to agree with the point or accept the opposing position. From the information you have gathered, you can take the next step.

3. Make a proposal. Your proposal should take into consideration what the other person needs or wants in this situation. If he accommodates you, is there something in it for him? You may have to be creative and flexible, breaking through the constraints of rules or traditions.

Marge, who worked as an accountant in a large urban high-rise, really wanted to have the office with the window instead of a partitioned work space. She appealed to her manager in terms that took into account his interests as well as her own. "If I can have this office, I'll be willing to store the overflow files. I'll also make the office available for the weekly meetings. And I'd be willing to share the space with the other nonsmoker in the office. That way, she'll be off your back about the new no-smoking policy. How about it?"

4. Make a counterproposal. If the other person won't accept your proposal, encourage him to come up with a different solution. People unfamiliar with negotiation may need some help getting started. Remind them that your objective is to understand their position and to find a compromise that both of you can live with. Here are some typical compromise solutions.

- "My way this time, your way next time."
- "My way when I'm doing it, your way when you're doing it."
- "If you do _____ for me, I'll do _____ for you."
- "Part of what I want with part of what you want."
- "Try it my way for a week and see. If you don't like it, we'll go back to the old way."
- "Split the difference."

You might even say, "I really want_____. This is really important to me. What would you need me to do to make it worth your while to go along this time."

Switch back and forth, listening, clarifying, and proposing until you both can agree on a solution.

The hardest part in negotiation may be getting started. You may first need to negotiate about negotiating. If you've had a long history of painful fights, or you have been angry and intimidating in the past, the other person may hesitate to even talk about the conflict. Try to determine why they resist an open discussion. Maybe they need reassurance that you will listen. They may feel safer if you set ground rules, such as a time limit, or make a prior agreement about not fighting or shouting, or decide to negotiate in the presence of a neutral third party.

Setting Limits

Think of the many requests made of you each day. Sometimes you agree to do things that are enjoyable to you. But some of the time you say yes when you want to say no.

The ability to say no is a crucial skill. It says to the world, "I am a person. I have needs, tastes, and preferences that are just as valid as yours. I can take care of myself." Saying no is a statement of your boundaries. Outside you are the needs and demands of all the people in your world. Inside are your own needs and desires. Being able to say no establishes that boundary. "No" is one of the first words you learned as a child, and one that first allowed you to make your needs known. "No, I won't eat my spinach." "No, I want to stay up." "No, I won't use the potty."

If saying no is such a basic and simple way of being assertive, why is it that many people have such a hard time doing it? Your early religious and moral training taught you to put others first. Those who give selflessly are admired. Those who look out for themselves are considered selfish. In some dysfunctional families, the children become the peacemakers and caregivers. Only by putting the needs of others first and denying their own needs can they survive. These lessons in survival stay with you long after they are useful or appropriate.

People with damaged self-esteem have special difficulty saying no. They feel unworthy. They have no right to their limits. They fear that saying no could mean losing a job or being abandoned by friends. By just going along, they hope to avoid disappointing or angering others.

But people who can't set limits may become chronically angry. They feel taken advantage of. Anyone can take their time, space, or money. They feel overrun and overwhelmed. An intimate relationship becomes a prison of limitless demands. They spend their time and energy on people and activities that don't give them pleasure and they end up having little time for things in life that bring real joy.

Shirley joined a carpool even though she preferred to take the train. Joan plays cards with her old friends every Tuesday even though she would prefer to take a quilting class. Tom accepts the job of United Fund organizer even though he hates dealing with office collections and doesn't have the time. Jill agreed to sew all the costumes for her daughter's dance recital because she doesn't "work" like the other mothers. All these people have difficulty setting limits and it makes their lives less productive, creative, and enjoyable.

Just Say No

In many circumstances, a simple "no" or "no thanks" is all that's appropriate or necessary. You don't owe the other person an explanation. You need not apologize. Keeping it simple will get the job done assertively. "No, I don't want a drink." "No, I don't need a vacation home in the Bahamas." "No, I don't want to contribute to the baby-shower present." Your pleasant but confident refusal conveys the feeling that you are not rejecting the person, just the request.

In other circumstances, you might want to give the other person more information. Complete limit setting has three components: it acknowledges the other person, states your position, and sets the limit. When you use the three-part statement, you don't have to get angry at demands ("What do you mean asking me for more money?"). You don't have to give advice ("If you kept your car maintained, you wouldn't be in this situation."). You don't have to blame ("If she'd plan ahead, she wouldn't keep me waiting for an hour."). You don't have to fix or solve the problem ("How will you get home now? I'll ask around and see if I can find someone else who can give you a ride.").

1. **Acknowledge the other person's needs.** If you are not sure exactly what is being asked of you, probe and get more details. What exactly is meant when the other person asks you to "help him move" or "support his program?" Acknowledging the other person's request assures him that you hear him correctly.

2. **State your position (your preference, feelings, or perception of the circumstances).** Be as confident and assertive as you can be. Do this without apologizing. Don't put yourself down. Just describe what is so for you. "I'm too tired tonight." "I have a previous engagement." "I decided that I'd rather drive my own car."

3. Say no. Say "No thanks...I don't want to...I'd rather not... This is not right for me...I've changed my mind...I won't be there."

Here are some examples of saying no.

- "I hear you need someone to watch your baby this afternoon while you go to the dentist. (*Acknowledgment*.) I wanted to spend this afternoon working in the yard while my boy is in school. (*Your position*.) I won't be available to help. (*Saying no*.) I sure hope you can find someone else."
- "I understand you need someone from our unit to go to that meeting. (*Acknowledgment*.) It can't be me. (*Saying no*.) I'm pretty busy with my own projects now, and I don't want to take the time off. (*Your position*.)"
- "I'm aware that you are sexually attracted to me. (*Acknowledgment*.) I enjoy the time we spend together, but the chemistry is just not there for me. (*Your position*.) A sexual relationship with you now wouldn't feel right for me. (*Saying no*.)"
- "I'm sorry that you feel that I'm being unfair. (*Acknowledgment*.) But I have to consider the needs of the business at this time and we just can't afford to lose you now. (*Your position*.) I won't okay your transfer. (*Saying no*.)"

You can't always plan ahead, but it might be useful to think of recurrent situations in your life where you need to set limits or say no. You might try to rehearse an assertive response using the three-part statement. You can practice saying no to a friend who often asks you for money or to your supervisor who expects you to work late or take work home. You can practice saying no to a relative or neighbor who drops in without notice, to committee work that takes up too much of your time, to telephone solicitors, and so on. When you are able to set limits, you can do more of the things you really enjoy.

Here are some more suggestions about saying no and setting limits.

1. Take your time. If you are someone who has had trouble setting limits and who automatically says yes, try delaying your response. You'll probably be able to think more clearly without the pressure of another person waiting for your answer. "I'll call you by the end of the week." "I'll let you know this afternoon." "Can I give you a call back in five minutes?"

2. Don't over-apologize. When you apologize for setting limits or saying no, you communicate to the other person and *to yourself* that you don't have the right to take care of yourself. You are saying "Forgive me for putting my needs before yours." Excessive apologies invite the other person to put more pressure on you to change your mind. Apologizing also inspires people to impose on you about other things so you can make it up to them.

3. Don't put yourself down. Some people can only set limits if they put themselves down. "I'm too weak, stupid, clumsy, poor, afraid." In the long run, saying "I won't" is better than saying "I can't." When you say "I can't," the other person will try to convince you that you *can do it*. You are then stuck trying to prove that you can't. When you say "No, I won't," the other person is less likely to argue.

4. Be specific. State exactly what you are and are not willing to do. "I am willing to help you move the furniture, but not pack or clean." "I am willing to drive you to work, but only if you can be ready by 8:15."

5. Be aware of voice and body language. Stand, or sit comfortably. Look the other person in the eye. Speak with confidence, your voice strong. Let your body and tone of voice match your assertive words.

6. Beware of guilt. After you say no, you might be willing to do something *else* for the other person. But take your time before offering. Be sure you are not acting from guilt. You don't want to obligate yourself to do something you will be sorry for later.

Dealing with Criticism

Criticism is painful. You can end up feeling wrong, judged, guilty, or afraid. And each of these painful emotions has the potential for triggering anger. "How dare she?" "He has no right."

For people sensitive to criticism, it doesn't matter if the issue is minor. It doesn't matter if the critic is someone whose opinion is unimportant. It doesn't even matter if the criticism is inaccurate. Just feeling criticized sets off a chain reaction—like a row of falling dominos, your self-esteem tumbles, your confidence drops, and you begin feeling extremely defensive.

Being criticized reminds you of what it felt like when you were a child, when you were corrected and judged by angry parents. As an adult, you don't want to reexperience the old feelings of being wrong, bad, even worthless. And you resent being made to feel like a child.

Being criticized makes it hard to feel perfect. Many people irrationally expect that they can do it all, do it right, and please everyone. So criticism is scary. If, as you imagine, others expect you to be perfect, you have to fear the slightest mistake. Any flaw, it seems, could lose you a job, a friend, and so on.

You may use anger to avoid and cover over the many painful emotions triggered by criticism. This was the case with Linda, a newly graduated RN. The occasion was her first three-month evaluation by her head nurse. Most of the evaluation was full of praise for her energy, her potential leadership ability, and her warm, professional interactions with patients. The evaluation also included this line: "When Linda gets behind in her work, she sometimes becomes rushed and careless. She needs to develop time management skills."

After the evaluation, Linda was depressed for a few days. Then she was so angry that she almost quit her new career. How did that happen to her?

First, she disregarded the majority of the evaluation (which was positive and praised her skills and strengths). She read the critical line over and over, focusing on the words "rushed and careless." Her internal monologue went like this: "Oh, God, this is awful. If I'm rushed and careless, I'll probably kill someone. How can I do this job if I'm afraid that I'll bump someone off? Good nurses don't rush patients. I rush around in a careless way. I must be a bad nurse."

Her self-deprecation spread well beyond the evaluation. "I'm not only a bad nurse, but a bad person as well. Imagine being sick and in pain and having someone rush you. How cruel to rush helpless sick people. Other people get their work done on time without rushing. Their patients are well taken care of and they finish on time. I'll never get it right. I'm a failure."

After several painful hours, Linda began covering her guilt and depression with anger. "Good God, this is an impossible job. I do my best but it just isn't good enough. What do they expect? They give me too many patients who are too seriously ill, and then complain if I can't breeze through the day. What does the head nurse know? All she does is pencil pushing. This job is impossible. I don't have to take it anymore!"

There is a way of hearing even hostile criticism that allows you to assess it, benefit from what is appropriate, and disregard what is not. Here are the steps you need to take.

1. Limit the damage. First, you can limit damage by stopping abusive, angry attacks from others. Even if you feel guilty about the situation, don't allow yourself to be verbally battered. Even if you're wrong, you don't deserve to be called names, threatened, or violated. Take "time out," or simply refuse to go on with the discussion if the attack continues.

Next, remind yourself that you are hearing one man or woman's opinion about a specific aspect of your behavior. The criticism is about what you do, not about who you are. Even if the other person is attacking and rejecting you, you don't have to join in. "This paper is not acceptable" does *not* mean that *you* are unacceptable. It does not mean that you are incapable of doing acceptable work. It does not mean that all of your past papers have been unacceptable.

Finally, you can limit the damage by accepting that perfection is impossible. There is no way you can do it all, do it right, all the time. Accept that mistakes are inevitable. There are times when you will be tired, distracted, misinformed, unmotivated, or rushed. By accepting that about yourself (and others), you will be less angry and less damaged by criticism. When faced with an angry attack, repeat to yourself the mantra "I am a good person, doing the best I can." Just keep saying it, over and over. For other coping mantras that might be useful, see Chapter 10 on coping through healthy self-talk.

2. Probe. Criticism can be constructive and valid. It may provide the feedback you need to grow in your relationships or your work. Actors, speakers, artists, and performers of all kinds seek constructive criticism from those they trust.

The only way to assess criticism is to probe. Make sure that you know exactly what the critic means. People are so uncomfortable with criticism that they often avoid questioning the critic. They're afraid of the painful emotions that criticism stirs. But only when you probe to understand exactly what the critic means can you determine if it's useful to you. Before you fly into anger, retreat in defeat, or collapse in agreement, make sure you know exactly what the critic is conveying. Dave, a recent high school graduate, just started a new job in construction. His foreman approached him and said, "You need to improve your attitude if you're going to get along." Dave asked him what he meant. The foreman elaborated. "The contractors notice when you come and when you go. You were 15 minutes late twice this week. It makes our whole team look bad and the other guys resent it." Dave learned that, on this job, coming to work late was interpreted as a "bad attitude."

Jim's wife was sick with the flu. Her criticism was attacking and angry: "You're just never there for me. All you care about is yourself." Jim asked what she meant. "Here I am, sick, and you show no concern for me at all. When you had the flu last week, I called you twice from work, I fixed dinner, and I stayed home from my karate class just to be with you. You just go on with your life with hardly a 'How are you?'" Now Jim has more information. His wife would feel more cared for if he did those kinds of special things for her. Jim doesn't have to accept or agree with her attack. But now he knows more about his wife and more about how his behavior affects her sense of being cared for.

Mat and Rich were old friends from grade school through college. Now that they are both working, they seem to be drifting apart. They have less time to do things together. Rich was surprised when Mat attacked him. He managed to control his hurt feelings long enough to determine what lay at the heart of some rather hostile criticism.

Mat: You've turned into quite a social climber.

Rich: What do you mean by "social climber"?

Mat: You're always hanging out with friends at work now, you hardly have time anymore.

Rich: What is it about my hanging out with work friends that bothers you?

Mat: You all vacation and party together. You go to their yuppie sports club. How can I compete? You'd rather hang out with them than be with the real people.

Rich: What do you mean by "real people"?

Mat: People from the old neighborhood, like me.

Rich: Since I've been working you feel like I've been going places and doing things with my new friends and we don't have as much time to do things together?
Mat: Yeah, I miss the old days when we did everything together. It's kind of lonely without you.

What started out sounding angry was really Mat's feelings of loss and jealousy and a need to be closer. Once you've determined exactly what the complaint is, you can start to evaluate its accuracy. The new nurse really did need to work on time management skills. The two old friends were really drifting apart and their relationship was changing. Dave, the construcion worker, was 15 minutes late twice last week. Jim did not pamper his wife when she was ill.

Recognize also the part of the criticism that is not accurate. Dave's lateness does not necessarily indicate that he has an "attitude" problem, but only that he didn't count on traffic delays. Rich was not snubbing his old friends and becoming a social climber. It isn't true that Jim is "never there" for his wife, only that it never occurred to him to pamper her when she was feeling ill. The new nurse's difficulty organizing her work doesn't mean that she was a bad nurse and a bad person, only that she is new and inexperienced.

One way to spot inaccurate, harmful criticism is to listen for generalizations. "You never _____." "I'm always the one who_____." "Everyone else knows about _____ but me." There are plenty of exceptions to such globalized statements. Look for them. Also be alert for global indictments that attack you as a person, not just complain about your behavior. When you hear yourself condemned as selfish or stupid or uncaring, refocus on the specifics of the situation. These attacks on your identity are wrong by definition. No one is totally anything. You are a complex person with many different (sometimes contradictory) motivations and needs.

3. Deflect. Here are four techniques you can use to disarm the critic and prevent escalation.

In *clouding,* you agree in part with the criticism, without accepting it completely. It requires that you listen carefully to the critic and agree with the part of the criticism that is accurate.

Critic: You are never around when I need you.

Response: I have been working a lot this month and I haven't been around as much in the evenings.

Critic: If you keep spending money at this rate, we'll be broke in no time.

Response: We have been spending more money since we moved into the new house.

Notice that you don't have to agree with everything. You don't have to buy that you're *never* around, or that you'll go broke. You acknowledge the grain of truth without accepting the entire exaggerated statement.

Another way to cloud is to *agree in probability*. "It may be..." or "You could be right..." are ways you can imply agreement without total capitulation. Using agreement in probability with the previous examples, you might reply:

"You may be right that I haven't been around much lately."

"It's probably true that we're spending quite a bit."

A third form of clouding is to *agree in principle*. The trick here is to accept the conclusion without accepting the premise.

Father to son: "If you don't work harder, you'll never get into law school." The young man can agree with the principle that hard work is necessary to get into law school. But he doesn't have to buy the *premise* that he isn't working hard. Here is how he might agree in principle: "You're right, you have to work hard to get into law school."

When you agree in part or in principle with the critic, the critic feels listened to and his opinion and concern is, in part, accepted. He'll be less likely to continue arguing to prove he is right and you are wrong.

Assertive preference is a way of shutting off the critic. Using this technique, you acknowledge the criticism but disagree with it. Don't feel you have to provide a long explanation. Just state that you prefer to do it your way. "I hear that you don't agree with how I'm handling this situation, but I prefer to do it this way." "I hear what you're saying. I guess we just don't agree on this point." "Thanks for your concern, but I'm willing to take the risk." This technique is used when you have the power to do things your way and you want the critic to back off and stop badgering you. It stops further discussion without attacking the other person and without getting angry.

Assertive delay is an important and powerful technique for responding to criticism without anger. If you take time out (even for a few minutes) you allow yourself to calm down, think, activate some coping strategies, consult with another, get support, gather information, and so on. When the critic is talking, you can just pretend that you are a tape recorder. Record, clarify, and understand the criticism. Don't feel you have to respond, apologize, fix the problem, or throw in the towel. You can delay responding until later when you can "play it back" in your mind, assess it, determine what is accurate and what is not. A few minutes alone can provide the perspective and awareness that you don't have when you feel under attack. "I hear what you're saying. Let me think about it and I'll call you in the morning." "What you're saying is important, but I frankly am feeling a little overwhelmed right now. Let's get together after work for coffee and we can talk some more."

Don't get pressured into responding if you're not ready. Don't try to get in the last word or get into an argument about whether or not you have the right to delay responding. Use your three-part statement for setting limits. "I understand that you are not happy with the job I've been doing (*acknowledgment*). I'm feeling like I need some time to think before I respond to you (*your position*). I'll call you tomorrow (*setting the limit*)."

A content-to-process shift is useful when the discussion is escalating into a battle, you feel that the critic is over or under-reacting to something, or you suspect the critic is not saying what's really bothering him. When you use the content-to-process shift, you stop talking about the issue (content) and talk about the angry feelings or your sense of being attacked (process). It is a way of putting on the brakes and exploring the quality of the interaction between you. "I don't know about you, but I'm kind of frustrated. We always get stuck in this sort of argument." "This is the third time today that you've criticized how I've handled the kids. What's happening?" "You say you're not upset about my cancelling our date, but you sound like you're almost in tears." "We always end up arguing about how much money to spend on new equipment. I'm feeling accused and attacked. What's going on between us that we end up feeling angry like this?" A content-to-process shift allows you to get to the real issue or the more important issue that lies at the bottom of a conflict.

The Payoff

People who are not able to communicate assertively are usually angry. They're angry because they are not able to ask for what they want or to protect themselves by setting limits. They are angry because they can't motivate others to cooperate or negotiate successfully. They blame instead of listen, they defend instead of problem solve. Your efforts toward becoming assertive will eliminate many anger-generating situations. Now you can begin to acknowledge your needs, ask for changes, set limits, and cope with criticism. This work will have an immediate payoff in the quality of your relationships.

13

Images of Anger

It's 12 noon. You've just seen two colleagues literally sneaking out of a conference rather than inviting you along for lunch. You recall their smiling, silly, smug expressions as they ducked out the rear door. You imagine telling them off, lingering over each sarcastic remark. You polish the scene, you relish the tone of contempt in your voice. You review delicious scenes where you snub them or ridicule them in front of a superior.

Imagery is a powerful trigger for your anger. Anger images are not limited to simple visual phenomena, but may include auditory or even kinesthetic experiences. You can fantasize about someone or something and "see" the scene. Or you can hear someone's voice with a certain inflection or "edge" to it. Or the "image" might consist of nothing more than a feeling in your body of tightened muscles or a remembered jab in your ribs.

Some anger images appear spontaneously. Like Marley's ghost in Dickens' *Christmas Carol*, they come back to haunt you night after night. But angry scenes don't just occur in nightmares. In the form of "day dreams," they can strike any time, anywhere—when you least expect them.

The most common type of anger image is intentionally generated. Many people indulge in replays of recent or old wounds laced with fantasies of retribution. This seemingly harmless pastime may sometimes lead to painful consequences. Each anger-generating scene keeps pushing the adrenalin button inside your body. Your anger escalates. Your dreams of retaliation grow more cruel. And the odds keep increasing that you'll act your anger out in ways that could harm a relationship.

Replay

Anger replays evoke feelings of hopelessness, helplessness, frustration, and deep psychological pain. The well-known Charles Atlas advertisement in which the skinny kid gets sand kicked in his face is a vivid illustration of this process. One imagines him going home to run the scene through a hundred times in his mind. Each replay brings a new surge of rage and hurt. Each replay makes him crave more deeply the perfect revenge.

Replaying painful scenes is one of the most popular forms of self-torture. Millions lose sleep nightly reliving the major and minor slights and disappointments in their lives. These kinds of scenes usually take on an "If only I had said or done..." format. Using the wisdom of retrospect, you reexperience the hurt, along with a sense of failure that you didn't respond differently.

Michael, a licensed clinical social worker, almost nightly relived the latest outrage with his teenage daughter. As if on a TV monitor, he watched the sneer, the flounce as she left the room. He listened to her shrill voice: "Your're a shit, Dad. A stupid shit. Get out of my way!" He heard himself telling her to grow up or move back to her mother's house. He imagined explaining that she'd been crippled by a mother who knew nothing about discipline and setting limits. He imagined telling her about the waiting cavalcade of loser jobs and loser men that she'd experience if she didn't shape up. She'd never succeed at anything. She'd just screw every skinhead punk who came along.

He felt triumphant. He felt right. He felt so angry that he was sick with it. His stomach churned. He felt hot. His shoulders were as tight as tow ropes. And he had a vague sense that something terrible would come of his rage.

Sally, a secretary working for a downtown business firm, ran a different kind of replay. The instrument of her torture was a malicious inner Walkman with a demonic will of its own. All day she would "record" in high fidelity every conversation or verbal interaction that had negative connotations for her.

She worked for a boss known for his critical, sarcastic manner. Hardly a day went by that she didn't get the opportunity to add some new assault on her self-esteem to her tape library. There were the daily jibes about her figure (she was slightly overweight). And the comments about her spelling: "Don't you own a dictionary?"

Her boyfriend, Phil, a sweet but inarticulate man, could be relied upon to make some faux pas. He commented on how "cute" she looked, when in fact she was trying to be "sexy." Once when she was experimenting with a new dark eye shadow, he asked if she was getting enough sleep. The demonic tape recorder picked up the insults, every word, every nuance of inflection.

At her leisure during a solitary lunch hour or a quiet evening at home, Sally would replay her tapes. As she heard again the critical or unflattering comments, she would feel her body begin to tense. An angry, gnawing sensation would start in her stomach and slowly begin to rise. If she was lucky, she would manage to turn off the machine. But usually, the on-off switch was stuck, and her rage headed in an upward spiral.

Retribution

Fantasies of retribution are especially appealing. In the safety of your own mind, you can deliver poetic justice of the most satisfying kind. The Hammurabi code of "an eye for an eye" is only the beginning.

Everyone has taken a turn at the game of "sweet revenge." Remember how the Charles Atlas ad ends? The "skinny kid" (now miraculously muscled) returns to reclaim his girl and rout the bully. The cartoon has the kid throw one bloodless, sanitized punch, but hints of a more violent retribution lurk just below the surface. Although fantasies like these may give you short-term satisfaction, in the long run they will end up making you feel chronically helpless and upset. Worse yet, repeated revenge fantasies tend to impair impulse control. You may act out your fantasies in ways that destroy any chance for real problem solving or healing in your relationships.

Anne, a Vassar graduate, was thrilled when she married a Harvard professor. But only a few years later the thrill was replaced by a deep sense of betrayal. Tweed jacket and all, Robert turned into a bit of a rake. He was enormously popular with the young coeds, flattering them, advising them, laughing with them. Amanda (English 2A) was the last straw for Anne. She came home early from potting class one day to find the two of them in the hot tub.

Rather than confront her husband, Anne withdrew. She withdrew both physically (as she literally ran back into the house) and emotionally. But the hot tub scene couldn't be shut out so easily. The sound of the couple's laughter rang in her ears and followed her everywhere.

For Anne, the most "civilized" solution to this problem was to indulge in discreet revenge fantasies. At first, she tried imagining a lover of her own. But no one she knew seemed really desirable.

Eventually she hit on the idea of a theatrical vengence. Dante's *Inferno* provided the backdrop, and Gilbert and Sullivan's *Mikado* the musical inspiration. For her "object all sublime," she conceived the striking image of Robert and Amanda being boiled in a vat of oil. This "hot tub" was ringed by demons brandishing pitchforks. If Robert tried to escape, he was painfully prodded back into place.

As usually happens, this fantasy did not succeed in diverting her anger but actually served to sustain it. Every time Anne heard her husband's laughter, it brought back the scene in the hot tub. This was immediately replaced by a vision of the demonic vat of oil, an image that heated her own blood as well. One Sunday morning while Robert was chuckling over the funnies, Anne "accidentally" spilled hot coffee in his lap. At a dinner party a week later, Robert's laughter was cut short when Anne "tripped" and spilled a tureen of hot soup down his neck and back.

Chuck, a warehouseman on New York's Eastside, had a relatively happy life until about 10 months ago. At that time, while backing his forklift toward a waiting truck, Chuck appeared to brush a pedestrian. The man fell down and started screaming. In Chuck's mind, he never touched the guy. All the hollering seemed like an Academy Award scam. An ambulance came, then the police. The guy kept screaming and pointing at Chuck: "He knocked me down, he ran over me..."

Now there's a lawsuit—against Chuck, his boss, the warehouse company (whose deep pockets appear to be the main target). Chuck hates the lawyer who took his deposition. He imagines how he'll handle that sleaze-bag on the stand. He imagines making anonymous threats on his life. He imagines visiting the "victim" and forcing him at gunpoint to walk without the cane and brace. He imagines videotaping the victim walking and playing the tape in the courtroom. He imagines shooting the lawyer's kneecaps with a shotgun. First the left, then the right one.

Every night Chuck would play his favorite scenes—the courtroom, the brandished gun. And night after night, by increments, he got angrier. Over time, the anger images began to loosen Chuck's impulse control. He bought a camera, intending to catch the victim walking without his cane. Chuck staked out the man's house and waited. Now his fantasies were going full bore. He'd confront the guy, he'd tell him what a "packed-with-shit scam artist" he was.

When the victim emerged from his house, Chuck forgot his photographic mission. He ran up to the man. He swore, he shouted, he punched him a good one. Now the lawyer has added assault and battery and $100,000 in punitive damages to the suit. Chuck's anger seems strangely blown out. He's doing something he never thought he'd do—seeing a psychotherapist for depression.

Taking Control

You do *not* have to be at the mercy of unbidden images that sneak up on you and turn your life into chaos. You do *not* have to be victimized by runaway fantasies that threaten to overwhelm you. You have a choice. And the choice is to take control.

Image Stopping

Perhaps the single most useful tool for dealing with anger imagery is a variation of thought stopping. The idea was first introduced by Bain in 1928 and adapted in the 1950s by Joseph

Wolpe and other behavioral therapists. More recently, Donald Meichenbaum (1977) has developed a technique of substituting *covert assertions* (relaxing thoughts and images) for the anger-triggering ones.

You can use this tactic to distract or "derail" the train of thoughts and images before it gets up a full head of steam. In a way, thought stopping is a kind of deterrent that lessens the chance that the same thought or image will emerge again. Negative images are cut off before they have a chance to do much damage. Instead, through relaxed, forgiving images, you can create a positive feedback loop that diminishes your anger.

The first step in taking control is to arrange for a *timed interruption*. Get an egg timer or alarm clock and put it next to a comfortable chair. Now sit in the chair and allow yourself to let your mind wander. When you find yourself beginning to entertain negative images or fantasies, open your eyes and set the timer for two minutes. Then close your eyes and allow the images to continue. When the bell goes off, shout "Stop!" out loud. As a way of reinforcing the experience, either snap your fingers or stand up quickly.

You will probably find that the images stop and are replaced with neutral thoughts. If the fantasies return within 30 seconds, shout "Stop!" again.

When you have mastered image stopping with a timing device, you are ready to start using a cassette recorder. First, record yourself shouting "Stop!" at random intervals. For example, you might leave gaps of 30 seconds, two minutes, one and a half minutes, three minutes, and so on between shouts. If you had trouble stopping your images in the previous exercise, then record yourself shouting "Stop!" several times in a row at each interval. Now you can substitute your tape recording for the egg timer while you allow your mind to entertain the negative images.

The next step is to practice *unaided thought interruption*. Allow your images and fantasies to proceed for a bit and then shout "Stop!" Keep doing this on your own time schedule until you are able to stop the fantasies several times in a row.

When you are able to completely interrupt a chain of images by shouting, you can start lowering your voice to a normal tone. When your normal voice proves effective, you can continue to lower your volume until you reach a whisper. The last step in this process is to "subvocalize," or to imagine hearing the shouted word "Stop!" You still move your tongue and throat as if you were saying the word, but without making a sound.

Using this tehnique you can now effectively stop intrusive images or fantasies anywhere or anytime (without drawing funny looks from the people around you when you "shout").

If you find that this technique is not completely successful, you can try two other strategies. The first is to carry a hand-drawn picture of an eight-sided traffic stop sign in your wallet. You can pull out the picture as needed, whenever intrusive images occur. In time, you will learn to visualize this sign mentally whenever you want to take control. A second technique is to place a thick rubber band unobtrusively around your wrist. When disturbing images come to mind, a simple snap will quickly bring you back to reality. Remember to subvocalize "Stop!" whenever you snap the rubber band.

The stop sign and rubber band may seem like bizarre gimmicks. But they are proven strategies for stopping unwanted thoughts and images. They work—which is what's really important in the quest for anger control.

Don't be discouraged if at first the images tend to come back very quickly. If you use thought stopping *each time* the anger-triggering image occurs, its frequency will greatly diminish within one to two days. The secret formula for success is consistency. Consistent use of the thought stopping technique will prevent the image from taking root.

Image Substitution

It is rarely enough to simply *stop* the offending images. Nature abhors a vacuum, and something must come in to fill the empty space. The best strategy is to plan ahead and have some *positive images* prepared and ready to put into action.

One of the most healing images is that of a sunny beach in your favorite part of the world. Whether it's a quiet cove on Kauai, the bay of Corinth, Stinson Beach, or even Coney Island, the effect is the same. The warm sun makes your whole body feel quiet and deeply relaxed. You smell the ocean and hear the sound of the waves as they come in and go out. And you know that the sea has been doing that, ebb and flow, since time began.

Lying there, totally at peace with the universe, you can imagine all your troubles washing out to sea. Sally imagined her boss being carried farther and farther out by the waves. His strident voice became fainter and fainter, until there was nothing left but the surf, the sea, and the cry of an occasional seagull.

Or you can imagine climbing a mountain to achieve a new perspective on your situation. Look down and see the people in your life as small moving dots. Michael saw his daughter and himself, moving from room to room in the house as they do their angry dance. From the mountaintop their battle seemed so far away, so silly.

Another option for Sally is a technique that helps her get through the day. When her boss starts getting critical and makes derogatory remarks, she fantasizes a white light. This is the fabled white light of acceptance, which allows people to hear unpleasant things without taking them in or feeling defensive. She imagines herself bathed in the light. Safe. Protected. Beyond the reach of her boss's hurtful jibes. In the light, she can finally see his pain, his humanity, his obvious frailty. In addition, by imagining a simple switch, Sally can turn on a white noise feature. This noise effectively masks or minimizes the sound or impact of negative feedback and creates a peaceful environment around her.

For some people, a cool blue light works best. Chuck's therapist has taught him to stop hot thoughts by imagining an ice blue light filtering down from the ceiling. The coolness is relaxing for Chuck, and he has an easier time letting go of anger images.

A different type of thought substitution involves the creation of images that help you to see the angry, provocative person from a new point of view. For example, Sally sometimes imagines her boss in a belittling way by seeing him naked or dressed in a clown suit with a big red nose. Chuck pictures the lawyer who took his deposition crippled or otherwise handicapped by greed. By looking closely, he can see a small and frightened child inside the aggressive antagonist. Anne, the professor's wife, gets some measure of relief by seeing in her mind's eye the positive aspect of her husband's personality. Her balancing image of him as a gentle, intelligent, and caring soul helps prevent escalation and encourages her to confront him directly. Michael has made some progress in rebuilding his relationship to his daughter by looking for her loneliness and fear. He sees her as small and overwhelmed by life, looking for support from every man she meets.

Alternative Scenarios

Perhaps one of the most empowering strategies for dealing with runaway fantasies is to exercise the option of creating an alternative scenario. This technique is an adaptation of the "dream re-entry" process reportedly practiced by the Semai, a Malaysian tribe legendary for their peaceful way of life.

To begin this process, you'll find it helpful to review your fantasy in detail. Write it down in a looseleaf notebook, as this will make it easier for you to rework it to your satisfaction. By reexamining the fantasy, you will be able to isolate the *choice points*, those places where the fantasy can most easily take a different "turn." A turn for the better usually involves a possibility of reconciliation or leads to understanding and acceptance of differences.

Plan ahead! Sketch out alternative scenarios. Imagine the possibilities for change in your antagonist's point of view. Begin by imagining the smallest possible change and gradually expand on it. When you've prepared yourself for the new adventure, it's time to begin.

Find a quiet time and place. This may be difficult to do, but it's essential because you don't want any interruptions. Refer back to Chapter 8 on controlling stress step by step, to the section that outlines the systematic process for relaxing your entire body. Start with your hands and forearms, move slowly through all the muscle groups of your body, and continue to relax.

When your body is finally fully relaxed and your mind is at rest, you can begin to imagine yourself walking down a gentle path that meanders through the trees. You follow the path to a clearing, a protected meadow in the middle of the forest. This is your special place. Take a moment to feel the warm sun on your body. Smell the green grass and notice the occasional butterfly.

On the far side of the meadow is a hollow with a stairway. Ten steps down slowly descend to your inner sanctum: a room secured by a massive oak door. You have the only key. Once inside you have complete privacy and complete control. The noisy, intrusive world is safely locked outside. Among the many amenities of this wonderful room at your disposal is the absolute control of the VCR and tape library.

Relax in the comfortable overstuffed chair. Lean back and turn on the TV monitor (with its 48-inch screen and Dolby sound). Videotapes autoload into the VCR (equipped with a state-of-the-art zoom feature, instant replay, freeze frame, slow motion, and edit). You have at your fingertips, built into the arm of the chair, the ultimate remote control. Now you can choose to review the fantasy of your choice.

Anne chose to see, back to back, the "hot tub" and "vat of oil" sequences. As you recall, this particular pairing caused her a lot of trouble, not to mention a trip to the emergency room for Robert. In the relative calm and security of this place, she experimented with new endings. Sometimes she edits the videotape and watches herself climb into the hot tub, looking terrific. Robert sees her and tells Amanda to leave. In another version, Robert sees the error of his ways (after a few minutes in the boiling oil). He now appeals to Anne for clemency and makes new promises of fidelity.

When he found himself in the safe environment, Michael did a lot of reediting. He saw himself asking his daughter about what hurts her, what she needs from him. He saw himself talking about his need to see her safe and OK. Sometimes he imagined giving her a gentle hug.

Another possibility is to create a cartoon. Sally makes an animated image of her boss which depicts his personal pain. The pain has a shape and a unique color. Sally's pain also has its unique shape and color. She watches these two creations side by side, interacting—and finds that new solutions occur to her from this seemingly silly show.

Your imagination is like a double-edged sword. With one edge it can create enormous pain and chronic arousal. The other edge can be used like a surgical scalpel, to heal and repair. Of course this process will not change objective reality. It may, however, allow you to go on with your life without becoming mired in habitual anger images. The important thing to remember is that you have a choice. You hold the sword in your hands, and can use it for the purpose which serves you best.

14

Anger as a Defense

Two boys square off in a schoolyard. One is larger and louder; he shoves the smaller boy. It was an error in judgment, because the smaller boy explodes like a grenade. He goes for the stomach, the groin, the chest. And when the bigger boy falls, he kicks him in the face and ribs. It's over in less than a minute. A teacher drags the smaller boy to a bench, where he sits waiting for the principal. The boy relives the scene again and again. He wonders what gave him the quickness, the strength, and most amazingly the courage to beat the bully up.

The answer of course is anger. The hormonal changes triggered by anger do five important things to protect you from attack. Anger provides:

- A feeling of empowerment. Suddenly you don't doubt yourself. You can do whatever needs to be done.
- Energy to cope. Not only do you have the confidence, but anger gives you the strength to mobilize yourself for action.
- A blocking mechanism for nonadaptive feelings such as fear and guilt. Anger drives out or obscures any feeling that might inhibit protective action. Anger's vector is always forward, to attack and push away the source of pain. There's no room for feelings that would slow you down at the moment of combat.
- Adaptive egocentricity. Anger allows you to forget the other person's needs. His or her pain doesn't matter. All that counts is your pain and your needs.

- The conviction of rightness. Anger strengthens the feeling that you are right and that whatever you do is justified. There is a temporary suspension of any sense of wrongness or badness in the self in order to maximize the commitment to self-protection.

Protection Versus Psychological Defense

The same five properties of anger that help you respond to attack adaptively make it very useful as a psychological defense. A psychological defense is something you do that obscures or covers an important inner experience. Anger is often used as a defense because it can block painful feelings such as anxiety or fear, hurt, guilt, shame, embarrassment, the sense of being wrong or bad or unworthy, loss, emptiness, frustrated desire, helplessness, and many others. Anger can be a buffer against feelings that you would rather not experience. The properties of anger that block fear and guilt, that make you self-centered and fill you with a temporary sense of rightness, can help you push away literally any feeling or inner experience that threatens you.

Using Anger for Defense

The easiest way to understand how anger works as a defense is to see it in action. Consider the following examples.

Defending against guilt. A woman points out to her husband that he spends so much time at business and Rotary Club meetings that he is a stranger to his children. He defends himself from the guilt with the trigger thought that his wife has turned his children into self-indulgent brats. "The whole house is a playpen," he says. "You let them wreck it, you live with it." Then follows the explosion.

Defending against hurt. Marjorie has her first major job with an ad agency. When she brings home a direct mail piece that she wrote for an important client, her father makes several nitpicking suggestions. Marjorie defends against hurt with a trigger thought: "He never changes. The same perfectionist shit." Abruptly she rises. "Thanks for the support," she says in a deadly voice.

Defending against loss. Sheila's best friend, Anne, is marrying and moving to Canada. Anne is preoccupied with finishing at work, packing, out-of-town guests, and last-minute details. Sheila defends against feelings of loss with a trigger thought that Anne is stupid and unliberated to sacrifice her career and friends for this one relationship. Sheila has to really fire up her anger to cover the enormity of the loss. Two days before the wedding she attacks Anne for "dumping everyone who ever cared about her." At the reception they barely speak, and Anne leaves town before the damage is repaired.

Defending against feeling helpless or trapped. Last year, Mateo had a heart attack. For 20 years he's worked as the only typesetter for a small weekly newspaper. He's expected to stay long, unpredictable hours to meet production deadlines. He has two girls in college and a feeling that his age and health history would make it hard to find new employment. The newspaper seems familiar and safe, but the deadlines create overwhelming stress. Mateo defends against the feeling of helplessness with the trigger thought that his girls wanted to go to "expensive party schools" even if it killed him to pay for it. He picks fights whenever his daughters come home to visit.

Defending against anxiety or fear. Tony screams and then spanks his two-year-old for venturing off the curb. The anger blocks the jolt of fear he feels that a car might hit his child.

Rebecca is afraid that Jim is slipping away from her. He calls less and their dates are spaced further apart. She defends herself with the trigger thought that Jim abuses women. He keeps her waiting as part of a game of deliberate mental cruelty. And Rebecca grows more remote with each date.

Andy is secretary of a union local. Recent bargaining reversals make him expect that he'll be voted out. He cuts off his anxiety with the trigger thought "They want everything, but they're too spineless to get it." He becomes increasingly abrasive with members.

Defending against the feeling of being bad, wrong, or unworthy. A driver waits at an intersection while a pedestrian saunters slowly in front of him. He feels rage. The pedestrian's message seems to be "You don't count, you're nothing." And that message ties directly into feelings he had as a child of being ignored and discounted. His anger defends him from all those feelings as he hits the horn and shouts through the glass.

A woman's boyfriend declines a sexual advance. Immediately she is flooded with feelings of being bad and unworthy. She defends herself with the trigger thought that "He's controlling, he's only interested in sex if he can be in charge." She rolls him over to tell him so.

A couple's daughter is caught stealing at school. On the way to a conference with the principal, they both feel inadequate as parents. They conspire to fight about who should take the car in for a tune-up as a cover for these feelings.

Defending against emptiness. Two graduate students are attempting to have a relationship. As the semester progresses, Arthur finds himself more and more out of contact with Jean. Their evenings are spent reading and working on papers. An emptiness, very much like the ache for attention and nourishment he felt as a child, begins to grow in Arthur. He withdraws sexually. He begins to compulsively do crossword puzzles. He buys a telescope to look into people's windows. When these lesser measures fail to hold the emptiness in check, Arthur covers it with the trigger thought that Jean doesn't care about him and simply uses him for stability to get through grad school. He screams this charge one night, and they actually have sex. But within a week things are the same as ever.

Defending against frustrated desire (sour grapes). A divorced dad spends Saturdays with his son. He yearns for the child during the week and rents the boy's favorite Tweety and Sylvester cartoons for the coming visit. During the cartoon, he wants his son to sit next to him, to be close. But the boy keeps jumping up to play and make noise. To block the pain of his frustrated desire, the father thinks, "He's acting wild." So he shouts, "You can't control yourself. Sit down now or I'll never rent cartoons again."

Nearly everyone has at some time used anger to defend against painful feelings. The problem comes when you make a habit of it, when the frequency and intensity of your anger defense begins to affect your health or your relationships. Some people become addicted to anger as a way to spare themselves any experience that is threatening or painful. The person who at root feels bad or worthless learns to blow up at the slightest criticism rather than experience even a moment of self-doubt. The person who is afraid to feel fear learns to attack and blame rather than endure a moment of anxiety.

The Addictive Nature of Defense

It's hard to let go of anger after you've learned to employ it as a defense. It always seems as if the anger is easier to feel than fear or hurt or guilt or emptiness. And of course it is. *At that moment.* All addictions feel good at the moment, all addictions serve to block pain, and all addictions offer a short-term feeling of control and well-being.

The problem with addiction is never in the moment, but in the aftermath. The long-term effects of chronic anger on health and relationships have been discussed in previous chapters. There is a third and equally damaging effect from addictive anger. *In everything except direct threat, anger tends to lead you away from appropriate action.* When you use anger to block painful feelings, you never get to deal with the feelings themselves. And you never get to address the problem that generated the feelings to begin with.

Anger keeps you from dealing with the source of fear. Fear derives from one of two things: misattributions (distorted and exaggerated perceptions of danger) or actual danger. Consider Irma's case as an example of misattribution. She was convinced that her 16-year-old son was a heavy drug user. She buried her fear underneath frequent outbursts about his clothes, choice of friends, sexual activities and, of course, his suspected drug use. Her son, whose drug use consisted of smoking marijuana once a week, dismissed her as a "person whose IQ approaches absolute zero." Anger prevented her from getting accurate information about her fears. She had no way of correcting her misattribution because her communications had a blaming rather than fact-finding function.

Anger not only prevents you from correcting fear-inducing distortions, it stops you from effectively coping with real threats. A man who had been mugged in a dangerous neighborhood railed against his company for relocating in the "knock-you-down-for-a-dollar part of town." For months he talked about the details of the mugging and the poor treatment he received from the police, made racial slurs, and began referring to every young man on the street as a "fucking thief." His anger prevented him from dealing effectively with the danger. There were choices he could make: he could buy a car, stop working late, arrange for a lift home, or even get a job in a safer part of town. He failed to explore a single one of these options because he wasn't motivated to. His anger was masking most of his fear; he simply wasn't scared enough to make an adaptive decision.

Anger keeps you from dealing with your pathological critic. This is the voice inside of you, spawned by hurt, neglect, and criticism from your parents, that attacks you for every flaw and imperfection. It's the pathological critic who makes you feel wrong and bad and worthless when you make a mistake or when you're criticized. It's the critic who internally abuses you when you fail to live up to your highest standards. Some people are in so much pain from their critic that they learn to turn it loose on the world rather than go on feeling worthless and bad. If they can just make the mistake someone else's fault, if they can just find some reason to attack and blame, they can shut off the chanting inner voice that keeps saying "bad, bad, wrong."

The trouble with using anger to calm your critic is that you never learn to talk back to its abuse. You never cope directly with the crippling things it says to you. Harold was a trombone player in a major symphony and a perfectionist about his playing. His pathological critic would denigrate an entire performance if his tone was unsatisfactory for a few notes. But he learned to shut these feelings off by focusing on the performance of other musicians in his section. He raged about sloppiness, lack of preparation, and "musical incompetence that should have been obvious at their audition." Expecting the worst from others became a psychological trademark. The real problem was never addressed: low self-esteem and a killer critic.

Anger keeps you from examining the values that generate your guilt. Guilt results from a collision between needs and values. Sometimes the values are healthy and appropriate; sometimes they are not. Arlene worked for an attorney who frequently was poorly prepared for hearings. She helped him by preparing one- or two- page summaries of the salient issues in each case before he appeared in court. Whenever he was embarrassed or lost a case, she blamed herself and then defended against the guilt by criticizing her daughter's school work when she got home. Anger kept Arlene from questioning her values. Was she really responsible for the incompetence of her employer? Was it her job to anticipate every pitfall of a case?

The other side of the coin is also true. Many people run from guilt generated by appropriate and healthy values. A man who had custody of his 15-year-old daughter was rarely home to supervise her. He dealt with his guilt by denouncing her as "undisciplined and irresponsible, a nightmare on 12th Street." Here the anger prevented a reexamination of his behavior and a square look at how his night life was incompatible with good parenting.

Anger keeps you from facing loss. Chronic anger prevents you from grieving, from letting go. You just keep replaying the sins and violations of the person who abandoned you. The short-term effect is that you don't have to feel sad. The long-term consequences are symptoms of unresolved grief and the inability to trust or bond with others. Serena was a topflight model who suffered minor facial scarring in an auto accident. She railed at the plastic surgeon's incompetence, filed a lawsuit, and dumped the boyfriend whose driving led to the accident. Anger helped to keep the grief away. She thought very little about a new career, about decisions that lay ahead. But her bitterness was palpable when she interviewed for jobs as a receptionist or salesperson.

Anger keeps you from saying what hurts. Angry people don't talk about their pain. They talk about the faults of others. No one knows how much they hurt, how wounded they are by a remark or gesture. While the short-term effect of anger is to block feelings of hurt, the long-term consequences are that no one ever learns to recognize or accommodate vulnerabilities.

Arnie feels hurt whenever his wife mentions his recent six-month period of unemployment. He sees himself as an incompetent breadwinner, and so he counters with a discussion of her spending habits or picks a fight about their inability to save. Arnie's wife never hears about his hurt, and the core problem is never communicated. The truth is that she would gladly change her behavior if she only knew.

Anger keeps you helpless by stopping problem solving. When you're angry it's hard to fix things. You feel like a victim; life seems out of your control. While the deep frustration of feeling stuck can be somewhat masked by anger, the impulse to blame or attack prevents you from real problem solving. As in the case of the man who was mugged or the model who was disfigured, anger works in the short term to keep feelings of helplessness at bay. The long-term consequence is that important decisions never get made. And your self-defeating behavior remains unexamined.

Anger keeps you empty. Angry damages the very relationships that are the source of nourishment. Laurie's husband is a sports addict; she hates the sound of football because she associates it with loneliness and isolation. But the more she complains, the more her husband withdraws into the games. Anger keeps Laurie from taking more effective steps to increase the level of intimacy in her relationship.

Coping with the Underlying Feeling

It's a hard thing to face, but your anger defense is more harmful than the pain that it's designed to obscure. To understand the role your anger plays in defense, go back to your anger log. Review every anger incident for the past three-week period. Analyze these events; ask yourself which feeling the anger covered. Write the feeling down in red ink next to each anger entry.

Now you have some hard data. You may notice that one or two feelings predominate. Or that you experience different underlying feelings with different people. One man found that he frequently felt guilt about his daughter but helplessness with his wife. Another reported feeling an underlying experience of fear in nearly every anger episode.

If you have trouble contacting the underlying feeling, ask yourself this question for each anger incident: "What would I have to feel if I *didn't* get angry in this scene?" Imagine yourself continuing the scene and the dialogue or action unfolding without the protection of your anger. Use your visualization skills to fully experience the sights, sounds, and sensations of the event. Without anger, what are you left to feel inside?

The work that lies ahead now may be difficult, and it will require a real commitment. It's time to begin to face and feel the emotions your anger has blocked. What follows are specific steps you may wish to take in working with these underlying feelings.

Facing fear. Step one is to identify your catastrophic thoughts. Examine the anger scenes where the underlying feeling is fear or anxiety. Fear is always generated by a catastrophic image or belief. What dangerous or painful thing are you expecting to happen? What vision of the future does your fear paint for you? What's the nightmare, the worst-case scenario? As you review situations where you've covered fear with anger, make a list of your catastrophic expectations. For some it will be the same fear over and over—for example, the fear of being rejected or humiliated. Others will have great variety in their catastrophic projections.

Now for each catastrophic fear that you uncover, try to restate your concern using three guidelines:

- Strive for accuracy rather than exaggeration.
- Be specific rather than general.
- Include your tools to cope if the worst should happen.

Raymond's catastrophic fear was that his supervisor was displeased with his work and planning to fire him and that he would end up losing his newly purchased home. He realized that a more accurate statement about his job was that he had no idea how his supervisor felt about him. His supervisor had asked him to be more prompt with sales reports, but there had been no other feedback. Raymond decided that he needed to do two things to cope. First, he needed to ask his supervisor for some informal feedback on his performance. Second, he needed a fallback plan to handle his worst-case scenario of losing his job.

Here's how Raymond restated his catastrophic fear: "I have no idea how my supervisor feels. The only feedback I have is that he wants the sales reports on time. I'm going to arrange a worst-case contingency plan with my parents for getting a loan if I can't meet house payments. Then I'll ask my supervisor how I'm doing."

In Maria's log, she found again and again the fear of being exposed as incompetent. She was enraged if her boyfriend said anything about her cooking, her driving, her use of makeup, or her parenting of her six-year-old daughter. The catastrophic fear was "Everyone will see how incompetent I am." Striving for accuracy, Maria reminded herself that her boyfriend generally liked her food, she had a good driving record, men obviously thought her attractive, and her daughter seemed basically loving and happy. In none of these areas had she been exposed as incompetent to the world. The only evidence against her were private observations made by her boyfriend. She decided to cope by forcing herself to hear out his criticism, acknowledge it, and point out to him any balancing realities. Maria restated her catastrophic fear like this: "I'm an adequate cook, I'm attractive, I'm a good driver, and my daughter is clearly happy. My boyfriend's criticisms are just between us, and no one needs to know about it. I can hear what he says, but I'll also tell him the balancing realities."

When it's clear to you that your perception of danger is very real and very accurate, put your energy into brainstorming new ways to cope. Here's a condensation of the problem-solving strategies presented in Chapter 8.

- List as many alternative solutions as you can think of. Quantity is better than quality. Don't evaluate your ideas, just keep them coming. The more fresh, unusual, or bizarre the better.
- When you have a list of between 10 and 20 alternative solutions, begin ruling out the obviously unworkable ones. With the solutions that remain, list the positive and negative consequences for each one. Make sure that the consequences include both short- and long-term outcomes.
- Now select one or more alternative solutions that you would like to try. Decide on the first step you need to take toward implementation.

The key to dealing with real danger is effective action. You need to make a decision and carry it out.

Facing the fear of unworthiness. This is perhaps the greatest psychological pain a human being can endure: the feeling of not being good, not being adequate. While its roots lie in your relationship to your parents, the feeling of unworthiness is promoted every day of your life by the constant attacks of your pathological inner critic. The first step to coping with feelings of unworthiness is to really hear what the critic is saying to you. Go back to anger situations where the underlying feeling was being wrong or bad. What were you saying to yourself? How is the critic putting you down?

It's time to restate what the critic is saying. Use these four rules:

1. Make the statement accurate rather than exaggerated.
2. Make it specific rather than general.
3. Use nonpejorative language.
4. Include balancing realities.

The critic always exaggerates, always generalizes, and frequently uses language that has demeaning connotations. On the other side of the ledger, the critic never points out your strengths, abilities, or good points. Jane's critic was always on her for being "ugly." Jane's sister and girlfriend frequently brought up the issue of her weight and endless dieting. Sometimes they joked, sometimes they asked serious questions about her eating habits. On each occasion, Jane seethed inside. Her angry trigger thoughts helped drown for a while the critic who was shouting, "You're fat, you're fat." Jane decided to state the critic's attack using accurate, specific, nonpejorative language: "I weigh 150. I'd like to lose 30 pounds." For a balancing reality, Jane pointed out to herself that she had not gained weight in two years, that she had bought an attractive wardrobe rather than waiting to lose the pounds, and that she liked certain parts of her body (her legs, eyes, and breasts). Jane resolved to use her new statement as a way of talking back each time her critic harangued her. It felt particularly important to her to make the balancing statements that acknowledge things that she valued in herself.

Special note. A deeply held belief in your badness may be a result of early trauma. People who were abandoned, neglected, or seriously abused often feel that the trauma happened because they were bad or because they invited it. If this feels true for you, it could be extremely helpful to see a trained psychotherapist.

Facing guilt. As you review the scenes in your log where anger covers an underlying experience of guilt, ask yourself this question: "What is the rule for how I am supposed to be or act that I violated in this situation?" You may have one rule that emerges again and again, or there may be a variety of rules that strongly influence your behavior. Whether there are one or many, these rules have a rigid, absolute quality. To break them is to be bad. These rules also stand in opposition to some important need you have. Otherwise, you wouldn't be acting to violate them.

Once you've identified a rule that generates guilt, you can begin to examine it. Is this your rule? Does it come from your own experience? Or is it the rule of a parent or some authority figure that you've accepted without question? Is the rule flexible? Does it allow for unusual or mitigating circumstances? Or is it written in stone without possible exceptions? Is the rule realistic? Is it based on real and likely consequences for your acts? Or is it based on strict, unbending concepts of what's right and wrong? Is your rule life affirming? Does it support taking care of yourself in a way that's healthy for you and those you love? Or is it life constricting, denying you access to important sources of nourishment and satisfaction?

You are feeling guilt because your needs are in conflict with a rule or value. Now ask yourself this question: Is your need more important in this situation than the rule? Should the rule be made more flexible, more supportive? You may wish to rewrite the rule so that you are allowed to pursue certain needs in specific situations.

If you feel good about your rule, if your value makes sense to you, then your guilt is a healthy response to behavior you want to stop. Your greatest enemy now is denial, the response of running away from a feeling that signals a need to change. The guilt is your ally, a necessary source of pain that can push you to make the tough choice between your rule and the behavior that conflicts with it.

If guilt alone is insufficient to motivate change, this can only mean that you don't have enough support to stop the harmful or inappropriate behavior. You may need to join an appropriate 12-step program or a support group to stop violence or improve your communication or deal with sexual acting out. Perhaps you need a training group such as those offered by parent-effectiveness programs. Many people get support by telling their friends about a problem and making a contract for specific changes. Regular check-in times are built into the contract and the friend agrees to monitor your progress.

Cheryl was guilty about blowing up at her children. She covered the guilt with more anger about the condition of their room, their slowness getting dressed, their dawdling over meals, and so on. She asked herself what rule she was violating to generate such guilt. She recognized that she felt a very strong prohibition against shouting at her kids. The rule seemed to be her own, rather than an old idea borrowed from her parents. The rule seemed flexible (it was okay for her to shout sometimes). The rule seemed realistic in that she felt that very negative consequences could develop for her children's self-esteem if she barraged them with angry criticism. The rule was also life affirming in that it supported her children's growth while allowing her to express needs and criticism in a nonpejorative way.

Cheryl decided that her rule was okay, and the guilt was appropriate. It was her behavior that had to change. She enrolled in a parent training group and found more effective ways to set limits than her old strategy of shouting.

Facing grief. When you become aware that anger is covering loss, you can arm yourself with this mantra: "He (or She or It) is gone. I am angry so that I won't feel the loss." If you say this each time that the anger emerges, you will gradually develop greater contact with your basic feelings of grief. Whatever the nature of the loss, your work now is to begin letting go. Set at least half an hour aside each day to mourn (or more if your loss is a recent or grave one). Mourning means reminiscing, appreciating, regretting, but most of all feeling the sadness of surrendering and giving up the lost person or object.

It is important to trust the grief process. People run from grief because they (1) resist pain and (2) are afraid of being overwhelmed and engulfed by the powerful feelings. The truth is that the human psyche is set up to experience grief (or any pain) in a sequence of waves. The awareness of a loss hits with crushing intensity. The pain goes on until you reach a natural shutting down process. There's a respite, a quietness, perhaps even a numbness in the middle of the pain. After the rest and numbness comes another wave, and so on. Grief can be enormous. But when it reaches overwhelming proportions, the natural shutting down process gives you time to get your breath. You can "work through" grief by letting the waves happen and remembering they will pass before their intensity overwhelms your abilities to cope.

Two years ago, Harold's girlfriend moved out. He is still angry and still talks about her to friends. He focuses on her withdrawal and her failure to communicate and on a conviction he has that she secretly planned to leave for many months. He counts her sins and transgressions like beads on a rosary of blame. But the real function of Harold's anger is to effectively block feelings of grief. While he holds on to her with his anger, he never has to face the loss.

Harold began his recovery process by using the mantra "She's gone, I get angry to stop feeling sad." He repeated this sentence internally each time he noticed himself slipping into his familiar obsession. He decided to set aside a half hour each day from 6:30 to 7:00 to mourn their time together. He assembled a group of pictures and mementos. Harold focused on the good that was lost and let the grief well up in him. Over time, he began to recognize that he could rarely sustain feelings of grief for more than five to ten minutes. He saw this as the natural limits of the wave and reduced his sessions of mourning to a shorter interval.

Facing hurt. Hurt ranges from feeling slightly neglected or discounted all the way to an overwhelming sense of abandonment. If you find a propensity to cover hurt with anger in your log, then anger should be a signal for you to ask yourself, "What hurts me?"

Hurt is either realistic or unrealistic. Unrealistic hurt occurs when a small slight or criticism triggers deep feelings of unworthiness based on your early relationship with your parents. If you feel that this describes your case, return to the section in the chapter on facing the fear of unworthiness. Hurt can also be a realistic response to a current slight, criticism, or rejection. Realistic hurt is usually far less painful. You still feel basically good about yourself, even though something is wrong with your current interaction. Sometimes hurt has both realistic and unrealistic components. The hurt that you feel when a friend arrives late may also trigger echoes of earlier experiences of neglect.

The active work in facing your hurt is to acknowledge it—openly and directly. Anger is always blaming and accusatory. It's focused on the other person. To communicate hurt, you must find a way to convey what hurts without implying that the other person is bad or wrong to have caused it.

Ariel was a short-order cook who felt close to most of the waitresses in the diner. Susan had an acerbic, biting humor that

Ariel usually liked, but also found grating at times. Whenever a customer sent food back, Susan would joke about Ariel's incompetence. "Eggs a little slimy, babe?" These remarks hurt. Ariel found herself reacting with trigger thoughts such as "You want to cook, bitch?" She grew more distant from Susan.

After Ariel began to recognize her use of anger to cover hurt, she would ask herself "What hurts?" whenever Susan's behavior triggered anger. She decided to express her feelings to Susan and settled on this response: "When you joke like that, it makes me feel bad about my cooking." It was important not to convey in the message that Susan was doing something wrong. Only that Ariel was feeling hurt and hoped that Susan would cool the cooking jokes.

Facing helplessness. Anger obscures the feeling of helplessness in two ways. First, it keeps you from experiencing how stuck you are by putting all your attention on the failings of others. You're so concerned with their selfishness, their mistakes, and their stupidity that your own sense of impotence is never fully faced. Second, by shifting the blame to other people, you don't have to take responsibility for your own decisions or failures to act that led to feeling so stuck.

Facing helplessness requires that you give up the crutch of blame. Anger won't change anything. People will keep doing what *they* need to do, not what *you* need them to do. The first step in facing helplessness is to take full responsibility for being stuck right now. Look back at the specific choices you made, both to act and not to act, that led you to your current circumstances. Right now you need to accept that the ways you chose to cope, your game plan, your strategy for getting your needs met, fell short of the mark.

Step two in dealing with helplessness is to generate a new set of coping options. If you've begun to face your own responsibility for being stuck, then you are ready to face the fact that *you are the only one who can solve your problem.* You are the one in pain, you are the one whose needs are unmet. You are also the one who knows best what you require to feel better.

To generate new options for coping, you should develop a clearly stated goal. What must you achieve to feel unstuck, to lift the burden of helplessness? Make sure that the goal is concrete and specific. Write it down. If you're having trouble formulating a goal, ask yourself what specific thing you want that you don't have or what source of pain you want remedied. Now brainstorm some alternative solutions and proceed with the problem-solving strategies described in the section on facing fear. If none of your solutions seem to offer much improvement over the current situation, it's time to go back to brainstorming. But this time involve your friends, your family, and any trusted adviser in the process of developing new ideas. Tell them that you don't expect them to give you the right answer, but that you just want to hear all the new ideas or perspectives that they can think of. Don't forget to remind them that wild and crazy ideas are acceptable too.

The third step in coping with helplessness is to take action. You have decided on a new coping strategy. You need to take the initial step toward implementing it. Decide now on what that step is and when exactly you will begin.

Joe had worked for the past three years as a gofer at a major newspaper. He was stuck on the lowest rung of the ladder and he blamed his boss for it. "He won't give me any responsibility. He trusts me with nothing. He's a condescending, rat-faced little man." Joe's first task was to begin taking responsibility for his own experience of helplessness. He looked back at the things he had done and not done over the past years. He had decided to take a high-paying warehouse job when he was 18, rather than go to college. He lost this job when he picked a fight with his boss. He had enjoyed a vacation paid for by unemployment insurance for the next six months and then taken his current job in desperation when his money ran out. He had wanted to go back to school, but felt intimidated by the effort that he'd need to make to hold down a nine-to-five job plus evening classes. He had also thought of applying for other jobs inside the newspaper, but had never really mobilized himself. He knew that he should do a resume, but had never written one.

Having taken responsibility for his current dilemma, Joe identified a specific goal. "I want to be a reporter. I want to see my byline." He generated over two dozen alternative solutions. Joe settled on starting night classes in journalism at a local community college. He planned to assemble a portfolio of writing that he could use later in job applications. The first step toward action would be calling the college to request an application packet.

Facing feelings of emptiness. Feelings of loneliness and emptiness are so painful that some people will do anything to block them from awareness. The key here, as with all the other difficult feelings, is to separate blame from pain. You need to experience your loneliness directly without linking it to a fault or failing in others. To accomplish this, you will need to literally encourage the feeling.

Since loneliness is extremely painful, you will have to arrange for it to come up in brief, manageable chunks. Set a time limit so that the feeling doesn't overwhelm you:

- Take a 10-minute walk on an isolated part of the beach.
- Sit alone for 10 minutes, concentrating only on counting your breaths.
- Spend 15 minutes in a place where you once felt happy and close to someone.
- Concentrate on exploring feelings of boredom and loneliness for 10 minutes just before turning to some distracting activity.
- Turn off the radio and TV and just sit in silence for 20 minutes in your living room.
- Resist your impulse to call someone. Notice what it's like to postpone the contact for 10 minutes or so.
- Place a chair in the middle of the backyard and sit in it for 15 minutes.

Some of these exercises will make you more aware of your loneliness. Paradoxically, some of them may generate a strange sense of calm. The important thing is to notice what you feel like when you're not running away from your experience by getting angry. When you can just feel your loneliness without blaming anyone, you're taking a big step toward improving relationships with others. At this point, you have two ways to go. One is to learn more about yourself by expanding the periods during which you contact your aloneness. You may learn that aloneness brings up other uncomfortable feelings: guilt, grief, or a sense of unworthiness. These underlying feelings may require special attention and working through (as described in earlier sections of this chapter). Or you may learn that your emptiness includes painful memories from the past. (You may find it helpful to seek professional help if these memories are disturbing or hard to shake.)

Your loneliness may just be an ache, a yearning for attachment. It may be a long-held dream of a certain kind of closeness and partnership. Here the second part for dealing with loneliness presents itself. If your loneliness does seem focused on a need for intimacy, then direct action may really help. It may be time to make a clear decision (frightening as it may seem) to join a hiking group or go to a single's dance or begin participating in a political action group. If you already have close relationships, yet are haunted by feelings of dissatisfaction, you may take action by initiating activities that promote closeness and intimacy. Create a candlelight evening of massage, a weekend in the country, an interesting sexual variation, a great dinner out, and so on. Just turning the television off so that you can talk may be an important decision. Whatever you decide to do, make sure that you take full responsibility for generating the experience that you want. You are going to have to lead; hopefully your friend or partner will follow. Years of blaming the other person can make initiating the hardest task in the world. Why should you suggest anything new when it's always their turn to do something, their responsibility to fix what's wrong. In truth, the only one who can make a difference is you. You need the closeness, and you will have to find a way to ask for it or create experiences of sharing that meet this fundamental need.

Maria's boyfriend is a tennis nut who plays two evenings a week and both mornings on the weekend. For Maria, the loneliness and anger were always interwoven. She considered his tennis playing to be selfish and compulsive.

In the intial stages of facing the emptiness, Maria began taking brief walks on the beach while her boyfriend played on the weekend. She practiced just feeling the loneliness without making him responsible for the pain. Somehow, by removing the anger, several solutions became clear to her. She decided to continue her walks on Sunday and sign up for a painting class on Saturday. She asked her boyfriend to spend one weekend afternoon taking a country hike with her. In this new shared activity, she found it possible to have a closeness that she looked forward to all week. The emptiness was still there sometimes, but Maria felt more confident in her ability to cope.

Making Your Own Plan

As you begin to let go of anger as a defense, you can experiment with suggestions offered in this chapter. Some will help, and some won't work for you at all. In time you may develop strategies of your own to deal with underlying feelings. What's important is to stick with your commitment to see through your anger to the feelings underneath and to find new ways of responding to parts of yourself that once lay buried under layers of blame and upset.

III

Anger At Home

15

Anger and Children

Vicki, seven months pregnant, sat in a cafe drinking cappuccino and talking to her friend, Bonnie. With them was Bonnie's 18-month-old, whining, squirming daughter. The two adults tried in vain to talk. Bonnie was so distracted trying to keep her baby restrained in the high chair that Vicki soon gave up any attempt at conversation. Vicki could feel her unborn baby moving within her, and she imagined how wonderful it would be when the baby finally arrived. Her baby would be calm—not fussy and crying all the time like Bonnie's. In this moment of perfect symbiosis, Vicki felt that her baby was close and quiet and perfect.

Before you had children, you might have had fantasies about how you would feel and act as a parent. You would strive to be loving and patient. You would explain, not order. You would discuss, not overpower. You may have been critical of other parents who were impatient, inconsistent, too lenient, or too strict. You certainly would never feel anger.

You now know how difficult it is to achieve those ideals. It is not necessarily true that if you love your children, if you are conscientious and aware, you will be immune to anger. You cannot automatically assume that you will always rise above the little upsets in parenting and handle conflict with intelligence and good humor. Being a parent tests your patience, your flexibility, wisdom, and endurance like no other career and no other relationship.

In a survey of Canadian parents (Minden 1982), 41 percent of the parents rated their parenting experience as negative and frustrating. Over half the parents in a study by Frude and Goss (1979) had lost their temper and hit their child "really hard." Another 40 percent feared that they might lose their temper and really hurt their child in the future. These were not troubled families with difficult children. The subjects who reported these feelings were "normal" parents with "normal" children.

When you look at the working conditions of your job as a parent, you can see why many parents feel exhausted and stressed.

1. Long hours. You are "in charge" every hour of every day (including weekends and holidays). If you work outside the home, your parenting job starts well before you leave the house in the morning and resumes the moment you come home. And it doesn't end at bedtime. Infants and babies may wake frequently during the night, and your sleep might be broken by a child who is ill or has a nightmare.

2. Children are incredibly messy. A lot of your time and energy is spent picking up, cleaning up, wiping up. Food, toys, clothing, and dirt spread thoughout the house. Even parents of children who are responsible about cleaning up their own toys find themselves involved with encouraging, supervising, training, organizing, and supporting the cleanup effort.

3. Children are noisy. A household with children is a house filled with laughter, screaming, crying. Children are constantly asking questions. Any activity that requires quiet, such as reading, phone calls, or conversation, is always a struggle.

4. Caring for children requires that you do many repetitive and time-consuming tasks. The laundry, shopping, and cooking never end. Children need you to transport them everywhere—to sporting events and dance classes and to the dentist.

5. Children are self-centered. They aren't usually aware that you are worn out, losing patience, or under a great deal of stress. Social skills, such as empathy or sensitivity to others, are learned over a long period of time.

6. Children push the limits. Normal children are constantly seeking autonomy. They want and need to do more for themselves, and they question your judgment and authority. From the two-year-old who has learned to say no to the rebellious teen, children push and challenge the rules in order to grow up.

7. Children need tremendous amounts of attention and approval. They compete with anything and anyone that takes you away from them. Their attention-getting strategies may be overt and obvious (look at me, see me, watch me), or covert and indirect (sibling rivalry, destructive behavior, low achievement at school).

8. Children require vigilance. They must be protected from immediate and potential dangers. Parents of young children must constantly watch the child, remaining alert for anything breakable, hot, sharp, or small enough to be swallowed. Parents of older children who play and travel away from home are always worried about bike or car accidents, the dangers of the playground, the dangers posed by strangers, and so on. No matter how vigilant you are, you never feel that your children are completely safe.

The Lessons of Anger

Marny sat with her two children in the playground. Joey, the four-year-old, seemed bored and restless. He would build a hill of sand and call to his mother to look at his "volcano." Marny would look over for a moment and then continue to talk to her friend. Joey's calls for attention occurred about every two minutes. Finally he went over to where his two-year-old brother, Tony, was filling cups with sand, and pulled the cups out of his hand. Sand splashed out of the cup and got in Tony's mouth and eyes. Tony screamed with surprise and pain. Marny flew into a rage.

"How dare you take his toys away? Stop being selfish. Give that cup back to him this instant." "No," Joey yelled, his hands curled into fists.

"Oh yes you will." Marny snatched the cups from him and then turned him around and spanked him on the buttocks.

Joey screamed. Marny noticed that other people in the park were listening to them, and she felt embarrassed as Joey's crying continued. She held him tightly by the arm as he tried to struggle away, and warned him, "Stop that crying. If you don't stop acting like a baby, I'll give you something to really cry about." Joey stifled his cries and sat alone, away from his mother. He muttered under his breath, "I don't like my brother. I won't be his friend, ever, ever, ever." What has Joey learned from this encounter? Certainly not sharing, not gentleness with a baby. By snatching the toys and spanking him, Marny has demonstrated that big people can do hurtful things to little people and that physical aggression is an option when you want something or when you are angry.

Joey is also learning about himself. He is developing a self-image that includes the fact that he is selfish, bad, and defiant. He can make his mother so angry that she acts in a rejecting way. Since he doesn't see Marny treating the baby this way, he is learning to dislike and feel less worthy than his little brother. He is also learning that having sad, hurt feelings and expressing them by crying is not okay and can, in fact, lead to even more trouble.

A case study of adolescent mothers (Crockenberg 1987) showed that angry and punitive mothers had children who were angry and noncompliant. These children also distanced themselves from their mothers. In her 1985 study of toddlers, Crockenberg found that when these toddlers were exposed to anger (rather than other negative emotions), they reacted with self-concern and angry defiance toward others. They also showed *less* concern for others and were *less* empathetic when witnessing the distress of others.

For children to learn kindness, they must be treated kindly. For children to discover alternatives to anger and aggression, they have to see these alternatives demonstrated. For children to be considerate of others, their feelings and needs have to be treated with consideration.

The Effects of Anger on Children

Because anger is almost ubiquitous in parent-child relationships, one may have the illusion that it is harmless. The truth is that anger's effect on children is devastating. It distorts their sense of self. ("I must be very bad to make Mommy so mad.") It makes them feel scared that they are not safe. It makes them feel that their lives are out of control. ("Who will take care of me? Who will protect me?") It makes them feel abandoned. Feelings of abandonment are particularly excruciating for children because their lives literally their depend on their parents' love and protection.

Each child learns to see himself as he is seen by his parents. Children who are frequently insulted, put down, or threatened tend to see themselves as mean, selfish, stupid, worthless. They are also more tolerant of abusive behavior from others and more susceptible to peer pressure.

Children have a great need to see their parents as all-powerful and knowing. It helps them feel safe. Because of this magical thinking, when parents are rejecting, angry, or abusive, children will blame *themselves* before they'll see their parents as wrong or mean or bad. Even children who have suffered severe abuse will often defend and protect the abusing parent. Robert Fire-Stone (1985) describes this as a "fantasy bond" —the illusion of a connection with the caretaker that will protect the child. This illusion of protection has an ironic effect. The more a child feels abandoned, the more likely he is to idealize and cling to his parents.

Bradshaw (1988) describes the bonding with an abusive parent this way. Children love their parents and are emotionally bonded to them, but abused children are *even more strongly bonded* because they feel worthless. Thus they idealize their parents' rules and judgments so as not to separate themselves from them. Children who develop poor self-esteem in order to maintain an idealized view of their parents continue to blame themselves long after they become adults. They continue to "parent themselves" in the same way that they were parented, according to Bradshaw. And they will also go on to parent their children in the same way. By this process, the toxic effects of abuse are carried to the next generation.

The Functions of Anger

As discussed earlier, anger helps you to block or discharge painful levels of stress. It enables you to defend against painful feelings of anxiety, hurt, guilt, worry, or loss.

Meg's 14-year-old daughter Kim was supposed to be home by 10:00 p.m. When Meg heard Kim's key in the lock at midnight, her anger discharged the pain of two solid hours of worry.

Eight-year-old Bobby was showing his dad a new trick he had learned on his skateboard. A car turned the corner and just narrowly missed hitting him. His father's anger at Bobby helped discharge the pain of anxiety.

Matt's mom was doing well in the hospital. But at 7:00 a.m. a nurse called to inform him that his mother had been moved to the intensive care unit. The pain of anxiety triggered an impatient outburst at his four-year-old as she dressed and prepared for school in her usual "slow as molasses" way.

Anger also helps block the stress of painful physical sensations.

After an hour of noisy and rough play, Martin's nerves were shot. When one of his children accidentally kicked him in the shin, he blew up and sent them all to bed.

Peggy was helping her daughter study for an important French test. At 10:00 at night Peggy was exhausted and found that she was being irritable and sarcastic to her daughter.

Anger also blocks the stress that develops when you are frustrated in your attempt to do something that you need or want to do. In Heusser's (1986) study of parents of young children, she found that frustration from interruptions was one of the most common sources of anger.

Nancy complains that she can't even go to the bathroom alone. Her toddlers follow after her. If she closes the door, they shout and bang and cry. By mid-afternoon, when both children are supposed to be napping, she finally sat down with her favorite magazine and a cup of tea. When her three-year-old woke the ten-month-old, she was in a rage. She slapped the boy and tossed him back into bed. Now, with the sound of both children crying, she felt even angrier.

Children suffer from fear of abandonment, but parents are also threatened by fear of being abandoned by their children. This often leads to anger.

Sue and her parents were in perpetual conflict during her senior year in high school. She wanted to work and share an apartment with her boyfriend after graduation instead of going to junior college and living at home. The threat of losing her fueled constant fights and bickering with her parents.

Justin looked forward to seeing his dad on weekends. As he excitedly packed his bags, his mother felt rejected. She suppressed this with a stream of irritable remarks.

Trigger Thoughts and Escalation

There is nothing automatic about anger. Pain doesn't make you angry at your kids. Thoughts, beliefs, and assumptions make you angry. These trigger thoughts, as you know, fall into one of two categories: shoulds or blamers. This is how shoulds and blamers trigger anger at your children.

Parents usually have specific beliefs about how life with children *should* be. For instance, "Children *need* a definite bedtime so that they can get enough rest." "Children *should* be able to help with household chores." "The family *should* eat dinner together every night." Children *should* always clean up what they mess up." "We *should* have no closed doors in this family." "After a certain time at night, children *should* be seen and not heard." "A family *should* pull together in times of stress."

When your rules and expectations (explicit or implied) are violated, it seems like someone has made a *deliberate break* with what is right or safe or moral. It is the perceived deliberateness of the infraction that makes parents angry. Remember Marny's anger at the playground? It isn't just that Joey grabbed the cups away from his brother. Marny triggers her anger by thinking "He wants to hurt the baby, he did it on purpose!"

Blaming triggers anger by making your pain the child's responsibility. Blaming also contributes to the illusion that children do "bad" things on purpose to make you mad, to frustrate or defeat you. But children are not responsible for your pain. They don't do things to be bad. Children have only one motivation for behavior: to satisfy basic needs. Their primary goals are to be fed, to belong, to be safe, to be significant, and so on. All their behavior is goal oriented. Although sometimes it is difficult to determine the goal of the behavior, you can assume that the behavior exists to satisfy some need.

Dreikers (1987) characterizes "misbehaving" children as discouraged children who may have mistaken beliefs about how to get their needs met. They may be discouraged about feeling accepted and significant. They may have the mistaken belief that they can only feel important if they have your full attention. They may have the mistaken belief that they can only feel powerful if they are the boss and get what they want. Blaming doesn't help children to behave more appropriately. It simply labels them as "bad" for trying, as best they know how, to take care of themselves.

Trigger thoughts happen so quickly that you may not be aware of how they fuel your anger. But if you review any anger-provoking situation, you'll find that (1) you had expectations that were not met, and (2) you believed that your child misbehaved deliberately (or even maliciously).

Remember Matt, whose mother was sent to the intensive care unit? His stress originated from the fear of loss. But his anger at his daughter was triggered by what he said to himself. "She knows I have to get out of here so she's slowing down to bug me."

When you find yourself getting upset, pay particular attention to the five self-deceptions that trigger anger at kids.

1. The entitlement fallacy. "I want something, so I ought to have it." Peter wanted everything to be perfect when he and his wife were entertaining his business associates. His anger at his children when they were messy and noisy at dinner stemmed from the belief that his children ought to be aware of his needs and cooperate. In fact, kids have no interest in impressing strange adults and probably wouldn't know how to impress them anyway. Children's behavior is *always* motivated by their own needs, not yours. They might have been more cooperative if they were cued into what was expected of them and were reinforced for doing so.

2. The fallacy of fairness. "Children should recognize the rights of others. It's only fair that others' needs should sometimes come first." Nancy believed that she *deserved* some break time to relax and that the children were being unfair in denying her legitimate need. In fact, children (especially young ones) are very limited in their ability to empathize or even be aware of needs other than their own. A parent-child relationship is, by definition, unbalanced and unfair. Nancy certainly needed a break from her children, but expecting fairness from young children is a hopeless case.

3. The fallacy of change. "You can make children different if you just apply sufficient pressure." Sue's parents believed that their disapproval would change her mind about moving in with her boyfriend after graduation. But their pressure only achieved the opposite result. Sue resented being manipulated and was more determined than ever to assert her autonomy by moving out. The constant bickering made her feel more withdrawn from her parents at a time when she could have used their support and understanding. Children, just like adults, resent and resist pressure, even if it's "for their own good."

4. Conditional assumptions. "If you really loved me, you would do what I want." Justin's mom felt rejected and angry when Justin showed obvious excitement as he prepared to go to his father's house for the weekend. She said to herself, "If he loved me, he'd hate that selfish bum for leaving us." The truth is that it's possible to love and care for someone and still not meet his or her needs. Justin's need to maintain his relationship with his father was immensely important to him. So important that he risked disappointing his mother.

5. The letting it out fallacy. The child who hurts you should be punished. Meg certainly felt like that when her daughter came home two hours late. It seemed like her daughter deserved every bit of anger and rage she wanted to express. This is a common and dangerous anger-generating belief. It often leads to overreaction, physical aggression, and feelings of being out of control. The underlying assumption is that "I will make you feel as bad as I feel." But expressing that kind of anger is terrifying and dangerous to the child. It can destroy your relationship with your children as they erect psychological barriers to protect themselves from your anger. The desire to "let it out" is very attractive, but parents who act out in anger do not get what they really want—considerate, responsible, cooperative children.

A word about physical punishment. Besides being dangerous and devastating to children, it just doesn't work. Hoffman (1970) studied the moral development of children and found that children who feared physical punishment tended to have less guilt, were less willing to accept responsibility, were less resistant to temptation, and had fewer internal behavioral controls than children who were not physically punished. Corporal punishment may even prevent the development of internal controls. The child may feel that it is okay to misbehave if he is willing to take the consequences (being hit). Children who are not physically punished must first understand why their behavior is wrong and then renounce it.

Another problem of controlling behavior through physical punishment is that the lesson learned is situation specific. For instance, a boy who is spanked for stealing will resist stealing again only if he is pretty sure he will be caught and punished again. Behavior that is controlled by fear rather than by internal controls must be maintained by fear as well.

Corporal punishment frequently leads to serious behavioral and emotional disturbances. Herman (1985) cites studies that show a correlation between corporal punishment and stealing, truancy, aggression, hostility, lying, depression, and low self-esteem. There must be a better way.

Your Expectations

What you expect of your children has enormous impact on your anger. Not the expectation of who and what they'll be when they grow up, but your values and needs as they affect the daily activities of family life. What you expect at family meals, at bedtime, regarding schoolwork, hygiene, and dress. What you expect around cleanup, friends, chores, and private time.

Why do certain expectations cause so much stress and anger? Sometimes you may expect things of your kids that are just not reasonable. You may have two expectations that are mutually exclusive or contradictory. Your child may not be capable of meeting your expectations or you may have expectations that are no longer appropriate for the age of your child. To begin to understand how your expectations affect every aspect of family life, complete the following exercise.

Exercise 1. Make a list of your childrens' activities and behaviors. The list might include such items as mealtime, bedtime, cleanup, playtime, time alone, noise, following directions, allowance, chores, fighting, homework, school performance, watching TV, sports activities, and so on. For younger children, you might also include potty training, sleeping in your bed, sleeping through the night, nursing, sharing, interrupting adults, and so on. The list for older children should include visiting other children, other children visiting you, overnights, parties, being alone in the house, dating, driving, working, makeup, music, and sexuality.

Next to each activity write a belief, value, or need that you associate with that activity. Your beliefs and needs together form your expectations of your child in each of these situations. List as many as you can.

Here are a few items from Rochelle's list to give you an idea of how your list might be constructed.

Mealtime: The family should eat together. One person should talk at a time. No playing with food.

Bedtime: I need the kids to go to sleep at a consistent, reasonable hour so that I can relax and have time with my husband.

Homework: Kids should take responsibility to do their own work. I try to be available if they need help, but I won't stand over them until it's done.

Television: Kids should not be allowed to space out watching TV without limits. I allow my kids to watch one hour of TV each evening, and they can watch anything they want during that hour.

If you have a partner, have him or her do this exercise also. Are you surprised by your partner's responses? How are they different than yours? Do those differences contribute to stress in your relationship?

Now that you have a list of all the issues that are relevant to you and your expectations about them, put a check next to the items that cause stress and conflict in your family. Which expectations are a source of fights? These are the items that you will want to work on later. But now you need more information.

Looking at Your Child

Sometimes it's hard to see your children as they really are. They remind you of yourself, or they remind you of someone else. Often they pick up labels that describe one aspect of their personality or developmental state. This kind of generalization can stay with them for a lifetime. Meg is the "princess." Bill is the "rebel." Cheryl is "16 going on 50." Even positive labels describe only one aspect of the child. Mike is the "smart one." Gary is an "angel."

These descriptions are a kind of shorthand that limit how you see your child. But of greater concern, they can trigger anger. You start with a generalization. "He's lazy." "She can't be trusted." "She's a bully." Then you become hyperalert to the behavior that exemplifies that generalization. You say to yourself, "Here she goes again. I don't have to put up with that," and so on. You fail to see even a single exception to the expected behavior. If your children accept the negative labels, they may live up to your expectations by persisting in that behavior, thus making you angrier.

Perhaps the most damaging part of labeling and generalizing is that you miss seeing your children as they really are. You miss seeing your son's potential, his talents. You miss knowing the things that motivate your daughter, that challenge her, interest her. Steve felt that his 12-year-old son was ignoring him. "He never hears me when I talk to him" (*generalization*). "He deliberately tunes me out" (*trigger thought*). What Steve failed to appreciate was that Joe had an incredible ability to concentrate. He loved learning math, especially algebra. He enjoyed working on his model planes and actually built a remote control plane by himself. He liked to read. He just didn't hear Steve (or anything else) when he was concentrating on these things. Labels were keeping Steve from seeing how focused and competent his son really was.

Exercise 2. One way to get a fresh look at your children is to describe them to someone who doesn't know them at all. The best way to do this is in the form of a letter. Think of someone you haven't seen since becoming a parent (like an old college friend or a relative who lives far away). In your "letter," describe your child as completely as you can. What is your daughter good at? What is hard for her? How does she relate to you, to her other friends? What does your son like to do? What is his best subject in school? What are his needs for privacy or social contact? How is he creative? How does your daughter deal with frustration? How does she express her feelings of affection or anger? How does she get support? What are your son's needs for order, for limits, for autonomy? How is he different from you when you were his age?

Make this exercise a real treasure hunt. Get more information and fill out your description by watching and listening carefully. Ask others who know your children—their teachers, parents of their friends, their siblings. You might find yourself looking at your children more carefully than you ever have before.

The goal of this exercise is to see who your children really are and become more aware of their specialness, their talents, their limits, and their potential. If you started with some over-generalizations, look for the exceptions to the "rules." Is your daughter careless? Or is she just easily distracted? Is she careless about everything? What things is she careful about? Take several days to complete the letter, adding to it over time, watching, observing, and gathering more information. When both you and your partner have done this exercise, share the letters with each other. Does your partner's letter differ much from your own?

Rachel's father saw her as being totally self-involved and unconcerned about the needs of other family members. She complained about her few chores. She'd stay on the phone most of the evening.

Rachel's door was often closed, and the closed door seemed symbolic to her father of how he felt shut out of her life. Every time he passed her door, he felt angry. He'd say to himself and to his wife, "She doesn't participate in this family at all, yet she wants us to give her an allowance, lend her the car, and pay for a college education. Well, who does she think she is?"

To research his letter, Rachel's dad started talking to her about things that were happening in her life. And he started to notice things. He noticed that although Rachel didn't want to accompany her parents to large family gatherings, she did enjoy going to the movies with them. Although she complained about her chores, she would occasionally take on a project without being asked. She decided to plant flowers in the front yard. She also helped hang wallpaper in the bathroom.

He noticed that her friends often confided in her, and she seemed to have great insight about them and their relationships. In fact, it seemed that she was very mature when helping others deal with crises and make decisions. When Rachel's dad was able to see beyond the limited view he had of her, he was less hurt when she did withdraw. He also had some information about how to create and preserve a connection to her during her teen years.

Seeing Clearly

Once you have completed the "letter," use the information and new awarenesses that you have discovered to make two lists. The first list is for the child's positive characteristics and the potential that he or she shows. These are areas that you need to recognize, support, and encourage. When you see your children's best selves, their talents and emerging abilities, you will be less likely to carry with you negative generalizations that create and intensify anger.

Make a second list of all the negative characteristics that annoy you, disappoint you, and tend to make you angry. Put a check mark next to the ones on the list that are especially irritating. Start with these "hot" items and ask yourself what makes them so irritating. Do they violate one of your important values? Is it behavior that reminds you of someone else? Does it remind you of yourself now or how you used to be? Does this behavior end up being embarrassing to you, or do you feel that others would disapprove of it? It is important to recognize how you bring your own history, values, and needs to a conflict situation. You can then replace your trigger thoughts ("This behavior is intolerable") with ones that are less anger-provoking and more accurate ("This behavior is embarrassing to me, or disappointing, or makes me feel that he is out of control").

Look again at the items on the negative list. Make note of the items that you probably won't be able to change. Here are some common reasons that certain behaviors might persist despite all your efforts to change them.

1. The child's basic nature. Children have their own personalities, tastes, preferences, sensitivities, and strengths. There is little you can do to make a shy child into a social butterfly by reminding, nagging, or pushing. The pressure that children feel to go against their basic nature might make them more withdrawn or inauthentic.

2. Fads and fashion. It is certainly useless to argue fashion, fads, hairstyles, and music with your children when these tastes are so strongly influenced by peer groups. You may limit how and when they listen to their music, but you won't talk them into liking yours or disliking their own.

3. States of development. Some behavior is almost inevitable at certain stages of development. Typical two-year-olds can be very negative. Being able to use the word *no* enables them to assert their autonomy and separate themselves from the world around them. Children go through stages of imaginary friends, fear of being alone, identifying with superheroes, fascination with movie and rock idols. Older children will predictably reject their parents' values and seek their own. It helps to read about child development, talk to other parents, and talk to your child's teachers. Check out what is typical behavior at certain ages so that you can see your child's behavior in the context of developmental norms.

Accepting that you won't change certain behaviors, that they are basic to the child or the developmental stage, may help you let go of blaming trigger thoughts.

Ask Why

You need to do one more thing with your list of negative behaviors: ask *why* this behavior persists. Any attempt to eradicate a behavior by punishments, restrictions, distractions, or indulgence is useless unless you look at what function that behavior has in the child's life. All behavior has a purpose. Ask yourself, "What need is being expressed by this behavior?" Look for basic needs like safety, attention, belonging, and approval. Then ask, "How can I help my child express that need in a more successful and acceptable way?" Do this for every remaining item on your negative list.

These questions move you beyond anger to real problem solving. Instead of saying, "How dare he do this to me?" (trigger thought), you say "What need does this behavior try to satisfy?" which establishes that your son acted as he did in a legitimate attempt to take care of himself. And that your job is to help him find healthier or more effective ways to meet those needs.

High-Risk Situations

Review your relationship with your children. See if you can find some pattern. Is there a particular time of day or day of the week that the conflict occurs? Is there a particular activity or issue that sets you off? Is there some predisposing event or feeling that sets the scene for later anger-generating interactions with your child?

A common predisposing factor is *fatigue*. Parents who come home tired after working and commuting have no time to revive. Their children may also be tired, hungry, and needy for attention. The after-work hours may therefore be a danger zone.

Another predisposing factor is feeling *rushed*. The early morning challenge of getting everyone out the door is a common source of chronic conflict.

Feeling *disappointed* in your child or feeling that your child compares poorly with other children can be a source of chronic anger.

Conflict can also become a habit around *control* issues. Are rules about food, bedtime, friends, dress, language, or curfew a source of conflict for you?

A common source of anger is *interruptions*. It is very frustrating to be interrupted when you're struggling to complete a task, concentrate, talk on the phone, or have a conversation with another adult.

Other contributing factors might include worry, symptoms of illness, interpersonal conflict, and literally any significant source of stress.

When you've identified that you are in a high-risk situation, one that traditionally leads to anger at your child, you are forearmed. You can plan ahead for the coping strategies that may be required. You can anticipate the impulse to blame or attack and prepare a less destructive response.

Reinforcement

All behavior persists because it is reinforced. You can only change your child's behavior by changing the reinforcers.

Positive Reinforcements

Positive reinforcement is a powerful tool to get children to change their behavior. The most powerful reinforcement of all is your approval and attention. This truth cannot be overemphasized. The child's goal is to be accepted and to belong. You are the one, through praise and support, who can provide the motivation for nearly any positive behavior.

You can shape behavior by positively reinforcing each step in the right direction. Let's say that you want your son to clean his room. As he goes toward his room, you could say, "Great, Jack, I see you're getting right on it. I appreciate not having to remind you." He picks up his dirty clothes and puts them in the hamper and you say, "It looks better already. You are doing a great job." And so on. If he slows down or stops, you can be encouraging with more praise and approval by saying, "You've done so well. Just a few more things and you'll be through." When the job is completed, you can make it even more reinforcing by praising him to others. "Jack did a beautiful job on his room, and he did it all by himself except for the puzzles. I'm really proud of him." Other reinforcers could be as simple as a gold star for a job completed or a special treat such as staying up later, reading a story, or some favorite food.

Older children respond to positive reinforcement as well. Teens, who may be in conflict with parents about many ideas, often complain that their cooperation is never noticed. Praise encourages cooperation. Just saying, "Thanks for getting home on time; I'm glad you're here," makes a teen want to please you again.

When you praise and reward behavior, you build a child's self-esteem. He can feel like a good, cooperative, capable, smart, important person and is more likely to continue behaving in ways that gain your approval.

Discipline and Consequences

Discipline is an important tool for helping children learn. It needn't come from anger and needn't involve revenge, threat, or aggression. Discipline that is reasonable, supportive, and consistent allows your children to learn and grow with their self-esteem intact.

But many parents only think about discipline when they are already angry. It is often imposed without thought or planning. "How many times have I told you not to do that? Now you'll be sorry." The next step is some shouted punishment that may alienate your child and actually make him *more* likely to misbehave in the future.

Remember that there is an imbalance of power in your relationship with your child. You are much stronger, and you are more articulate. You make the rules, you control the resources, you are in charge. You have the power to impose any punishment or restriction you want, and the child has no direct recourse. This imbalance of power makes it all the more important that punishments be implemented without a lot of anger.

When you're angry, you are more likely to make rash, extreme, and inappropriate decisions. You're more likely to make threats and use violence. You're more likely to hit, squeeze, push, or shake a child. Your body is surging with adrenalin, your judgment is impaired, and your response is likely to be dangerous—physically and psychologically. "If you as much as lay a finger on that baby, I'll break your hands." "If you're not home on time, you'll never see that boy again."

Imposing negative consequences without anger is possible. Here are some suggestions.

1. Natural consequences. Every action has its consequence. It is a fact of life. If you don't put gas in the car, it won't run. If you miss eating breakfast, you feel hungry. If you don't take your jacket, you'll be cold. Natural consequences aren't imposed by any authority, but arise inevitably from the situation. Allowing the natural consequence to occur to children may be the easiest and least anger-provoking form of discipline. If you don't get involved with trying to save them from natural consequences, they will learn the lesson without feeling criticized or manipulated by you. You can even be sympathetic to their problem and encourage them to do better next time. "It's hard when you have to leave the house in your pajamas and dress in the car because you didn't dress in time at home." "You must be terribly disappointed that the school won't let you play on the team because of your report card." "I was sorry to see you forgot your lunch. You must have been hungry all afternoon."

There is no need to threaten or rub it in. Children are capable of figuring out how to change their behavior so that the consequences won't recur. Even though it might make you uncomfortable to think of your daughter going hungry or going to school unprepared, even though you are tempted to "save" her, remember that when you prevent natural consequences from occurring, you are *reinforcing* the problematic behavior. If you deliver her forgotten lunch to school, she is less motivated to remember it next time. If you take responsibility for completing her homework, it becomes your homework. When you allow natural consequences to occur, you teach your children the real facts of life—and they learn to own and solve many of their own problems.

2. Reasonable consequences. Sometimes, of course, allowing natural consequences to occur is neither reasonable nor safe. You can't let a small child play in the road to learn how dangerous cars are. You may not be able to allow a child to miss school because he has overslept. In such cases, you have to create negative consequences for the behavior. The negative consequences should be reasonable, appropriate, timely, and consistently applied. Here are some guidelines for creating reasonable consequences.

(a) Consequences should take into account the age and ability of the child. If you take television away from a five-year-old for one day because he hit another child, he might learn something about impulse control. Bigger punishments create unnecessary deprivation for a child that young.

(b) Whenever possible, consequences should relate to the offense. If your child has lost or broken something, the consequence should involve saving or earning the money to replace that item. If your children are roughhousing in the car, the consequence might be to stop driving and wait until they have settled down. If the children are fighting over a toy, the consequence might be the loss of the toy while they work out how they are going to share it. If your child doesn't complete a chore in the time allotted, the consequence might involve losing a part of her allowance or delaying some other activity until the chore is done.

3. Time-out. This can be an effective strategy in handling younger children who are being noncompliant, having a temper tantrum, or are acting in other antisocial ways. A short period of time (five minutes, for instance) in a boring but safe environment (a room with no TV or toys) enables children to reassess their behavior and choose to act differently so that they can reenter the social environment. It also enables you to regain control of the situation without getting upset. Explain to the child that the consequences of certain behaviors result in five minutes of time-out and that he can choose to change his behavior or not. Place a portable egg timer outside of the door to keep track of the minutes so that it is the sound of the timer and not you who determines when he gets out. He can come out after the set period of time if he is willing to follow the rules (no hitting, help cleaning up, willingness to share, quiet play, and so on).

4. Avoid long-lasting or delayed punishments. Long-term restrictions mean that you are tied to enforcing the consequence long after children have forgotten what they are being punished for.

5. Make sure that your children know exactly what is expected of them. Define what you mean by "behave in the restaurant." Also make sure that your children are capable of what you want. Is your five-year-old daughter really able to "sit still" for a half hour? If you expect your son to clean the kitchen, does he know how to fill the dishwasher and turn it on? Does he know that you also want him to sweep the floor?

6. Tell your children in advance what the consequences of misbehavior will be. This way they can make a reasonable decision about how they will act. Then, when it's time to impose the consequences, children are less likely to protest or try to convince you to change your mind. You don't have to get angry or prove that they are wrong. Reasonable consequences, clearly communicated, lower the stress level in your family.

7. Once you have established a reasonable consequence, don't continue to harp or nag about it. Avoid teasing, reminding, or rubbing it in. Nora knew that the consequence for any driving violation was that she would lose her use of the family car for a month. John knew that if he hit his sister with the robot arm, it would be taken away for an hour. Sue and Millie knew that if they didn't finish their homework by 8:00 p.m., they would not get to watch their favorite TV show. The beauty of reasonable consequences is that *it's your child's choice:* appropriate behavior or face an unpleasant outcome.

8. Consequences should be consistently applied. Do what you said you would do every time. If you aren't consistent, then your children will be constantly testing you. And they'll have little motivation to change their behavior. One time they are punished for something that is ignored the next time. When you are inconsistent, you are forced to "really get angry" in order to be taken seriously.

Don't threaten a consequence that you are not prepared to carry out. If you say "No more fighting in the car or I'll turn around and take you home," then be prepared to do it—even if you are disappointed as well. If you say "Get dressed so we can leave by 8:15, or you'll need to finishing dressing in the car," be prepared to enforce the consequences—even if it's raining.

You'll probably not have to impose the consequence more than once or twice before your child will get the point that you mean it. It's the consistency, not the strictness or severity of consequences, that make them effective.

Putting It All Together—Solving Problems

Exercise 3. Now return to the recurrent problems that tend to cause stress and fighting in your family. By following the six steps listed below, you can begin to work toward a solution that will change old patterns of conflict. Do this exercise when you are not feeling angry or frustrated, so that you can be creative and optimistic about solving the problems.

1. *The problem.* State the problem in behavioral terms. Be very specific about the exact behavior that causes the conflict.
2. *State what need you think the child is expressing by behaving this way.* Is the child trying to satisfy her need for attention, safety, approval, or autonomy? Is she frustrated, bored, or overwhelmed? You may not know for sure what need is being expressed, but try to figure it out using your knowledge of your child's personality, needs, interests, and motivating drives. You may need to get more information from your son, his teachers, or others who know him. You can also get information from reading about other children who are at your child's level of development.
3. *What value or expectation of yours is being violated?* Earlier you wrote down some of your beliefs, values, and expectations relating to your child's behavior. Apply what you learned to this particular situation.
4. *How can you help your children express their needs in a more acceptable way?* Try to be creative and open minded. There doesn't have to be a winner or a loser. You may be able to find an alternative way to take care of everyone's needs. It might mean that you compromise. It might require changing your priorities or doing things differently. It

might require that you let go of some expectation that causes or intensifies stress.

5. *Positive reinforcements.* How can you motivate your children to want to change their behavior? What would make them want to cooperate?

6. *Negative consequences.* What consequences would your children want to avoid by changing their behavior? Would allowing a natural consequence to occur work? Can you create a reasonable consequence that would motivate your child to change?

Here are two examples of how these six steps can be used to solve problems.

Dinner time was a disaster for Caroline, Fred, and their two small sons, ages four and six. Both parents preferred that the whole family eat together, but this preference was not a high priority. Fred didn't get home until 6:30 most nights. By the time they all sat down to eat it was 7:00 and both boys were irritable from being hungry and tired. Caroline and Fred were tired as well, and had little patience for the mess and noise and fighting that ensued. Neither child was very skilled at using utensils, and they usually spilled food on the table and floor. Caroline and Fred found themselves correcting, warning, threatening, and finally sending one or both boys from the table. This is how they used the six steps to assess the problem and work toward a solution.

1. *The problem:* The children are messy and noisy and they fight at the table.

2. *The need being expressed by this behavior:* The children are hungry and tired. Neither child knows how to use utensils properly. Both children fight because they are competing for attention from their parents.

3. *Values and expectations violated:* The whole family should eat together without fighting. Children should be able to use utensils and not make a mess.

4. *How can the children express their needs in a more appropriate way:*

- Feed the children earlier on weekdays and let them join the adults for dessert. The family would eat together on weekends.
- Have the children take turns talking at the table and don't allow interruption.

5. *Positive reinforcements:*
   - Have children practice using utensils in a way that is enjoyable. For instance, they could practice using a soup spoon by eating ice cream "soup." They could practice using a knife and fork to eat brownies.
   - Make the conversation interesting and enjoyable for them at the dinner table and let each child take a turn talking without being interrupted.
   - Acknowledge and praise improvement in table manners.

6. *Negative consequences:*
   - Require that the children clean up and sweep up any spilled food after a meal.
   - If there is any fighting, they will have to leave the table.

Ten-year-old Zack had always been shy and small for his age, but he was agile and very coordinated. The previous summer he had learned how to ride a skateboard. He devoted a lot of time to practicing until he was the best skateboard rider in his class. Along with his competence in skateboarding came confidence and new friendships with other boys who enjoyed this sport. His father, Jerry, was concerned that Zack would be seriously injured if he fell and bought his son a helmet and protective pads. Zack promised his father that he would not ride in the street and would always wear the protective gear on the skateboard.

One rainy day Jerry saw his son riding in the middle of traffic without his helmet or pads. His first inclination was to burn the board. But skateboarding provided a lot for Zack—challenge, confidence, and the respect of other boys. This is how Jerry used the six steps to assess the problem and work toward a solution.

1. *The problem:* Zack riding his skateboard in the street without protective gear and deceiving his father about it.

2. *The need being expressed by his behavior:* Zack's need to be accepted by his peer group (by riding unprotected) is greater than his need to be honest with his father or his need for safety.

3. *Values and expectations violated:*
   - Children should be honest with their parents.
   - Children should not ride without protective gear and should not ride in the street. (Both expectations had a high priority for Jerry.)

4. *How could he express his need in a more appropriate way?*
   - Jerry would try to get others in Zack's peer group to wear helmets and pads. He could call the parents of the other children and encourage them to buy pads and helmets for their kids.
   - Encourage Zack to participate in other sports where he would probably excel (wrestling, gymnastics) and gain more confidence and prestige.

5. *Positive reinforcement:*
   - If Zack will wear his helmet and pads when riding his skateboard, Jerry will take him and a friend to a skate park where he can practice on the ramps and tracks. (Protective gear is required in these parks.)
   - If Zack will wear his helmet and pads, Jerry will buy him a subscription to a skateboard magazine so that he can learn more about professional skateboarders.

6. *Negative reinforcement:*
   - If Zack is caught riding in the street or without his protective gear, he will lose his skateboard for a week.

The Anti-Anger Prescription

1. Your relationship. The first and most important step in avoiding anger at your children is to establish and preserve a good feeling between you. If children feel safe and accepted at home, they are less likely to act out and misbehave. They prefer to maintain the feelings of warmth and respect between you.

You communicate your acceptance by listening, spending time together, and sharing activities that are fun. Share yourself as well. Children of all ages enjoy hearing stories from their parents' childhood and stories about themselves at an earlier age. Spending time alone with your child helps establish good feelings. Each child needs time when he or she doesn't have to compete with other children or activities for your attention. When you make time for your daughter, you are saying to her, "You are important. I want to know what you think and feel." When you listen, you learn about your child's perceptions, fears, motivations, and limits. You can more accurately predict problem situations and avoid them. You can more frequently recognize the pressures your son is under in his efforts to manage his own life. When he does misbehave, you're more likely to understand why and indulge in fewer trigger thoughts.

2. Be aware of your stress. Watch out for the danger times when you are under stress and are more likely to be annoyed by the common frustrations of parenting. After work or when you're tired are two typical times when you should be on the alert. Other times to be careful are when you are in pain or don't feel well, when you are rushed, or when you are angry at someone else. Children, unfortunately, are easy targets for your anger at these times.

Some parents come home from work in a physically aroused state, looking for a fight in order to discharge their stress. If this happens to you, absolutely avoid difficult or conflict situations with your children during these danger periods. If bath time is a battle, skip the bath. Don't add to your stress by taking on more obligations or starting new projects, even if you think you ought to. Delay, avoid, or cancel whatever is not absolutely necessary.

3. Communicate to your children that you are feeling stress (upset, frustrated, worried, unhappy). Even very young children can understand that you are upset and they need to be careful around you. You may also communicate what they can do to help or at least not add to the problem.

"I need a half an hour of quiet now."
"I'm worried about Grandma because she's sick. I need you to be quiet and not interrupt me while I call the hospital."

"That man at the garage really made me mad. I'm very grumpy right now, but I'll be better in a few minutes."

Communicating clearly about your own emotional state helps the kids learn about you, your limits, and your needs. It also teaches them how to express their own needs and limits in appropriate ways. If they are frustrated or stressed, they'll learn to ask for what they need without being angry or aggressive.

4. Take care of yourself—right away if possible. Do something that will lower your stress level. A hot bath, a phone conversation with someone who is supportive, or just taking off your work clothes and sitting down with a cool soft drink and listening to some music can take the edge off and help you feel more able to cope.

5. Be prepared for a disaster and avoid it when possible. If you give a three-year-old a glass of milk, there is some chance that she will spill it. If she is sitting on the old couch, you will feel annoyed. If she spills it while sitting on the new couch, how would you feel? If you know that you'd "go nuts," then *don't let her drink milk on the new couch.* How would you feel if your son lost your jacket at the school dance? Would you be somewhat disappointed? How would you feel if he lost your old, favorite, irreplaceable, cherished denim jacket that you had since college? If you think you would be "out of your mind," then *don't lend him the jacket.* Know you own limits and avoid feeling pushed beyond what is tolerable. By doing that you avoid setting yourself up for pain and the stress that causes anger.

6. Plan ahead. You can probably predict and prevent some problems if you plan ahead. Plan ahead by letting the children know exactly what is expected of them. What exactly do you mean by "Don't bother me now" or "Don't give the sitter any trouble"? Plan ahead by helping children cope. Long car rides are stressful for everyone. Snack food, quiet activity toys, story or music tapes that they enjoy, frequent stops—all help to make a trip more pleasant.

You are aware of your child's particular strengths and limits. Avoid putting your son in a situation where you can predict that he will feel pushed beyond his limits or capabilities and be likely to misbehave. Let him feel prepared by explaining and rehearsing what will happen in a new situation (first day of school, first visit to the dentist). Some children need more physical activity.

Some need less stimulation. Some children need very clear limits and are always testing you. Some kids get extremely irritable when they are hungry or tired. It is up to you to discover what makes each child tick, what situations will be most difficult, and how you can help your son or daughter cope and be successful. Not only is each child different, but his or her needs will change as he or she gets older. Planning ahead means staying attuned to a child's unique and changing needs.

Seeing Red

The above suggestions in the anti-anger prescription will help you control and limit feelings of anger at your children. But when you do get angry, you need some guidelines to help you cope, avoid the danger of escalation, and recover.

   1. Don't touch your child when you are angry. The adrenalin charge in your body makes it difficult to gauge the amount of force you are using and your physiological arousal could easily turn to aggression. This is no time for a spanking! When you are angry, it is safest to have your son go to his room or otherwise separate himself from you on his own power. If this is not possible, you should leave. If your children are old enough to leave alone, take a walk around the block. If you cannot leave them alone, sit outside the house, or sit in your car (do not drive!) where you can easily hear or see them. If you must handle a child to put him in his crib or restrict him to a safe environment, do so in a calm and controlled way. Move in slow motion and be aware of any overreaction. Do not shout or slam the door. These actions increase the adrenalin charge and the risk of losing control.

   2. Combat your trigger thoughts. Replace them with self-talk that is calming and comforting to you. "I can control myself." "I am really worn out, and I need a break." "I don't need to make a decision now, I'll think of a solution when I'm calm." "I can get help figuring this out later." See Chapter 10 on coping through healthy self-talk for more suggestions about keeping control when you're angry.

   3. Get support. It may help to talk to another person, but avoid complaining about your child to someone who will fan the flames of anger. It doesn't help to hear "You're right, what a little beast. I would never put up with that kind of behavior." You might make an agreement with a friend or relative whom you can call when you feel really stressed. Choose a person who will allow you to ventilate and just listen or will help you calm down *without* agreeing with you, arguing, or giving advice.

4. Use time-out when necessary. (See Chapter 9.) When you are angry, you may be fearful that what you do or say may be damaging to your child. You need time to calm down, regroup your resources, and look at things with a new and calmer point of view. If your child is old enough, explain the concept and rules of time-out when you are *not* in conflict. Establish what signal you will use to call time-out, how long you will be away, when you will return, and what you expect of him or her. When you are gone, use the time to calm down or expend the physical energy generated by the anger. Brisk walking, hitting a pillow, aerobic exercise, or crying are all good ways of releasing the pent-up energy that goes along with anger. Some household tasks are very conducive to discharging anger, such as vacuuming the rugs, polishing, hammering, or mowing. A cup of tea, listening to a favorite album, or spending a few minutes reading can help you recover. Do not try to solve the problem. Your aim is to recover from anger, not find the solution.

5. Stick with "I" messages and avoid blaming, sarcasm, insults, or generalizations. Attacking statements intensify your angry feelings. Angry attacks on children are devastating to their self-esteem and do not inspire regret or cooperation. Long after the fight is over, the insults that children have heard will linger in their memory and affect their image of themselves. Stick to the point. If you are confronting your son about teasing his brother, don't bring up difficulties he is having at school or his failure to feed the dog that morning.

6. Listen. Repeat what you heard your child say to make sure you heard it. Ask if you got it right. If not, ask your child to explain again the part you missed. Listening to your daughter's position doesn't mean that you agree with it. When people feel heard, they are less resistant and provocative.

7. If you feel overwhelmed, call a parent stress hotline. The counselors who answer phones are supportive, not critical—they know the stress you are under. They can handle the immediate problem as well as refer you to other community resources. Sometimes just talking to someone on the phone or reaching out for help will lower your arousal level and enable you to better cope. Parents having difficulty coping with a child's demands can call CHILD HELP (1-800-422-4453), a 24-hour national hotline that provides phone counseling. Parents Anonymous provides support for distressed parents. They have over a thousand chapters and also staff a toll-free hotline (1-800-421-0353).

Making It Happen

Your relationship with your child is different from any other relationship in your life. As a parent, you are responsible to teach your children, socialize them, and prepare them to be able to live in the world successfully without you. In no other relationship are you 100 percent responsible to set the limits and provide both discipline and love. In no other relationship is the other person so dependent and vulnerable. In no other relationship are the effects of anger so devastating and the importance of finding ways to solve problems without anger so important. The fact that you are reading this book indicates that you are aware of the importance of finding a way to live with your children without feeling so angry so much of the time.

Making changes in any relationship takes patience and perseverance. Children expect their parents to act a certain way. When you change your style of communication and respond to conflict or stress without lashing out, they may be surprised—even confused.

The changes you make may seem strange or unnatural to you at first. It may take a while to get used to allowing natural consequences to occur instead of stepping in to rescue the child. It may take time to get used to planning reasonable consequences instead of blowing up and feeling guilty later.

Parent support and education groups (Parent Effectiveness Training, Tough Love, Positive Discipline) can put you in contact with a network of supportive teachers and other parents who are going through similar experiences with their children. You are not alone. When you hear how other parents cope with similar problems, you can gain a better perspective on your own.

Family therapy may be helpful to identify problems and patterns that trigger anger. It can be a place where everyone in the family can participate in exploring solutions and finding alternatives.

There will be times when you are successful in changing your usual responses to stress and you don't get angry. There may be times when you fall into the old anger-generating habits—mind reading, trigger thoughts, and negative attributions. At these times you may wonder if it's too late to change old patterns. But even long-established negative patterns can change. Sometimes even the smallest changes in the language that you use or the things you tell yourself when you get upset can make a tremendous difference in how you feel and how you cope. The effort you expend will help protect the most important thing in your life—your kids.

16

Spouse Abuse

by Kim Paleg, Ph.D.*

Jim couldn't find his blue striped shirt. "Damn! Not again!" He
stormed into the kitchen where his wife, Alison, was cooking
his breakfast. "I didn't have time to iron yesterday," she began.
Jim grabbed the omelet pan from her hand and hurled it across
the kitchen. "Pay attention when I tell you something!" he
screamed. Her meekness infuriated him even more as she
shrank against the refrigerator and edged toward the kitchen
door. He became enraged. He punched at her wildly, then
grabbed her and threw her out of his way before marching back
into the bedroom to finish dressing and slam out of the house.

Vicki told her husband of her mother's intended visit. Joe
hated his mother-in-law's visits; he always felt excluded by the
two of them talking and laughing—about him, he often
thought. And Vicki knew how he felt, so why was she doing this
to him again? He was livid. The argument escalated rapidly
until Joe screamed, "If she steps one foot in my house, I don't
know what I'll do." He slammed out of the room, returning a
few minutes later carrying his shotgun. Vicki watched with
terror as Joe sat and cleaned the gun, staring white-faced and
threatening.

* Kim Paleg is a supervising psychologist at Haight Ashbury Psychological
  Services in San Francisco. In private practice, she specializes in couple
  and family psychotherapy. Dr. Paleg is co-author of *Focal Group Psychotherapy* (New Harbinger Publications). She received her Ph.D. from the
  California Graduate School of Marital and Family Therapy.

Julie was tired after a long week of working hard. Her boyfriend, David, was due to arrive any minute; Julie was hoping he'd like the idea of ordering a pizza and cuddling in front of the TV. He didn't. "You never want to do anything anymore," he complained. "Don't be silly," Julie retorted, "I'm usually the one who makes the suggestions for going out." David knew that was true, and he knew he was being silly, but he hated hearing it from Julie. He already felt inferior in comparison with her; she was more articulate and had a better memory, and when they argued he always lost. Suddenly he was furious. "Why do you always have to argue?" he yelled. "Why can't you just do what I want for a change?" David stood, clenching and unclenching his fists. Suddenly he swung around and punched the wall about two feet from her head, skinning his knuckles and making a hole in the wall. Then he turned and left.

When anger escalates out of control, violence and abuse can easily result. The line between what's abusive and what's not is often difficult to determine. Sometimes the line is crossed without either person being totally aware of the transition. It seems clear that Alison was being abused when her husband punched and threw her against the wall. But what about Vicki? Was her husband being abusive when he sat, white-faced and menacing, cleaning his shotgun? Or what about Julie's boyfriend, who broke her wall instead of her jaw? In truth, these are all examples of abuse. Abuse occurs any time someone is induced to act in ways that they would not otherwise have chosen to act, by violence, threats, or intimidation. Abuse includes not only habitual beatings, but the occasional slap or shove and even the threat of such behavior.

It has been estimated that one out of every two American families experiences some form of domestic violence each year. One family in five experiences violence on an ongoing basis. More often than not, the abusing partner is the man, and the victim, the woman.

Sometimes an abusive incident will occur once and never be repeated. Jan described one argument with her husband where she accused him of not caring about her feelings. She'd had a fight with her boss that day and wanted Tony's comfort and support. Tired from his own day, Tony at first retreated behind his newspaper. After a while he became defensive and counter-attacked. As Jan's frustration mounted, she not only lashed out at Tony verbally, but physically as well. Tony caught her fist in mid-punch and threw her backwards, where she fell heavily, hitting her head on the coffee table. Both were horrified and shaken. Now, eight years later, Jan reports that the shock of that incident left an indelible mark on their relationship and provided the necessary restraints to ensure that no further violence would occur.

At the other end of the scale, Sarah described from her hospital bed a nightmare of five years of almost daily beatings. She and Peter had had heated arguments in the year following their marriage. There had been some violence—a few slaps, a shove or two—but she'd never thought of it as abuse. The first major beating occurred when they'd returned home from a party where, according to Peter, Sarah had flirted with "anything in pants." After this, escalation was rapid. Every argument and every disagreement led to a beating, and soon Sarah began to dread the sound of Peter's car in the driveway. The last episode left Sarah in the hospital with a ruptured spleen and the realization that if something didn't change she might soon be dead. Sarah's case demonstrates an important fact about abuse: left unchecked, abuse tends to escalate into increasingly violent episodes.

The first time violence occurs, it's usually a shock to both partners. The victim feels stunned: how can someone who supposedly loves her treat her this way? She rationalizes that it must have been an exceptional, isolated incident in which he overreacted. The abuser validates this perception, promising that it will never happen again. Wanting to believe him, the victim searches for what she might have done wrong to cause her partner's reaction so that she can avoid triggering him again. In this way they convince themselves that it's not a problem and minimize the seriousness of the episode.

Patterns of Abuse

Various theories describe the cycle of violence. Walker's (1984) three-step model includes (1) the phase of tension building, (2) the explosion or acute violent episode, and (3) the remorse phase. During the tension building phase frustrations gradually mount. Spouses often report being aware that things are leading to a blowup. Sometimes the tension becomes so intolerable that the eventual violence is a relief. When the explosion or acute violent episode occurs, the victim might be pushed, grabbed, held, slapped, shoved, kicked, bitten, choked, punched, hit with an object, or threatened or attacked with a knife or a gun. The remorse phase occurs in the period after the violence, when the abuser often feels embarrassed or humiliated about his loss of control. He swears it will never happen again and finds ways to reassure his partner of his devotion. This period has also been called the "honeymoon phase." Jim would bring Alison flowers and gifts; Joe would take Vicki out for a romantic dinner at a fancy restaurant. Over time, less and less remorse is shown, and the couple experiences more frequently repeated periods of tension building and violence.

Deschner's (1984) model is more complex and consists of seven phases. The first phase is that of mutual dependency. In abusive relationships, partners often rely on each other for the satisfaction of all their needs, emotional and otherwise. When there are no outside sources of reward, having a need frustrated by a spouse becomes much more serious. Any irritating event (the second phase) such as dinner not being ready on time or a shirt not being ironed can lead rapidly to the third phase, where each partner attempts to force the other to meet his or her needs through coercion. The "last straw" decision (phase four) occurs at the point at which the abuser feels that the stressful situation is no longer tolerable. He feels as if he's exhausted his alternatives and has to resort to expressing his anger and frustration in violence. At this point, he gives way to the primitive rage that is the hallmark of phase five. Phase six provides the abuser with reinforcement for his battering. Since the abuse results in an immediate cessation of whatever was causing the stress, violence is reinforced as an effective way to deal with frustration and pain. For the victim, the end of the battering provides negative reinforcement. Phase seven is the repentence phase. Both partners are initially shocked at the outbreak of violence. The batterer swears earnestly that it will never happen again and attempts to prove his love and devotion. The victim is only too willing to believe him. For the victim, this honeymoon phase can reinforce the cycle of violence. This phase may be the only time that she ever feels close in the relationship and experiences her partner as warm and loving. It's also a time when the power in the relationship shifts temporarily to the victim, and this reversal of roles is also very reinforcing. After repeated battering episodes, the seven steps are often truncated to more rapidly completed cycles of buildup (phase three) and attack (phase five).

Why Does Abuse Occur?

Societal Factors

Complex answers to the question of violence include factors outside the family as well as within it. In this society, violence is a part of daily life. As a child, you watched cartoons that showed brutal violence between the cartoon characters that seems to do no lasting harm. Wile E. Coyote is killed and reborn an average of five times in each Road Runner episode. As an adult, you see violence in the media and read newspapers that describe countless incidents of violence here and around the world.

In all but nine states across the U.S., paddling is allowed in schools. This paddling can be hard and is inflicted on both teens and small children. Once again the message from society is that violence solves problems.

The socialization process also increases a propensity for violence in men. Males are taught that to be considered "real men" they must be strong and tough and ready to defend their manhood at any time. They're discouraged from talking about feelings that could be perceived as "weak," such as fear, sadness, neediness, or hurt. To deal with vulnerability and pain, some men turn to alcohol and drugs; others simply bury the feelings under episodes of explosive rage (see Chapter 14 on anger as a defense).

Women are given a different set of instructions. It's okay for women to express vulnerable feelings, but they are encouraged to be passive and "ladylike" in their interactions with men. Direct expressions of anger are discouraged. Thus in any violent exchange, women are more likely to be victims and men to be abusers.

Society also reinforces the forceful domination of women by men in many subtle ways. Religious doctrine emphasizes the superiority of men and assigns women an adjunct role. Family law until recently gave men rights over their wives as though they were possessions (including the right to beat them when necessary). Only a few states today have laws prohibiting rape in marriage. Many people in law enforcement still don't acknowledge spouse abuse or marital rape as crimes. An economic system in which women are paid less than 65 cents for every dollar paid to men keeps women financially dependent on their husbands. These often unquestioned social characteristics contribute to the inequality of a relationship that gives one sex power over the other and makes spouse abuse possible.

Family Factors

An important piece in the puzzle of domestic violence is the abuse that each partner may have experienced in his or her own family of origin. As a child, your earliest role models were, of course, your parents. If you saw your parents engaged in an abusive relationship, you may have acquired a template for future relationships. As a boy, you may have learned that anger is most effectively expressed in violence and that violence is useful as a means of influencing or controlling others. As a girl, you may have learned that your lot in life is to be subjected to such violence. Recent research (Strauss, Gelles, and Steinmetz 1981) indicates that men who grew up with violent parents are 10 times more likely to batter their wives than men who weren't exposed to violence in their family of origin are. Additionally, men who received heavy physical punishment as teenagers become batterers at a rate four times that of men who weren't punished physically.

If you were abused as a child, it's likely that the violence affected how you view yourself. Most children believe that they deserve what happens to them, and so you may have developed the deep belief that you were not a very worthwhile person. Feelings of unworthiness can contribute to low self-esteem and a dependency on others for validation. Both of these factors can produce a heightened vulnerability to frustration and criticism.

Characteristics of Batterers

Men who batter represent a wide spectrum of age, race, religion, socioeconomic status, education, and career. However, some characteristics are present across the board. For the most part, the abuser is a man who doesn't feel very good about himself, believes that he's not very worthwhile, and looks to others for reassurance. He holds traditional views about sex roles and looks to his partner for nearly all of his emotional support and nurturance. If he doesn't feel good about himself, he's likely to suspect that others may feel the same. So he anticipates rejection and he can perceive almost anything as a rejection. Since he finds it difficult to express feelings of hurt and disappointment, he's more likely to respond with anger. Responding to perceived insults with violence increases his negative feelings about himself and makes the cycle all the more likely to recur. His limited ability to empathize makes it difficult for him to understand his wife's feelings. He has little or no insight into her pain and fear, so his violent acting out goes unrestrained.

Pathological Jealousy

Another related characteristic of a man who abuses his partner is pathological jealousy. If he's dependent on his spouse for all of his emotional groceries, then he may be constantly terrified that she'll leave him for another man. After all, if she can see that he's as worthless as he often feels, then she would naturally want to be with someone else. The fear of abandonment underlying jealousy typically provokes irrational suspiciousness and frequent questioning and accusations. Mary's husband monitored her activities in and out of the house. He insisted on driving her to work every day and picking her up in the evening. He grilled her about her social contacts at the office. On weekends he refused to allow her to visit friends and strictly limited her use of the phone.

Pathological jealousy can also lead to sexual violence. Rape frequently occurs in battering relationships. Some men force their partners to have sex with them as a way of feeling reassured about their own sexual identity. Some equate physical and psychological abuse with sexual arousal and desire sex in the aftermath of a beating.

Isolation

One of the most important characteristics of battering relationships is their isolation. The more anxious and in need of reassurance the man becomes, the more likely he is to bond tightly with his partner. Outsiders are seen as threats to his control and to his relationship. He may forbid her to go out without him, to exercise, to meet with friends, or to do the weekly grocery shopping. He may restrict her money and her phone contacts with friends and family. Eventually he may even monitor her mail. Gradually the partners become more and more isolated, which in turn increases their dependency on each other for most emotional and practical needs. Increasing dependency usually leads to decreasing flexibility in meeting the demands of everyday life. That means more stress. And the more stress, the greater the chances of conflict and eventual violence.

The abuser tends to lack the skills both to ask for what he wants and to say no to his partner. He holds society's stereotype of what it means to be a man, which includes the ability to control his wife and not to be "henpecked." Thus his self-esteem is bruised again and again when he's unable to live up to all of his standards. The result is a building resentment and a growing willingness to use violence to get his needs met. Violence becomes a way of controlling and incapacitating the partner. He's less threatened by her independence and the possibility of her leaving him. He feels more powerful and more in control. In this way, violence is positively reinforced, increasing the likelihood that it will be used again.

Instrumental Aggression

One of the most frightening and dangerous types of abuse, which is usually seen in long-term battering relationships, is called "instrumental aggression." In most cases of abuse, each violent episode is accompanied by a rush of primitive rage, during which the batterer feels out of control. Afterwards he may feel embarrassed and remorseful, temporarily upset about his behavior and determined to prevent its recurrence. But sometimes the violence is so rewarded that it becomes ingrained as a habitual way of getting what's wanted. It's no longer simply an out-of-control rage response, but a calculated way of gaining a desired reward. The violence becomes "instrumental" in gaining the reward.

This batterer seems to show no emotion during the violence and no remorse afterwards. This is a man who can beat his wife daily for no apparent reason and no longer seems to be responding to any internal feeling of anger or rage. He is unlikely to give up the habit, even in treatment, since he sees it as a justified and useful tactic for getting his needs met.

Drugs and Alcohol

Drugs and alcohol are involved in more than 80 percent of violent episodes (Sonkin, Martin, and Walker 1985). Alcohol lowers inhibitions against violence, while heavy use of drugs like cocaine increases paranoia, which increases the likelihood of violence. Some men attribute their violence to the drugs or alcohol, claiming to feel out of control when under their influence. In most cases, however, the man has been abusive before the substance became a problem. And since he often aims for places that don't show—breasts, stomach, base of the spine, parts of the head hidden by hair—he apparently knows what he's doing. Considerable control is required to wound only where it won't be seen.

Military Men

Men in the military have added factors that contribute to problems with anger and violence. These men are given specific training in the use of violence and combat skills that become part of their day-to-day lives. When the conflict occurs at home instead of on the battlefield, it's not surprising that violence can result. In addition to the indoctrination process, military men and their families also experience a number of other stresses. Most military personnel tend to hold traditional sex roles, where the man must be strong, competent, and in charge. But the work is hard, long, and poorly paid and frequently involves experiences that lead to feelings of humiliation or powerlessness. These factors may all increase the need to feel in control at home. Families may be separated for extended periods of time while the men are on tours of duty. Absence of regular contact makes it harder to maintain marital and parental relationships. Moreover, the pattern of moving from place to place makes it difficult to establish and maintain friendships for everyone in the family. This in turn leads to increased isolation, one of the most important factors in battering relationships.

Estimates of the percentage of batterers that have had prior military experience range from 58 percent (Walker 1983) to 90 percent (Eisenberg and Micklow 1979).

The Battered Woman

There are many myths about the woman who remains in a battering relationship. Some people suggest that she is less a victim than a masochist who enjoys being abused. Or that she causes her partner to become violent. The battered woman has been described as passive, manipulative, and compliant. These notions are confirmed for some by the fact that women often return home to the abusive situation after a brief respite in a battered women's shelter.

The truth is that the woman who remains in a battering relationship does so because she sees no way out. Often she's financially dependent on her husband, untrained for any profession, and unable to support herself and her children. Frequently the man will threaten to kill her or her children, family, or friends if she leaves. And if the beatings have been severe enough, she may have good reason to believe him.

The potential for violence forces the woman to accept her husband's rigid view of her role, since this course is plainly safer for her than that of provoking his rage by acting any other way. So it's not hard to see why she is often seen as more traditional in her attitudes and more willing to accept a passive, compliant, "feminine" role. One recent study (Walker 1984) found that many battered women are actually more liberal in their sex-role attitudes than the norm. But when faced with an angry, potentially violent man, the woman will try to appease him and calm his anger. Over time, this behavior becomes the automatic response to anger—anyone's anger.

Since any direct expression of her own anger is likely to result in violence, the battered woman must resort to a more indirect way of voicing her feelings. She may say yes to her husband's requests, but find ways of sabotaging his plans without any indication of deliberate intention. While this behavior could be labeled manipulative or passive-aggressive, it clearly helps her meet important needs while protecting her from abuse.

Abuse and Self-Esteem

By far the most devastating effect of physical or psychological abuse is the impact it has on the victim's self-esteem. The woman's realization that she has lost her ability to protect herself can result in constantly feeling afraid and off balance. She becomes hypervigilent, watching for any sign from her husband that might lead to anger and a beating.

After the first violent episode, a woman may convince herself that it was a mistake and that it will never happen again. Then it happens again...and again. She can no longer escape from the sense that her love and trust has been violated, nor the terror of being unable to trust her own perceptions. After all, if this man was abusive before she met him, why couldn't she see it? And if he wasn't, what does that say about her? Is there some part of her that provokes violence, or worse, that deserves violence?

Feeling unable to prevent the abuse, the victim often develops a "learned helplessness." Time and time again the woman's attempts to stop the cycle of violence are ineffective. She comes to believe that she is unable to change anything, and so she simply stops trying. Instead, she learns to behave in ways that help her avoid the violence. She hides her feelings—sometimes even from herself—and assumes a passive, compliant role.

The feeling of helplessness can also lead to a tendency to deny and minimize the seriousness of the abuse. If the abuse isn't so severe or frequent, then it's not so terrible to be stuck in the relationship. This rationalization helps reduce the fear to a tolerable level. Sometimes the woman tells of her abuse to a friend or acquaintance, pastor or doctor, whose response is to minimize her complaints or not take them seriously. No one likes to acknowledge violence in an outwardly "lovely couple." But this response invalidates the woman's experience while reinforcing her denial. Doreen was told by her pastor that her husband was a "good man" and that she should be more understanding of the pressures he was under. Her doctor offered her a prescription for Valium.

In addition to all of these assaults on her self-esteem, the woman may be constantly belittled by her husband. During the buildup and abuse phases, she may be subjected to endless accounts of her faults and failings. Her husband may even blame her for the violent episodes, telling her that if she were a better wife (cook, mother, housekeeper, lover) the abuse wouldn't occur. After a while, it's not surprising that many women get profoundly depressed, even while maintaining a cheerful exterior facade. Often the depression is manifested in physical symptoms: back pain, headaches, menstrual problems, and low energy.

Who's Responsible?

So what keeps the abusive cycle going? Contrary to the myths described above, women do NOT cause or provoke spousal abuse. It's never the woman's fault that she's the victim of violence. No matter what she does, she never "deserves" to be beaten—no one does. There is absolutely no justification for violence. No matter how angry a man is, there are always alternatives to violence, and his choice of violence is quite simply that: his choice. Even if the man feels that he has no other resources in dealing with his anger, he is never justified in using violence. He alone is responsible for the abuse, and unless he acknowledges his problem with anger and wants to stop his violent behavior, the outlook for the relationship is grim.

Nevertheless, both partners *are* responsible for the stress and conflict in a relationship, and the woman can and often does behave in ways that provoke frustration and anxiety in her partner. Every relationship can be thought of as a unique dance, with each partner engaging in complementary steps that maintain the nature and direction of the dance. The battered woman can't stop the abuse, and attempting to do so only reinforces the erroneous belief that somehow she's to blame for the violence.

Her partner must address his abusive behavior and learn new skills in anger management. But if she wants to stay in the relationship, she must also learn new skills in dealing with conflict.

Can Things Change?

The first question that must be addressed is whether there is any hope of the relationship changing, or whether the only logical option for the woman is to leave. If the history of violence in the relationship is short and the frequency and severity of the beatings are low, then the chances of success are increased. As the abuse becomes more entrenched and habitual, it becomes more resistant to change.

There must also be motivation to change. Does the batterer acknowledge his problems with anger and violence? Does he feel sorry after each abusive episode and wish to change sincerely enough to work on developing new behaviors? Is he willing to admit his problem to helping professionals and work with them long enough to stop the cycle?

The presence of remorse is an important indication of motivation. If the batterer shows no remorse after an episode of violence, then you may be dealing with a case of instrumental aggression. If so, the only reasonable option may be to work toward leaving. Finally, ongoing substance abuse weighs heavily against the possibility of stopping the violence.

Leaving

If your partner refuses to acknowledge his problem with anger and violence or refuses to work with others toward ending it, there may be very little that you can do to change your situation other than leave. Making the decision to leave can be extremely difficult. If you've found yourself going around and around in a struggle to decide, do an exercise suggested by Ginny NiCarthy in her book *Getting Free* (1982). Make a list of your fears of the worst that can happen if you leave. Be specific. Will you get so lonely and depressed that you'll take an overdose of sleeping pills? Will you be unable to provide for or discipline your children alone? Under each fear, write the reasons that it's *likely* to happen and the reasons that it's *unlikely* to happen. Then make a list of the worst that can happen if you stay with the abuser. Consider the most likely bad things to happen if you stay. Include the physical and psychological damage to you and your children. Remember the last time you were battered and list the things that you were afraid would happen then. Maybe you were afraid of being killed or of killing your partner. Maybe you feared being permanently injured. Do you get enough from the relationship to risk these things? Comparing the lists and weighing the different items on each can sometimes make the decision a little easier.

Without a job or any means of support, leaving can be a terrifying prospect, especially if you have children. There's probably a battered women's shelter in your community or nearby (listed in your local yellow pages under "Crisis Services") whose staff would be willing to talk to you. Call them and find out what resources are available for you and your children with respect to financial and legal aid, housing, and job training. If there are no shelters listed, call the National Coalition Against Domestic Violence crisis line: 1-800-333-SAFE (24 hours a day, seven days a week) for referrals. Seek an assertive lawyer who specializes in spouse abuse cases. Some lawyers will offer low-cost services, and some will work on a contingency basis. Look under "Legal Aid" in the phone book, or ask your local shelter for a referral. Try to solicit help and support from friends and family. Although you may feel reluctant to ask others for help, most friends would rather help you leave before you're injured than see the nightmare continue. But be careful of those people who, with the best of intentions, might attempt to "save your marriage" by informing your partner of your plans or whereabouts.

Protecting Yourself Now

One of the first and foremost considerations for you if you're a victim of domestic violence is safety for you and your children. Whether or not you ultimately decide to leave the relationship, you may still be at risk right now. Your husband might agree that he has a problem with anger and be committed to changing his behavior. But he isn't going to change overnight. It's crucial that you have a place where you and your children can go when you feel you're at risk. Friends or relatives are good options, but if your partner decides to look for you, these places may be at the top of his list. Battered women's shelters are another alternative. They provide crisis counseling and safety from an abusive situation.

Make a plan to exercise this option. Set aside some money, an extra set of car keys, and any personal business documents you might need for the few days or longer that you might be away. It might help to have a small overnight bag packed and ready for the occasion—preferably stored at a friend's or neighbor's house. If children are involved, include some toys for them. When you feel in danger, get out fast. Don't hang around wondering if there's something you've forgotten. Although unconfirmed, statistics suggest that the highest risk period for homicides against women is while leaving. You can always return at a later date with police support to collect anything you need.

If possible, call the police when violence has occurred. In some places, the police are required to respond to calls and make an arrest if a felony has been committed. Beating someone, even one's wife, is usually a felony. Arrest has a sobering effect on offenders and tends to reduce the recidivism rate, even when the offender is released within 24 hours. Prosecution further lowers recidivism, even if no conviction occurs. The court may require that the batterer attend counseling to address the problems. It may also issue a temporary restraining order (TRO) or stay-away order that forces the batterer to keep away from you and the children. These orders can be issued by the court without an arrest or prosecution proceedings and don't even require the involvement of a lawyer.

Find out what kind of police support exists in your area. Unfortunately, in some places the police are reluctant to respond to domestic violence calls and often wait for several days before coming to the house. The staff at your local women's shelter should be able to tell you whether this is true in your community.

When Children Are Involved

Sometimes the decision to stay or leave involves considerations about children. You may be concerned about disrupting your children's lives or depriving them of a father. You might fear being unable to provide for them in the way you'd like. Some women try to postpone leaving till their children are all in school, are toilet trained, have all left home, or have reached some other landmark. And sometimes it works out for the best. But staying in a frightening, violent situation can often be more harmful for children than any temporary disruption or material deprivation.

You might be afraid that your partner will gain custody of the children if you leave or try to punish you by hurting them. Unfortunately, these fears are sometimes justified, and custody and visitation rulings are often unfair. Think through your plan of action with a lawyer who specializes in domestic violence cases.

If the children are being abused, the decision to stay or leave becomes even more crucial. Child abuse can be just as subtle and difficult to identify as spouse abuse. It can include constant belittling and threats of violence as well as physical beatings. Usually, all the battering in a family is done by the one violent person. And you may feel just as helpless to protect your children as to ensure your own safety. If so, leaving the relationship may be the only option that offers the safe environment that children need. Call the children's protective service agency in your area or the National Child Abuse Hotline, operated by Childhelp USA: 1-800-4-A-CHILD (24 hours a day, seven days a week). These agencies can help you clarify your options and provide counseling and referrals.

If you are abusing your children, recognizing that you have a problem with your own anger is the first step. You may be angry at their father for his abuse of you and unable to express it to him. Or you may be jealous of the fact that the abuse is only directed at you and not at them. Or your tolerance for conflict may be very low as a result of having to live in a constant state of stress and vigilance. In any case, your abuse, although understandable, is unacceptable. Once you're out of the violent situation, this abuse might automatically stop. Meanwhile, call

Parents Anonymous: 1-800-421-0353 (open seven days a week) or the hotlines listed above for crisis counseling and referrals. Although it will be difficult to make the calls, you will probably feel relieved to finally get help in dealing with your children more effectively. Reading the following sections on resources for batterers can give you some tools in dealing with your own frustration and anger. Counseling and support groups can increase your parenting skills and improve your ability to set limits.

If You Stay: Seeing the Cycle

If you decide to stay and work on the relationship, there are several factors to explore. The following suggestions assume that the batterer has acknowledged his problem with anger and violence and is actively working on changing his behavior with the help of a professional. If not, the chances of the violence stopping and the relationship improving are minimal.

Although the ultimate decision to use violence is solely the batterer's responsibility, the conflict that precedes the violence often involves both partners.

Think about the cycle that usually occurs in your relationship. When do you become aware that violence is inevitable? Can you detect early warning signs? Does the man drink heavily before a violent interaction? Does he get upset about innocuous events? Maybe he gets silent and withdrawn. What goes on immediately before that "point of inevitability"? Review Chapter 9 on stopping escalation to see how aversive chains develop. These may begin with a relatively trivial exchange and rapidly and predictably escalate to the expression of anger and violence. The more links (or interchanges) on a chain, the more likely violence will result. The last link that often precedes a violent outburst is called the "trigger behavior," a link that usually stirs up feelings of abandonment or rejection in the abuser.

There are many possible links that can build aversive chains, including a variety of verbal behaviors (blaming, threatening, complaining), nonverbal sounds (groaning or sighing), tone and quality of voice (mocking, cold, loud), facial expressions (scowling or frowning), gestures (shaking a fist), and body movements (turning or moving away, throwing something). Think back over the past several incidents that have occurred in your relationship. Try to identify the different links in the chain and see if you can detect patterns. Does your partner always get furious when you try to defend yourself against his accusations? Does he seem to respond negatively to your visible signs of fear? Do things get worse when you attempt to end the interaction by walking away from him? There are usually (but not always) a series of progressive stages that precede a violent outburst.

Changing the Cycle

Once you've begun to identify the early warning signs that indicate potential violence, you can begin to use the "time-out" model described in Chapter 9. (If your partner is in treatment, he may already have been introduced to the concept.) At the instant you recognize a warning sign that an aversive chain is beginning, call "Time-out" and make the T sign with your hands. It helps to discuss the procedure ahead of time, at a moment when tension is low, and reach an agreement about who's going to leave first, where each of you are going to go, and for how long. Because anger is often triggered by feelings of rejection and abandonment, your partner may prefer to be the first to leave in order to avoid the experience of being "left." Since there is a risk that when the next episode occurs your partner might forget or simply not care that he made an agreement with you, you should be sure to make plans for your own safety. Come back and check in with each other at a specified interval after the time-out. Be careful that you're not putting yourself in danger again by coming back. You might arrange to initiate the check-in with a phone call in order to assess the level of anger still present.

Rechanneling

Another technique described in Chapter 9 is that of rechanneling. More subtle than time-out, this technique redirects the sequence at a critical junction or "weak link" in the aversive chain. A weak link is a point in the chain where a new behavior could be most easily substituted for the old.

Examine the patterns you were able to detect in your relationship. At what points might you be able to say or do something different? Vicki knew that her husband, Joe, felt left out whenever her mother came to visit. She felt guilty about enjoying time with her mother away from Joe, yet knew she didn't want to give up those special times. Vicki identified a weak link at the point when Joe said, "Oh great! Just what I need! That old bag visiting again." Instead of her usual defensive, blaming response, Vicki realized that she could have acknowledged how left out Joe felt at those times and offered to try to include him in some of their activities. For Julie, a weak link existed at the point at which she said to her husband, "Don't be silly!" in a patronizing voice. The scene might have been rechanneled with acknowledgment and compromise: "I guess you were really looking forward to going out tonight. Maybe we could compromise and go to an early show?"

Rechanneling can only be effective if your partner is also involved in substituting new behaviors for his old violent patterns. While identifying the weak links and attempting alternative behaviors can often alter the pattern of conflict, the responsibility for changing the violent response still remains strictly with the man. Unless your partner is actively working on finding his own weak links in the chain, your efforts may be futile. If your partner is uncommitted to making the necessary changes in his behavior, you might wish to reconsider whether staying in the relationship is the best decision after all.

One very important part of changing your old pattern of isolation and mutual dependency is for you to join a group for women who've been victims of domestic violence. The battered women's shelter in your area can probably give you referrals to such groups. In the group, you can establish relationships with other women and get support for the decisions you make about your relationship. You can practice assertive behaviors and explore the potential impact that dancing such different steps will have on your relationship.

Psychological Fallout

The psychological aftermath of being in an abusive relationship often resembles the post-traumatic stress syndrome that many war veterans experience. You may feel that you're constantly under seige because the memory of past violence and the uncertainty of when it might occur again lead to a state of constant fear and anticipation. Common symptoms include anxiety, fear, depression, shock, anger, inappropriate compassion, guilt, humiliation, confused thinking, intrusive memories, uncontrolled reexperiencing of traumatic events, rigidity, lack of trust, suspiciousness, hypervigilance, and increased startle response to cues of possible violence. A professional counselor who's been trained to assist victims of abuse can help you slowly heal the hidden wounds that remain after the physical scars have disappeared.

Discovering Your Needs

You need to explore and discover what *your* needs are, so that you can learn how to be more assertive in attempting to meet them. Abusive relationships are characterized by mutual dependency, where the batterer expects that all his needs will be met by his partner. As a consequence, the victim begins to stifle her own needs and desires and to focus on those of her partner. Eventually, even her awareness of those needs dims. Rediscovering your own needs and desires and learning how you can meet them can lead to increased feelings of competence and independence. It won't stop the abuse, but knowing what you want to change can push you to get help or get out.

Challenging Beliefs

It's important to evaluate the abusive patterns you may have learned in your own family of origin and relearn healthier, more self-affirming patterns. If you were abused as a child or witnessed abuse between your parents, you may have learned that violence was an unavoidable part of life. You will need to challenge your beliefs and assumptions about how you deserve to be treated in a relationship. Do you deserve to be abused? Do you deserve to be "punished" for doing something for yourself that your partner doesn't like? Does any adult have the right to punish, physically or otherwise, another adult?

Strengthening Self-Esteem

Most importantly, you need to restore your feelings of worth. Your abusive partner has probably attacked your basic value as a person as well as your behavior. It's difficult to hear frequent attacks without, on some level, starting to agree. Perhaps you already had secret doubts about your worth; perhaps you already criticize yourself for certain failures. Everyone has a critical inner voice. But when that voice constantly attacks and berates you, it can do tremendous damage to your self-esteem. To assess the strength of your inner critic, make a list of the things that you did right today. Add everything that you feel good about. If you can't think of very many things, chances are that your critic is working overtime.

The first step in strengthening your self-esteem is to identify the critic and determine exactly what it says to you. Because the attacks are so frequent and familiar, they may be hardly noticeable. Try to hear what your critic is saying when you've made a mistake, when your partner is criticizing you, or when you're feeling depressed or down on yourself. Keep a notebook and write down exactly what's said, from single words ("Idiot!") to whole sentences ("If I hadn't been such a stubborn fool, I might not have made such a stupid mistake").

Notice whether the criticisms are general or specific. General criticisms are those that make a global judgment about you or your behavior ("What a slob!" "Boy, are you stupid!" "You never do anything right!"). Criticisms like these are destructive because they don't allow any room for improvement, but simply hack away at any feelings of worth. Specific criticisms are limited to a particular incident or behavior. They don't condemn you totally as a person for each minor mistake or failure ("I didn't express myself very assertively with Dennis today;" "the promo piece wasn't catchy enough").

Go back over your list of things the critic has been saying to you. Analyze each attack. Is it general or specific? Is it a global indictment or does it refer to a specific situation without condemning you as a person? Try substituting a simple statement of fact for each criticism. Use language that's specific (avoid words like *never, always, everything*) and nonpejorative (avoid adjectives that have negative connotations like *lazy, illogical, stupid, stubborn, crazy*). Sally was able to substitute, "I forgot Fred's birthday and sent him a card that was a few days late," for, "What a fuckup! You never remember anything on time!" Pat changed, "You're such a manipulative bitch!" to "Sometimes I don't express my needs directly to Larry because I'm afraid he might respond with anger and violence."

Now try and find exceptions or strengths that correspond to the critic's statements. Pat could see that although she didn't express herself directly with Larry, she had no difficulty with her mother or sister. Sally acknowledged that although she forgot Fred's birthday she had remembered everything else on her list of things to do for the week. This last step is particularly important in the pursuit of higher self-esteem.

Some of the strengths you identify can be turned into positive affirmations. Make a list of qualities and abilities that you like about yourself. Remind yourself of your strengths when the critic goes on the attack.

Once you've begun to hear the critic and practiced writing down the criticisms, analyzing them, and substituting more realistic and self-affirming statements, you can begin to practice the process without writing. The more you practice, the sooner you'll begin to feel less depressed and more positive about yourself.

Seeing a Professional

While there are many things that you can do to take care of yourself, a professional counselor can make an important contribution to your recovery. A variety of counselors have been trained in helping victims of spouse abuse. You can find marriage and family counselors, psychiatrists, psychologists, social workers, and religious counselors in your local yellow pages. More specifically, domestic violence programs can be found under the headings of "Crisis Intervention Services" or "Social Service Agencies." Suicide prevention or child abuse hotlines can also be helpful. Keep in mind the fact that some professionals, like many others in society, believe that a man's wife and children are his possessions and that he has the right to treat them as he chooses. Check with the local battered women's shelter or with the local chapter of NOW (National Organization of Women) to discover which counselors hold attitudes that will benefit your progress.

If You Use Violence

If you're a man and want to change your pattern of anger and violence, the most important step is to GET HELP. Changing the cycle of violent behavior is difficult at best, and virtually impossible without outside help. A treatment group for offenders is probably the most helpful, and can be found in the yellow pages under "Crisis Intervention Services" or "Social Service Agencies." You could also call the National Coalition Against Domestic Violence (1-800-333-SAFE) for referrals. A group setting is especially helpful in breaking the isolation and mutual dependency that exist in most abusive relationships. It can also provide a forum for developing and rehearsing anger-management skills.

Individual counseling can also be useful. If you're in the military, there are usually counseling services on the base which are set up to address problems that active duty personnel and their families experience. Or check out your regional military hospital or branch clinic. The chaplain can also sometimes be a useful source of referrals.

Remember that your willingness to enter some sort of treatment program is the best sign of your commitment to changing your violent behavior. Without this commitment, the chances of change occurring are remote.

Substance Abuse

If you use alcohol or other drugs, it's essential that you evaluate how these substances contribute to the abusive pattern in which you're involved. If you're in doubt about the impact that alcohol or drugs have, then go to a treatment center where you can get the assessment and help you need. Look in your local yellow pages under "Alcoholism Information and Treatment" or "Drug Abuse Information and Treatment." If you need more intensive treatment, hospital-based programs offer short-term in-patient care, while residential programs provide longer term assistance. Attempts to change violent behavior are unlikely to succeed if you continue to abuse drugs or alcohol.

Anger Control

There's little hope of managing your anger within the context of your relationship unless you are committed to the belief that there are no justifications for violence against your partner under any circumstances. No matter what the provocation, she does not deserve to be hit. Since violence is a behavior that you learned, it follows that you can also learn nonviolent alternatives.

Anger-control skills involve five major components: (1) taking responsibility for your pain and stress, (2) giving up blame and challenging the thoughts that trigger anger, (3) identifying the physical early warning cues and patterns of escalation, (4) learning stress-reduction behaviors, and (5) learning assertive, problem-solving communication.

Taking Responsibility

The first step in managing your anger and violence is to understand the two-step model of anger (Chapter 5) and the principle of personal responsibility (Chapter 6). This principle suggests that you are responsible for the outcome of all your interactions. It's stressful not to get what you want or need, and it's easy to mask the resulting feelings of frustration and helplessness by blaming the other person for your pain. But you are the only one who knows your exact desires and needs. The other person is aware of his or her needs, and is doing the best that he or she can at the time to get those needs met. Trying to force the other person to change with anger or violence is destructive to each of you and to the relationship. Only by changing your own behavior can you produce a more satisfying outcome.

It doesn't make sense to ask who's responsible for your pain. When needs conflict, as they often do, it's inevitable that one or both partners will be frustrated or disappointed. What does make sense is to use your anger or frustration as a cue to ask yourself, "What hurts?" and, "Since I'm responsible for my pain, what can I do to fix it?" Try different strategies to discover the ones that work best for you. If a strategy fails, don't fall into the "helpless victim" role—try another. Each time his mother-in-law visited, Joe felt angry and left out. He blamed Vicki for his frustration and believed that she should change things. That only led to resistance from Vicki and escalation of anger on both sides. When Joe asked himself the two questions, he realized that what hurt was feeling excluded. He decided to explore ways *he* could change the situation. He might suggest activities that included the three of them. Or he could spend some time really getting to know his mother-in-law so that he understood more of her jokes and idiosyncratic humor. Or he could plan fun activities for himself so that he wasn't sitting at home waiting when they were out together.

Owen found himself furious every time Betsy smiled at another man. His jealousy was reaching pathological levels. When he asked himself "What hurts?" Owen identified feelings of fear and insecurity. He was interpreting Betsy's smiles as interest in having an affair and was terrified at the potential of losing her—her time, attention, and love. If he were to take full responsibility for changing the situation, Owen would realize that he had several choices. He could express his concerns directly to Betsy and ask for reassurance. He experienced less jealousy when his level of stress was low, so he could practice his stress-reduction techniques. Finally, he could avoid situations that he could predict might trigger his jealousy.

Giving Up Blame

There are many ways of coping with the stress and frustration of not getting your needs met. Blaming is one of them. You decide that your pain was caused by someone else. Underlying blame is the belief that other people *should* be feeling, thinking, or behaving differently. The fact that they're not makes them bad, wrong, and deserving of punishment. Chapter 7 describes how these "blamers" and "shoulds," added to the stress itself, trigger anger.

The problem with this process is that the people you're judging rarely agree with your rules about what's right and wrong and what they should and shouldn't be doing, feeling, and thinking. While any kind of should can trigger anger, Chapter 7 describes several that are extremely damaging in intimate relationships. Review in particular the entitlement fallacy ("I want it very much, therefore I should have it"), the fallacy of fairness ("If my needs aren't met, it's not fair"), the fallacy of change ("If I just apply enough pressure, I can make you change and meet my needs"), conditional assumptions ("If you really loved me, you'd meet my needs"), and the letting it out fallacy ("If you don't meet my needs, you deserve to be punished with my anger").

The important blamers to understand are good-bad dichotomizing ("What you do to me is either good or bad, right or wrong"), assumed intent ("You're deliberately not meeting my needs in order to hurt me"), magnifying ("Things are really terrible, awful!"), and global labeling ("You're such a *****!").

In order to change your pattern of anger and violence, you need to combat these trigger thoughts. First, think back over the past few incidents that provoked an anger response. What stress were you experiencing before the particular incident occurred? What needs weren't being met and what method did you use in your attempt to meet those needs? Notice the pattern of escalation from frustration to anger to violence. If you haven't already started an anger journal, begin one now. Whenever you feel angry, write down what you're saying to yourself. Identify the trigger thoughts that you were using from those listed above. And finally, rewrite your original statement so that it is more realistic and no longer contains the distorted trigger thought.

Adrian's first entry in his anger journal was, "This house is a bloody pigsty! And she knows it drives me crazy coming home to such a mess after a long day at work!" He identified his trigger thoughts as assumed intent, magnifying, and the fallacy of fairness. After some consideration, Adrian rewrote his original statement. "I don't like it when the kids' toys are scattered around the living room when I come home. I assume Melanie is doing the best she can because other than the kids' stuff the house is pretty neat. And it's quite a handful trying to pick up after three children. Maybe we need to talk about hiring someone to help with the cleaning."

Stopping Escalation

You may have attempted to control your violence by trying not to get angry. What usually happens under these circumstances is that the anger you feel builds up and eventually explodes into more violence. You need to become aware of your anger at the stages *before* it builds to an explosion. Most men are only aware of very high levels of anger, those that would score above 5 on a scale of 1 to 10. Lower levels of anger, which you probably call annoyance or irritation, are the ones most likely to get ignored until they build to an explosion. Read through Chapter 8 again and learn the physiological cues that go along with early anger. Think back to recent times when you were frustrated or irritated. How did your body feel? Did you begin to feel tension in your jaw or neck? Did your hands ball into fists? Did your stomach feel tight or twisted? Go back to your anger journal. Each time you're angry or frustrated, write down the physiological cues you notice, the intensity of the anger on a scale of 1 to 10 (10 being high anger), and the situation that made you angry. Once you've identified your particular early warning signs, you can begin to make changes in the pattern of escalation that usually follows.

The most effective way to stop escalation is to employ the timeout model. Using Chapter 9 as a guide, discuss with your partner how each of you will initiate a time-out, who's going to leave first, where each of you is going to go, and the length of the interval you'll be gone. It's essential that you call a time-out at the first sign of escalation. It's also crucial that if your partner calls a time-out before you're aware of feeling angry or even irritated, you respect her need to disengage from the discussion. Because your anger is the biggest threat in these situations, you should be the one to leave the house. You probably learned years ago that only cowards walk away from a fight. But the really courageous person is the one who can recognize a no-win, potentially disastrous situation and walk away without resorting to violence.

Stress Reduction

In Chapter 8, you read how anger and relaxation are physiologically incompatible. Anger involves an increase in physiological tension, while relaxation leads to a decrease in tension. It's impossible to be relaxed and angry at the same time. If you can use your early warning signs of tension as a cue to relax, you can reduce the possibility of escalation even further. Chapter 8 describes several techniques for effectively reducing stress. Read the chapter again, and practice each technique several times before going on to the next one. In this way, you can determine which ones work best for you. Then practice. Relaxing, like any other skill, requires a certain discipline and commitment.

The next step is to identify the situations that produce tension. If you've been keeping your anger journal, you're probably already able to see patterns. Perhaps your job is the most stressful component of your life right now, or perhaps your family or social demands. Perhaps a series of apparently minor setbacks has produced enough irritation and frustration to result in a state of chronic stress. Knowing your particular patterns will enable you to prepare yourself ahead of time and approach the situation as calmly as possible. Relaxation is most effective when used as a preventative measure. It's far easier to relax tight jaw muscles or a knotted stomach than it is to combat the tension accompanying overwhelming rage.

Adrian noticed that as soon as he walked into his living room and saw his children's toys scattered around, his neck and shoulder muscles began to tighten. Rather than making his habitual response of "This house is a bloody pigsty!" Adrian sat down on the couch and took several deep breaths. Even before he started examining the trigger thoughts that elicited the old reaction, he noticed a sharp reduction in his level of tension.

Simon found that a fast, five-mile run to the beach and back during a time-out cleared his head and worked the tension from his muscles. To his surprise, he found that lying down and meditating for 15 minutes was equally effective. Eventually, Simon discovered that he could reduce the need for time-outs at home by setting aside a couple of brief periods during the day for meditation. Combating his stress at work led to far less escalation at home.

Communication

Since anger and violence are often fueled by the stress of unmet needs, it's important to learn more appropriate ways of meeting those needs. You were probably never taught how to express your needs clearly and assertively. You might hope that others will know or guess your needs by the subtle cues you give and then get frustrated and angry when they guess wrong. The less you're able to verbally express yourself, the more likely you are to resort to violence when frustrated. Problem-solving communication recognizes the validity of both partners' needs and the importance of compromise. Before continuing, make sure you've read and understood the concepts described in Chapter 12 on problem-solving communication.

1. Making requests. To express your needs assertively, you must first be able to define those needs. When you're feeling angry or frustrated, ask yourself that old question, "What hurts?" Then ask, "What do I want in order to fix it?" Formulate a statement that begins, "I feel..." and continues, "...and I want..." Take responsibility for your needs without blaming; "I feel lonely and want a hug," is more assertive than, "You're always so cold and distant." Say "I'm feeling bored and I'd like to go to a movie tonight," rather than, "You're so boring! You never want to go out anymore."

Sometimes you'll need to describe the problem before getting into your feelings and needs. State the problem simply, exactly, and nonpejoratively. Just the facts, without blaming or making a case. "The TV usually goes on after dinner (*fact*). I feel a bit overwhelmed by the noise and I'd like to keep it off until nine."

Try to restate questions as statements. Questions are often perceived as criticisms or attacks and can lead to defensiveness and escalation. Say, "I feel anxious about running late for work when breakfast isn't ready on time," rather than, "Why can't you ever have breakfast ready on time?" "When you question my judgment in front of the kids, I feel embarrassed and humiliated... I'd rather you talked to me in private," will probably lead to less defensiveness than, "What the hell do you think you're doing, making a fool of me in front of the kids?"

2. Setting limits. Saying no clearly and directly is probably very difficult for you. You may fear that your partner will reject you if you refuse a request. Or you may have been told as a child that it's selfish and thoughtless to refuse a request. Some people say yes verbally, while saying no with their actions by completing the request slowly, ineffectively, and resentfully. These people are often chronically angry and feel exploited and unappreciated. Eventually a simple request might trigger an explosion of anger or violence. This is the kind of no that does damage to relationships. You might feel so afraid of not being able to say no that you say it all the time with an intensity that borders on violence. Setting limits *assertively* reduces the likelihood of anger and violence. It also ensures that when you do say yes you'll feel better about offering help willingly rather than grudgingly.

Think about the last time you said yes when you wanted to say no or said no in a way that felt excessive. Imagine yourself in the same situation using the three-part statement described in Chapter 12—acknowledgment, your position, and saying no. George responded to Michelle's request with, "I know you'd like me to take the kids to school tomorrow morning (*acknowledgment*), but I have to be at work for an eight o'clock meeting with the board (*your position*). I can't take them (*saying no*)." Practice saying no, first in easy situations, then in increasingly difficult ones.

3. Negotiation. In any relationship there's bound to be conflict. No two people have identical needs. There will always be times when one partner's wants conflict with the other's. Giving up your needs or trying to force the other person to give up his or hers isn't very effective in the long run. It leads to anger, resentment, and often violence. Negotiation involves reaching a compromise that feels relatively satisfying to you both. It can be seen as a logical extension of the process you've already begun. You became aware of feeling angry, so you ask yourself, "What hurts?" and, "What do I want to fix it?" You may also ask yourself, "What are my limits?" Once you have a clear idea of what you want, present it to your partner. At this point, you must listen carefully to her needs and objections. It's often difficult to hear someone present needs that differ from your own without feeling criticized and getting defensive. Remind yourself that you're entitled to your needs and that your partner is entitled to hers.

When each of you has presented your needs, look for a compromise. Propose something that addresses both your concerns. If the first suggestion doesn't work, come up with another. Encourage your partner to come up with her own proposal. When negotiating, never say a flat no. Always offer a counterproposal so that you can continue to search for compromise. In the previous example, George was very clear and assertive in his response to Michelle's desire that he take the kids to school. Had he given his usual type of response, the interaction would have looked like this:

George: Jesus! You can't take them again? Well I can't either! So you'd better find some way to get them there.

Michelle: But my sister's arriving tomorrow...

George: Whoopee for your sister. Isn't she capable of even getting herself on a bus? Is she as dumb as she looks?

Michelle: That's a crummy thing to say about Joan! All I'm asking is...

George: Forget it! I said no and that's it!

Instead, the interaction continued:

Michelle: Well, my sister's flying in from Florida tomorrow morning. Her plane arrives at 8:25 and I'd like to meet her at the airport. (*Statement of needs.*)

George: What if I pay for her to take a taxi from the airport? (*Suggested compromise.*)

Michelle: No. I'd rather meet her in person.

George: What do you suggest?

Michelle: Perhaps I could call Andrea and see if she would take them to school with Kevin. If you could drop them at her house, you'd still have time to get to work before your meeting.

George: Well, if you can get them ready before you leave, I'm willing to take them to Andrea's.

If you practice these negotiation techniques, you won't have to get angry or violent to get your needs met. You'll be able to develop solutions that are satisfying to you both.

4. Dealing with Criticism. Being criticized always hurts, and usually results in the desire to react defensively or counterattack. In your relationship, you probably find yourself criticizing and attacking. Your reaction may be partly the result of feeling attacked yourself or feeling unable to get your needs acknowledged. Chapter 12 describes how being criticized can make you feel inferior, imperfect, guilty, and worthless. It also describes how you can respond to criticism more effectively. You can limit the damage to your self-esteem by blocking the attack, reminding yourself that the criticism is just one person's opinion, and accepting that perfection is impossible. Evaluate the criticism for anything accurate in it that you can use or learn from. At the same time, recognize the part of the criticism that isn't accurate. Respond by agreeing with what's true and ignore the rest. Initially this may be difficult, and you may want to use a time-out to prevent escalation.

In battering relationships, the woman is often too frightened of incurring further violence to express her anger at the abuse she's already experienced. As you begin to work on taking responsibility for the abuse and making changes in your behavior, your partner may feel safer to express her feelings. You may find yourself being subjected to all the rage and anger that your partner has been stuffing for years. It's essential that you don't get pulled back into the pattern of defensiveness and counterattack that led so rapidly to violence. Call time-out as soon as you feel yourself getting tense or angry. Allow yourself to calm down, then approach the situation again using the skills described above and in Chapter 12.

Self-Esteem

Most batterers feel ashamed of their violence and the fact that they can't control their behavior. In addition, they often suffer more global feelings of unworthiness. If you were abused as a child, you're even more likely to think that you're somehow bad or worthless. It's important that you learn to separate your behavior (which might be inappropriate and need changing) from you as a person. Go back and reread the section in this chapter on strengthening self-esteem. Begin to identify the internal critical voice that attacks you for your mistakes and imperfections. Keep a notebook in which you record all the things your critic says, from single words to entire monologues. Are the criticisms general indictments of you as a person ("You're a lying son-of-a-bitch")? Or are they specific references to specific behaviors ("What you just said was an exaggeration and a putdown")? Examine each of the critic's statements and substitute something more factual, less judgmental. Now identify your strengths and the exceptions to the criticisms. Use these to develop some positive affirmations and repeat these to yourself as often as you can. Incorporate them into the anger-control techniques described above. When you first become aware of feeling angry or stressed, you'll ask yourself, "What hurts?" and, "What do I want to do to fix it?" You might decide to take a time-out, do some relaxation, or assertively verbalize your feelings and needs. Using your positive affirmations at these times will give you added confidence to carry out your choice. Remind yourself that you're a worthwhile person, that you're doing the best you can, and that you can cope with stressful situations without resorting to violence.

When Violence Stops

When violence stops in a relationship, other problems don't disappear. Problems with dependency, isolation, and communication are common in abusive relationships, but can't be dealt with effectively until the violence has ended. Once the batterer has taken the responsibility for changing his violent behavior, you can work toward developing a healthier relationship based on mutual respect and affection.

This book offers some resources toward that end, but the process of change will most likely be slow and painful. After years of violence, you'll need to slowly reestablish trust in the relationship. The victim may need to see the batterer consistently choose nonviolent behaviors for some time before she can begin to relax her vigilance and trust the reality of the changes. It will take a lot of practice before you are both able to clearly express your feelings, both positive and negative. It takes practice to approach inevitable conflict with equanimity and assertively negotiate for satisfaction of your needs.

However, with a commitment on both sides to a healthy relationship, and with help of the resources listed in this book, you can develop a different kind of relationship than the scared and hurtful one you now experience.

Appendix

RCR Group Protocol

Selection of Group Members

Success for an RCR group depends on appropriate selection. Pregroup interviews should be conducted. Ask questions about the duration and quality of relationships. Attempt to rule out personality disorders, particularly borderline conditions. Since RCR groups are less effective for clients struggling with generalized anger, attempt to determine if the anger is generalized (free-floating hostility that can attach itself to any situation) or limited to specific situations or settings. Ask questions to determine if the client enjoys his or her anger, nurtures it, relies on it, or is otherwise invested in maintaining an angry stance. Clients who find their anger to be highly rewarding tend to be less successful RCR group members.

Group Structure

Groups should consist of 5 to 10 clients. Groups with more than 10 members offer each client too few opportunities for role playing, questions, and shared experiences. Groups should meet for one and a half to two hours over a six- to eight-week period.

The Anger Log

During the pregroup interview, ask clients to keep a daily anger log. Each anger incident should be listed and rated on a 1 to 10 point scale (1 is minimal anger, 10 is the angriest the client has ever felt). Emphasize that the anger log is an indispensable part of treatment and must be conscientiously maintained.

If you wish to do pre- and post-group testing, it is recommended that you use Charles Spielberger's excellent State-Trait Anger Inventory (Spielberger, Jacobs, Russell, and Crane 1983)

Session 1

Overview of RCR

1. Six pre-learned strategies for adaptively coping with angry encounters.
2. Strategies are divided into active and passive responses.
3. RCR will help you to cope even when extremely angry.
4. RCR will enable you to learn adaptive reactions that help solve problems rather than escalate tension.
5. RCR will keep you from getting stuck with a response that isn't working and make it more likely for you to find a response that will get you what you want.
6. RCR will help you experience anger as a signal to cope and try a new response rather than as a signal to intensify attack.

Describe each of the RCR responses. Emphasize that not all of the six responses will be appropriate for a particular anger situation. Emphasize the concept of switching from one response to another to cope with growing anger or escalation. While a single anger-control strategy often fails during provocations, the ability to use a variety of strategies or responses in succession increases the likelihood of resolution.

Key Attitude

The key attitude is problem solving rather than avenging. An avenger wants to punish and injure the offending party to the same degree that he or she has been hurt. Pain must be paid back. A problem-solving attitude assumes that the conflict is a matter of conflicting needs; there is no right or wrong about it. Each person's needs are legitimate and important. The goal is to work toward agreement through discussion and compromise.

Hand out RCR Response Sheet.

1st RCR RESPONSE: Ask for What You Want

1. Pre-learn opening line:

"I'm feeling (What's bothering me is) _____. And what I think I need (or want or would like) in this situation is _____."

2. Rules.

    a. What is bothering you (your feeling) is optional. Include this if you think it is important information to help the other person to be more responsive, or if the other person is an intimate who deserves to know your reactions.

    b. Ask for something behavioral, not attitudinal.

    c. Ask for something specific, limited to one or two things.

    d. Develop a fallback position, i.e., the minimum change that would be acceptable to you. This gives you room to negotiate.

3. Role-play by therapists to model RCR.
(Include this section if the group has co-leaders.) Emphasize concept of voice control: keep voice low in volume without much inflection. So often voice tone and volume communicate anger, blame, contempt, sarcasm, and so on. Voice control guards against escalations that are triggered by meta-messages in your tone of voice.

4. Client visualization.
Some groups find visualization difficult or unproductive. If this is the case, drop the visualization component and emphasize role plays. Homework should then focus on practicing the RCR response in vivo in low impact situations.

    a. Brief lesson in visualization. Practice a beach scene, bringing in visual, auditory, and kinesthetic aspects of scene.

    b. Clients visualize a scene from their anger logs that grew out of some unmet or frustrated need. Clients visualize using RCR response and having success.

Visualize second scene: initial RCR response is rebuffed but they are successful when offering fallback position.

5. **Discussion of visualization.**

    a. Discuss visualized scenes and any problems clients encountered generating need statements.
    b. Therapist helps clients who had trouble generating need statements and fallback positions to do so.

6. **Client role-play.** Using scene from his or her anger log, client takes role of provocateur. Second client practices RCR response after learning what presenting client wanted. Therapist coaches the provocateur and the client practicing RCR.

7. **Therapist discusses importance of expressing wants and needs.** Asks clients if there are concerns about what it's okay to ask for.

Homework

1. Pick three scenes from anger log (low, medium, and high). Generate need statements and fallback positions for each one.
2. Practice visualizing each scene, using RCR response 1, successfully each day. Start with low impact scene and progress to high impact scene.
3. Learn RCR response 2.

Session 2

Review response 1. Discuss any problems experienced with homework.

2nd RCR Response: Negotiate

1. **Review opening line:**

"What would you propose to solve this problem?"

(*Note:* If clients don't feel comfortable with phrasing of opening line, let them modify it so that it feels right for them.)

2. Rules.

    a. If you get resistance or a worthless proposal, offer your fallback position.

    b. If you hear a proposal that has possibilities, begin negotiation. Look for compromise. Examples:

- "Let's do this part of what you want, this part of what I want."
- "My way this time, your way next time."
- "If you do _____ for me, I'll do _____ for you."
- "Let's split the difference."
- "Try it my way for a week. If you don't like it, we'll go back to the old way."

    c. Compromise can only be reached when the solution takes into account BOTH people's needs.

Repeat sections 3, 4, 5, and 6 as described in first session.

3rd RCR Response: Self-Care

1. Pre-learn opening line:

"If (the problem) goes on, I'll have to (self-care solution) in order to take care of myself."

2. Rules.

    a. The self-care solution should have as its main goal *meeting your needs*, not hurting the other person. This isn't something you do to the other person, it's something you do for yourself.

    b. Emphasize that this is your way of solving the problem yourself, not a pushy ultimatum, not a punishment.

Repeat sections 3, 4, 5, and 6 as described in the first session.

Homework

1. Using three scenes from anger log (low, medium, and high), visualize using RCR response 2 successfully.
2. Using same three scenes, generate self-care statements and visualize using them.
3. Practice visualizations each day.
4. Learn RCR response 4.

Session 3

Review RCR responses 2 and 3. Discuss any problems with homework. Emphasize that responses 1 through 3 are "active" responses, while 4 through 6 are "passive" responses.

4th RCR Response: Get Information

1. Review opening line:

"What do you need in this situation?"
"What concerns (worries) you in this situation?"
"What's bothering (hurting) you in this situation?"

2. Rules.

a. Use this response when someone is angry at you and there's something behind their anger you don't understand.
b. If you don't already know what their need or worry is—GET INFORMATION.

Repeat sections 3, 4, 5, and 6 as described in the first session.

5th RCR Response: Acknowledge

1. Pre-learn opening line:

"So what you want is _____."
"So what concerns (worries) you is _____."
"So what bothers (hurts) you is _____."

2. Rules.

a. Use when someone has given you a clear message about his or her feelings.

b. Expect the other person to correct or modify what you said if you didn't get it right. Then re-acknowledge the new information.

c. Acknowledgment is not just to let people know you hear them, it is a way to clarify and correct your misconceptions.

Repeat sections 3, 4, 5, and 6 as described in the first session.

6th RCR Response: Withdrawal

1. Pre-learn opening line:

"It feels like we're starting to get upset. I want to stop and cool off for a while."

2. Rules.

a. Keep repeating, like a broken record, if you get resistance. Acknowledge the other person's desire to keep the discussion going or acknowledge his or her general distress, but keep repeating your withdrawal statement.

b. Physically leave the situation. Don't just leave the vicinity.

c. With intimates, give a specific time at which you'll return to resume the discussion.

Repeat sections 3, 4, 5, and 6 as described in the first session.

Homework

1. Pick three scenes from anger log (low, medium, and high) and visualize using RCR responses 4 and 5.
2. Visualize same three scenes, but add needing to use RCR response 6 (withdrawal).
3. Do visualizations every day.
4. Review opening statements of responses 1 through 6 each day.

Session 4

Review homework and discuss any problems.

Switching

1. **Rules.**

   a. Memorize all opening lines. Test yourself daily.
   b. Whenever possible, rehearse in advance active response numbers 1 and 3. Decide if you wish to include your feelings about the situation. Then formulate your request and your fallback position. Make sure it's behavioral and specific. Also try to generate a self-care response. Ask yourself how you can take care of the problem *without* the other person's cooperation.
   c. Continued anger or escalation are your signals to SWITCH responses. Don't get stuck if a response isn't working. Move on to what you feel, intuitively, is the next best option.
   d. Don't be afraid to repeat responses. You may wish to return, several times, to questions that get more information. You may wish to acknowledge what you're learning about the other person's experience. And as the discussion progresses, you may wish to invite another round of negotiation.
   e. If you don't know what to do next, try shifting from active to passive responses (or vice versa). If you've been focusing on getting information, try expressing your own needs now. If you're stuck in fruitless negotiation, consider asking for information.
   f. As a rule, start with active response 1 (asking for what you want) when you're angry or want something changed. Start with passive response 4 (getting information) when the other person is angry and on the attack.
   g. Keep shifting among responses until the problem feels resolved or further communication appears pointless. If you're still angry and stuck, go to one of the exit

responses (either self-care or withdrawal).

2. **Coping thoughts: to be used whenever you feel your anger increasing.**

   a. "Take a deep breath and relax."
   b. "I have a plan to cope with this. What's the next step?"

Role-Play Switching

Divide the group into pairs.

1. **Using Anger Logs:**

   a. Start with low-rated provocation from a client's anger log.
   b. Instruct the client to play him or herself and the second client to pay provocateur.
   c. Therapist acts as coach for each client. Cues coping by reminding provoked client of two key coping thoughts. Reminds client of opening lines of RCR if forgotten. May suggest switching to a new RCR response. Provoking client is coached to resist until three or four different RCR responses have been made.
   d. Provoked client uses anger as a cue to switch and chooses which RCR response to try next.
   e. Role play should end with successful resolution.

Homework

1. Review all opening lines on a daily basis.
2. In vivo homework:

   a. Using scene from anger log; pick low-risk individual with whom you have had conflict. Visualize using RCR with that person. Plan out Need Statement and Fallback Position.
   b. Actually engage in RCR exchange with that person.
   c. Record results in anger log.

Sessions 5, 6, and 7

Repeat the role-play switching exercise from session 4. Encourage clients to switch back to old responses already tried. They can acknowledge or negotiate or ask for what they want more than once. As clients become more proficient at RCR, begin using medium, then high impact anger scenes from logs.

Homework for Sessions 5 and 6

Use same homework assignment as in Session 4. Have clients pick a medium-risk person to use RCR with each week. Remind clients to record results in anger log.

Bibliography

Alexander, F. "Emotional factors in hypertension." *Psychosomatic Medicine*, 1939, 1:175-179.

Ardrey, R. *The Territorial Imperative*. New York: Atheneum, 1966.

Baer, P. E., F. H. Collins, G. C. Bourianoff, and M. F. Ketchel. "Assessing personality factors in essential hypertension with a brief self-report instrument." *Psychosomatic Medicine*. 1969, 7:653-659.

Barefoot, J. C., W. G. Dahlstrom, and R. B. Williams. "Hostility, CHD incidence, and total morbidity: A 25-year follow-up study of 255 physicians." *Psychosomatic Medicine*. 1983, 45:59-63.

Bateson, G. "The frustration-aggression hypothesis and culture." *Psychological Review*. 1941, 48:350-355.

Benson, H. *The Relaxation Response*. New York: Morrow, 1975.

Berkman, L., and S. L. Syme. "Social networks, lost resistance, and mortality: A nine year follow-up study of Alameda residents." *American Journal of Epidemiology*. 109:186-204.

Biaggio, M. K. "Anger arousal and personality characteristics." *Journal of Consulting and Social Psychology*. 1980, 39:352-356.

Blumenthal, J. A., R. Williams, Y. Kong, S. M. Schonberg, and L. W. Thompson. "Type A behavior and angiographically documented coronary disease." *Circulation*. 1978, 58:634-639.

Bradshaw, J. *Bradshaw on the Family*. Deerfield Beach, Fl: Health Communications, 1988.

Bry, A. *How To Get Angry Without Feeling Guilty*. New York: New American Library, 1976.

Burns, D. *Feeling Good: The New Mood Therapy*. New York: William Morrow, 1980.

Cannon, W. "Bodily changes in pain, hunger, fear and rage." New York. Appleton-Century-Crofts, 1929.

Cautela, J. "Covert modeling." Paper presented at the fifth annual meeting of the Association for Advancement of Behavior Therapy, 1971.

Crockenberg, S. "Toddler's reaction to maternal anger." *Merril-Palmer Quarterly*. 1985, 31:361-373.

_____. "Predicators and correlates of anger toward and punitive control of toddlers by adolescent mothers." *Child Development*. 1987, 58:964-965.

Davis, M., E. R. Eshelman, and M. McKay. *The Relaxation & Stress Reduction Workbook*. 3rd ed. Oakland, CA: New Harbinger Publications, 1988.

Dentan, R. K. *The Semai–A Nonviolent People of Malaya*. New York: Holt, Rinehart & Winston, 1968.

Deschner, J. P. *The Hitting Habit: Anger Control for Battering Couples*. New York: Macmillan, 1984.

Diamond, E. L. "The role of anger and hostility in essential hypertension and coronary heart desease." *Psychological Bulletin*. 1982, 92:410-433.

Dinkmeyer, D., and G. McKay. *The Parent's Handbook: Systematic Training for Effective Parenting*. Circle Pines, MN: American Guidance Service, 1982.

_____. *The Parent's Guide: A Systematic Training for Effective Parenting of Teens*. Circle Pines, MN: American Guidance Service. 1982.

Dollard, J. R., L. W. Doob, N. E. Miller, and O.H. Mowrer. *Frustration and Aggression*. New Haven: Yale University Press, 1939.

Doty, B., and P. Rooney. *Shake the Anger Habit*. Redding, CA: The Bookery, 1987.

Dreikers, M. D. *Children: The Challenge*. New York: E. P. Dutton, 1987.

Ebbesen, E., B. Ducan, and V. Konecni. "The effects of content of verbal aggression on future verbal aggression: A field experiment." *Journal of Experimental Psychology*. 1975, 11:192-204.

Eisenberg, S. E., and P. Micklow. "The assaulted wife: 'Catch 22' revisited." *Women's Rights Law Reporter*. 1979, 3:138-161.

Elliot, F. "The neurology of explosive rage: The dyscontrol syndrome." *The Practitioner*. 1976, 217:51-60.

Esler, M., S. Julius, A. Zweifler, O. Randall, E. Harburg, H. Gardiner, and V. De Quattro. "Mild high-renin essential hypertension: Neurogenic human hypertension?" *New England Journal of Medicine*. 1977, 296:405-411.

Feshbach, S. "The catharsis hypothesis and some consequences of interaction with aggression and neutral play objects." *Journal of Personality.* 1956, 24:449-462.

Firestone, R. *The Fantasy Bond.* New York: Human Sciences, 1985.

Freud, S. [1923] *The Ego and the Id.* Translated by Joan Riviere. New York: W. W. Norton, 1962.

Friedman, M., S. St. George, S. O. Byers, and R. H. Rosenman. "Excretion of catecholamines in men exhibiting a particular behavior pattern (A) associated with high incidence of clinical coronary artery disease." *Journal of Clinical Investigation.* 1960, 39: 758-764.

Friedman, M., and R. H. Rosenman. *Type A Behavior and Your Heart.* New York: Alfred A. Knopf, 1974.

Friedman, M., and D. Ulmer. *Treating Type A Behavior—and Your Heart.* New York: Alfred A. Knopf, 1984.

Frude, N., and A. Goss. 1979. "Parental anger: A general population survey." *Child Abuse and Neglect.* 1979, 3:331-333.

Gordon, T. *Parent Effectiveness Training.* New York: New American Library, 1975.

Gressel, G. E., F. O. Shobe, G. Saslow, M. DuBois, and H. A. Schroeder. "Personality factors in essential hypertension." *Journal of the American Medical Association.* 1949, 140:265-272.

Hadley, J., and C. Staudacher. *Hypnosis for Change.* Oakland, CA: New Harbinger Publications, 1985.

Hamilton, J. A. "Psychophysiology of blood pressure." *Psychosomatic Medicine.* 1942, 4:125-133.

Hansson, R. D., W. H. Jones, and B. Carpenter. "Relational competence and social support." *Review of Personality and Social Psychology.* 1984, 5:265-284.

Harburg, E., S. Julius, N. F. McGinn, J. McLeod, and S. W. Hoobler. "Personality traits and behavior patterns associated with systolic blood pressure levels in college males." *Journal of Chronic Diseases.* 1964, 17:405-414.

Harburg, E., J. C. Erfurt, L. S. Hauenstein, C. Chape, W. J. Schull, and M. A. Schork. "Socio-ecological stress, suppressed hostility, skin color, and black-while male blood pressure: Detroit." *Psychosomatic Medicine.* 1973, 35:276-296.

Harburg, E., E. H. Blakelock, and P. J. Roeper. "Resentful and reflective coping with arbitrary authority and blood pressure: Detroit." *Psychosomatic Medicine.* 1979, 41:189-202.

Harris, R. E., M. Sokolow, L. G. Carpenter, M. Freedman, and S. Hunt. "Response to psychogenic stress in persons who are potentially hypertensive." *Circulation.* 1953, 7:572-578.

Haynes, S. G., M. Feinleib, and W. B. Kannel. 1980. "The relationship of psychosocial factors to coronary heart disease in the Framingham study, Part III: Eight year incidence of CHD." *American Journal of Epidemiology.* 1980, 3:37-58.

Hazaleus, S., and J. Deffenbacher. "Relaxation and cognitive treatments of anger." *Journal of Consulting and Clinical Psychology.* 1986, 54:222-226.

Herman, D. "A statutory proposal to limit the infliction of violence upon children." *Family Law Quarterly.* 1985, 19:1-52.

Heusser, C. "Parental anger: An examination of cognitive and situational factors." Ph.D. diss., University of Waterloo, Waterloo, Ontario, 1986.

Hoffman, . "Moral development." *In Carmichael's Manual of Child Psychology,* edited by P. Mussen. New York: Wiley Publications, 1970.

Hokanson, J. E. "Psychophysiological evaluation of the catharsis hypotheses." In *The Dynamics of Aggression,* edited by Megaree and Hokanson. New York: Harper & Row, 1970.

Jones, W. H., J. E. Freeman, and R. A. Gasewick. "The persistence of loneliness: Self and other determinants." *Journal of Personality.* 1981, 49:27-48.

Kahn, H. A., J. H. Medalie, H. N. Newfield, E. Riss, and U. Goldbourt. "The incidence of hypertension and associated factors: The Israel ischemic heart disease study." *American Heart Journal.* 1972, 84:171-182.

Kahn, M. "The physiology of catharsis." *Journal of Personality and Social Phychology.* 1966, 3 (3):278-286.

Kaplan, S., L. A. Gottschalk, E. Magliocco, D. Rohovit, and W. Ross. "Hostility in verbal productions and hypnotic dreams in hypertensive patients." *Psychosomatic Medicine.* 1961, 23:311-322.

Kellner, R. M. T. Buckman, M. Fava, G. A. Fava, and I. Masuogiacomo. "Prolactin, aggression, and hostility: A discussion of recent studies." *Psychiatric Developments.* 1984, 2:131-138.

Konner, M. *The Tangled Wing.* New York: Holt, 1962.

Lazarus, R. S., and S. Folkman. *Stress, Appraisal, and Coping.* New York: Springer Publishing Co., 1984.

Leakey, R. *The Making of Mankind*. New York: E. P. Dutton, 1981.

Lerner, H. G. *The Dance of Anger*. New York: Harper and Row, 1985.

Lewis, H. K., and M. E. Lewis. *Psychosomatics: How Your Emotions Can Damage Your Health*. New York: Viking Press, 1972.

Lorenz, K. *On Aggression*. New York: Bantam Books, 1971.

Mallick, S. K., and B. R. McCandles. "A study of catharsis aggression." *Journal of Personality and Social Psychology*. 1966, 4:591-596.

Mann, A. H. "Psychiatric morbidity and hostility in hypertension." *Psychological Medicine*. 1977, 7:653-659.

Maranon, G. "Contribution a l'etude de l'action emotive de l'adrenaline." *Revue Francaise d'Endocrinologie*. 1924, 2:301-325.

Mark, V. "Sociobiological theories of abnormal aggression." In *Violence*, edited by I. L. Kutash et al. San Francisco: Jossey-Bass, 1978.

McKay, M., M. Davis, and P. Fanning. *Thoughts and Feelings: The Art of Cognitive Stress Intervention*. Oakland, CA: New Harbinger Publications, 1981.

_____. *Messages: The Communication Book*. Oakland, CA: New Harbinger Publications, 1983.

McKay, M., and P. Fanning. *Self-Esteem*. Oakland, CA: New Harbinger Publications, 1987.

Meichenbaum, D. *Cognitive Behavior Modifications*. New York: Plenum Press, 1977.

Miller, A. *The Drama of the Gifted Child*. New York: Basic Books, 1981.

_____. *For Your Own Good—Hidden Cruelty in Child-rearing and the Roots of Violence*. New York: Farrar, Straus, and Giroux, 1983.

Miller, C., and C. Grim. "Personality and emotional stress measurement on hypertensive patients with essential and secondary hypertension." *International Journal of Nursing Studies*. 1979, 16:85-93.

Miller, N. E. "The frustration-aggression hypothesis." *Psychological Review*. 1941, 48:337-342.

Minden, H. A. *Two Hugs for Survival*. Toronto: McClelland and Stewart, 1982.

Monat, A., and R. Lazarus, eds. *Stress and Coping: An Anthology*. 2nd ed. New York: Columbia University Press, 1985.

Mullin, R. E. *Handbook of Coginitive Therapy Techniques.* New York: W. E. Norton.

Neidig, P. H., and D. H. Friedman. *Spouse Abuse: A Treatment Program for Couples.* Champaign, IL: Research Press, 1984.

Nelson, J. *Positive discipline.* Fair Oaks, CA: Sunrise Press, 1981.

New York Times. "Cynicism and mistrust linked to early death. Thursday, January 17, 1989.

NiCarthy, G. *Getting Free: A Handbook for Women in Abusive Relationships.* Seattle: The Seal Press, 1982.

Novaco, R. *Anger Control: The Development and Evaluation of an Experimental Treatment.* Lexington, MA: C.D. Health, 1975.

Ornstein, R., and D. Sobel. *The Healing Brain.* New York: Simon and Schuster, 1987.

Patterson, G. R. *Coercive Family Process.* Eugene, OR: Castalia, 1982.

Paul, J., and M. Paul. *If You Really Loved Me.* Minneapolis: CompCare Publisher, 1987.

Pino, C. *Divorce, Remarriage, and Blended Families.* Palo Alto, CA: R. & E. Press, 1982.

Rosenman, R. H. "Health consequences of anger and implications for treatment." In *Anger and Hostility in Cardiovascular and Behavioral Disorders,* edited by M. A. Chesney and R. H. Rosenman. Washington, DC: Hemisphere Publishing Co., 1985.

Rubin, I. R. *The Angry Book.* New York: Collier Books, 1969.

Rule, B. G., and A. R. Nesdale. "Emotional arousal and aggressive behavior." *Psychological Bulletin.* 1976, 83:851-863.

Scaramella, T. H., and W. A. Brown. "Serum testosterone and aggressiveness in hockey players." *Psychosomatic Medicine.* 1978, 40: 262-267.

Schachter, J. "Pain, fear, and anger in hypertensives and normotensives." *Psychosomatic Medicine.* 1957, 19:17-29.

Schachter, S. *Emotion, Obesity, and Crime.* New York: Academic Press, 1971.

Schachter, S., and J. Singer. "Cognitive social and physiological determinants of emotional state." *Psychological Review.* 1962, 69:379-399.

Schwartz, G. E., D. A. Weinberger, and J. A. Singer. "Cardiovascular differentiation of happiness, sadness, anger, and fear following imagery and exercise." *Psychosomatic Medicine.* 1981, 43:343-364.

Selye, H. "A syndrome produced by diverse noxious agents." *Nature*, 1936, 138:32

Shekelle, R. B., M. Gale, A. M. Ostfeld, and O. Paul. "Hostility, risk of CHD, and mortality." *Psychosomatic Medicine*. 1983, 45:109-114.

Sonkin, D. J., and M. Durphy. *Learning To Live Without Violence: A Handbook for Men*. Rev. ed. San Francisco: Volcano Press, 1985.

Sonkin, D. J., D. Martin, and L. E. Walker. *The Male Batterer: A Treatment Approach*. New York: Springer Publishing Co., 1985.

Spielberger, C. D., G. A. Jacobs, S. Russell, R. S. Crane. "Assessment of anger: The State-Trait Anger Scale." In *Advances in Personality, Vol. 2*, edited by J. N. Butcher and C. D. Spielberger. Hillsdale, NJ: Erlbaum, 1983.

Straus, M. "Leveling, civility, and violence in the family." *Journal of Marriage and the Family*. 1974, 36:13-29.

Strauss, M. A., R. H. Gelles, and S. K. Steinmetz. *Behind Closed Doors: Violence in the American Family*. New York: Anchor-Doubleday, 1981.

Tavris, C. *Anger–the Misunderstood Emotion*. New York: Simon & Schuster, 1982.

_____. On the wisdom of counting from one to ten. *Review of Personality and Social Psychology*. 1984, 5:270-291.

Walker, L. E. "The battered woman syndrome study." In *The Dark Side of Families: Current Family Violence Research*, edited by D. Finkelhor, R. J. Gelles, G. Hotaling, and M. Straus. Beverly Hills, CA: Sage Publications, 1983.

_____. *The Battered Woman Syndrome*. New York: Springer Publishing Co., 1984.

Weisinger, H. *Dr. Weisinger's Anger Work-Out Book*. New York: William Morrow and Co., 1985.

Weiss, R. *Marital Separation*. New York: Basic Books, 1985.

Whitting, J. W. M. *Becoming a Kwoma*. New Haven: Yale University Press, 1941.

Williams, R. B., T. L. Haney, K. I. Lee, Y. Kong, J. A. Blumenthal, and R. E. Walen. "Type A behavior, hostility, and coronary atherosclerosis." *Psychosomatic Medicine*. 1980, 42:539-549.

Wolff, H. S., and S. Wolf. "A study of experimental evidence relating life stress to the pathogenesis of essential hypertension in man." In *Hypertension: A Symposium*, edited by E. T. Bell. Minneapolis: University of Minnesota Press, 1951.

_____. "Stress and the gut." *Gastroenterology*. 1967, 52:2.

Wolpe, J. *The Practice of Behavior Therapy*. Oxford: Pergamon Press, 1969.

Wood, C. "The hostile heart." *Psychology Today*. 1986, 20:9.

Other titles that may interest you:

Last Touch: Preparing for a Parent's Death, $11.95
Consuming Passions: Help for Compulsive Shoppers, $11.95
Concerned Intervention, When Your Loved One Won't Quit Alcohol or
      Drugs, $11.95
Redefining Mr. Right, $11.95
Dying of Embarrassment: Help for Social Anxiety and Social Phobia, $11.95
The Depression Workbook: Living With Depression and Manic Depression,
      $13.95
Risk-Taking for Personal Growth: A Step-by-Step Workbook, $11.95
The Marriage Bed: Renewing Love, Friendship, Trust, and Romance, $11.95
Hot Water Therapy: Save Your Back, Neck & Shoulders in 10 Minutes a Day
      $11.95
Older & Wiser: A Workbook for Coping With Aging, $12.95
Prisoners of Belief: Exposing & Changing Beliefs that Control Your Life,
      $10.95
Be Sick Well: A Healthy Approach to Chronic Illness, $11.95
Men & Grief: A Guide for Men Surviving the Death of a Loved One, $11.95
Love Addiction: A Guide to Emotional Independence, $11.95
When Once Is Not Enough: Help for Obsessive Compulsives, $11.95
The New Three Minute Meditator, $9.95
Getting to Sleep, $10.95
The Relaxation & Stress Reduction Workbook, 3rd Edition, $13.95
Beyond Grief: A Guide for Recovering from the Death of a Loved One, $10.95
Thoughts & Feelings: The Art of Cognitive Stress Intervention, $13.95
The Divorce Book, $11.95
Hypnosis for Change: A Manual of Proven Techniques, 2nd Edition, $12.95
The Deadly Diet II: Recovering from Anorexia & Bulimia, $11.95
Chronic Pain Control Workbook, $13.95
Rekindling Desire: Bringing Your Sexual Relationship Back to Life, $12.95
Visualization for Change, $12.95
Starting Out Right: Essential Parenting Skills for Your Child's First Seven
      Years, $12.95
Lifetime Weight Control, $11.95
The Anxiety & Phobia Workbook, $13.95
Love and Renewal: A Couple's Guide to Commitment, $12.95
The Habit Control Workbook, $12.95

Look for these titles at your local bookstore, or call **toll free, 1-800-748-6273**, to order books or request a free catalog. Have your Visa or Mastercard number ready. Or send a check for the titles you want to New Harbinger Publications, 5674 Shattuck Avenue, Oakland, CA 94609. Include $2.00 for the first book and 50¢ for each additional book, to cover shipping and handling. (California residents please include appropriate sales tax.) Allow four to six weeks for delivery.

Prices subject to change without notice.